GOD'S
NEW MAN

GOD'S
NEW MAN

*The Election of Benedict XVI
and the Legacy of John Paul II*

PAUL COLLINS

continuum

Continuum
The Tower Building   15 East 26th Street
11 York Road   New York
London SE1 7NX   NY 10010

www.continuumbooks.com

First published 2005

British Library Cataloguing-in-Publication Data
A catalogue record for this book is available from the British Library.

ISBN 0 8264 8015 2

Designed by Phil Campbell
Typeset in Malaysia by Syarikat Seng Teik Sdn. Bhd.
Printed in Great Britain by MPG Books Ltd, Cornwall

CONTENTS

ACKNOWLEDGEMENTS

Writers are always dependent on the people to whom they speak and whose books and articles they read. Many people have contributed to this book by writing about and talking through with me the major issues surrounding the contemporary papacy. But I am especially in the debt of some.

Two of the best informed people in Rome are Gerard O'Connell and John L. Allen of the *National Catholic Reporter*. Their knowledge, experience of the Vatican and its ways, and their generosity and friendship during a number of visits has been extraordinary. The regular translated columns of Sandro Magister of *L'Espresso* are always a source of information and opinion that is available nowhere else in English.

In London I am deeply in the debt of John Wilkins and Austen Ivereigh, both formerly of *The Tablet*. Austen was particularly helpful with material about Latin American Catholicism, as was Ivo Sefton de Azevedo in Brazil who put me in touch with Frei Betto and Antonio Carlos. Special thanks also to Michael Walsh, Simon Bryden-Brooke and Judith Champ.

The International Movement We Are Church organised the media briefings in which I participated at the time of the election of Benedict XVI. Special thanks to Isaac Würst and Luigi De Paoli and to Anthony Padavano and Maureen Fiedler.

In Australia I have talked the issues through with many people, but especially Bishop Patrick Power, Kevin Walcot, Professor John Malony, Jane Anderson, Geraldine Doogue, John Hill, Michael McGirr, John Madden and Father Paul Stenhouse. In the United States I have talked to Mary-Louise Hartman and Patrick Connor. Thanks also to Mary Cunnane and to the staff of Melbourne University Publishing, especially Sybil Nolan, and to Robin Baird-Smith at Continuum.

Finally, thanks to my wife, Marilyn Hatton, for living so long and so patiently with popes and the Vatican. Her love and support are endlessly generous.

Paul Collins
Canberra, June 2005

INTRODUCTION

Morto un papa, se ne fa un altro—'When a pope dies,
they make another one' (Roman saying)

There is a certain bluntness in the way the Romans talk about the papacy. You really can't blame them: in one way or another they have had to deal with this institution for more than 1700 years, and for much of that time they have been economically and politically dependent upon it. We have just seen one pope die and another elected by that most narrow and exclusive of franchises, the Sacred College of Cardinals. So what is the legacy of John Paul II, and what are the prospects for Catholicism under Benedict XVI's papacy?

To make sense of these questions we need to understand the broad perspective in which the contemporary papacy finds itself. The simple fact is that the Catholic church has been at a crossroad since the 1960s. As the first years of the new millennium roll by, it is still trying to sort out the best course to take in the contemporary world. Many older Catholics have known nothing their entire lives but an ongoing crisis in Catholicism. And most of them don't think this is such a bad thing: it has made them adaptable, open, alert, their spirituality and commitment focused on living with uncertainty, ambiguity and change. What has happened in the church mirrors the wider process of change in developed Western culture and social structures.

Catholicism, and particularly the papacy, lived—at least theoretically—in a pre-modern mind-set before the election of Angelo Roncalli as Pope John XXIII (1958–1963). A man of historical insight and rare courage, and probably the greatest pope since Paul III (1534–1549), Pope Roncalli launched a revolution in Catholicism, the Second Vatican Council, which sat through four sessions from 1962 to 1965. Attended by all the world's bishops and leading theologians, it dragged the Catholic church, part of it kicking and screaming, out of the early nineteenth into the mid-twentieth century. Although Vatican II's intentions were crystal clear by 1965—to open the church to the contemporary world and to enter into a serious but critical dialogue with it—there was enough ambiguity in its documents to leave the way open for a 're-interpretation' by those who never accepted its primary intentions. As a result there has been an ongoing struggle within Catholicism over the interpretation of the Council and its implications for Catholic life. This struggle came to a head in the exceptionally long papacy of John Paul II.

The actual task of initially implementing the Council fell to Paul VI (1963–1978). His biographer correctly calls him 'the first modern pope'. This was not because he was a great media performer or communicator, or because he brought about obvious radical change in church structures. In fact, in his time he seemed quite conservative, cautious and ambivalent. But he understood the nature of the main challenges confronting Catholicism in the modern world and he was prepared to try to deal with them. Following John XXIII, he took radical stances on world poverty, hunger and the massive imbalances between the developed world and the poor and marginalised. He also had an instinctive understanding of the way democratic systems work, and he was one of the first Western leaders to try to open up a systematic dialogue with the Soviet Union in an attempt to gain some freedom for Catholics and people caught in the occupied countries behind the Iron Curtain. Even in terms of the government and constitutional structure of Catholicism, he was prepared, at least to an extent, to share papal power and authority with his fellow bishops through the world synod. However, emotionally and theologically, he found him-self unable to shift on pivotal practical questions, such as contraception and priestly celibacy. We tend to remember him because it is these decisions that have led directly to the massive crisis of credibility the church faces on sexual and ministerial issues. In other words, official hierarchical views are completely out of touch with the actual life experience of Catholics in the areas of sexuality and the ministry and life of priests.

Then in October 1978, along came Karol Wojtyla, Archbishop of Cracow, who took the style of John Paul II. Was he the second 'modern pope'? At first sight he certainly seemed to be. Here was someone willing to travel the world and to use all the modern means of communication, who seemed to talk more frankly than any pope before him about topics like sex and the body. Wojtyla was a man who believed in exercise, mountain-climbing and the outdoors. He was a 'real man', not a wizened-up Italian cleric in a long black dress. He even installed a swimming pool at the papal summer residence at Castel Gandolfo, south-east of Rome. 'It's cheaper than another conclave (papal election),' he commented.

But he had not been pope for long before careful observers of the papacy began to wonder: was he really a modern man with a critical openness to the world like Paul VI, or was there something else operative? It soon became clear that his views on the church's ministry were quite traditional, even idiosyncratic. The distinction between priests and laity was to be re-enforced, and priests were to remain a celibate, separate, clerical group. If they left the ministry and attempted to marry without permission —only obtainable through a highly intrusive process lasting several years, and which even then was not always granted—they were excommunicated. Later he also rejected, and even tried to suppress, all discussion of the ordination of women. In fact, the whole move towards what could be called a more 'collegial', consultative church was gradually stopped in its tracks. The world synod of bishops became no more than a cipher where views that dissented from the prevailing opinions of the Vatican were uttered only by 'brave' bishops and certainly never recorded in official reports. The tendency to appoint an increasing number of intelligent and ministerially creative bishops, begun in the time of Paul VI, slowly dropped off as the Wojtyla papacy advanced. Increasing numbers of unimaginative conformists were appointed to the hierarchy, and John Paul II's own constant travel tended to lessen the authority of local bishops, who came to be seen as representatives of 'head office' with the pope as a kind of 'world bishop'. This is a complete distortion of the traditional and historical role of the pope. In terms of relationships with the other Christian churches and the other great religious traditions, John Paul II was a master at big events, such as the Assisi prayer days when he brought together religious leaders, such as the Dalai Lama, from all over the world. But at the same time, he encouraged his watchdog of orthodoxy, Cardinal Joseph Ratzinger, to go after those theologians who were sincerely trying to build a theological basis for dialogue among the great religious traditions of the world.

This is not for one moment to deny that the Wojtyla papacy did many positive things for the church. John Paul was deeply conscious of the Holocaust and no pope has done more to try to heal relationships between Jews and Catholics. He was born in Wadowice, just 30 kilometres from Oswiecim, a town known in German as 'Auschwitz'. He grew to young manhood in Cracow under the vicious Nazi occupation of Poland, and he saw first-hand what happened to the Jewish people. He has also tried to build relationships with the Orthodox churches of the East (such as the Greek and Russian churches) so the church 'could breathe with both lungs'. In the latter part of the papacy, and especially since 9/11, the Vatican has striven very hard to prevent antagonisms growing between Christians and Muslims, and has worked to build bridges between moderate Islam and Catholics. He visited Africa, with all its massive problems including AIDS, far more than any other world leader. He was also a major participant in the destabilisation of the old Soviet system, and he played a key role in the overthrow of Communism in Poland.

All of this political activity on behalf of his own country has to be seen, of course, within the perspective of the attack on those Catholics in Latin America who were carrying on their own struggle for freedom from poverty through the so-called 'base communities' and against oppressive right-wing military regimes. The Vatican's banning of liberation theology and forcing clergy who participated in politics to leave the priesthood, for example, in Nicaragua, was certainly one of the least attractive aspects of the Wojtyla papacy.

What has become clear is that John Paul II had a distinctly idiosyncratic view of Catholicism. At the core of this was his conviction that God had chosen him especially, under the patronage of the Blessed Virgin Mary, as the one to guide and even to save Catholicism in the turbulent period after Vatican II. The attempt on his life in May 1981, and his survival, seemed to reinforce this in his own mind. And the sheer length of his papacy meant that he was able to impress his peculiar agenda on the church to a considerable extent.

So how are we to assess John Paul II? Is he, as his biographer George Weigel says, 'John Paul the Great', the equivalent of Popes Leo the Great (440–461) and Gregory the Great (590–604)? Or are his accomplishments considerably more modest? Will he be seen, in a much more accurate historical perspective five or ten years hence, as a pope of real significance, or as one whose importance derives from the fact that he was incumbent for a very long time? That is what the first part of this book is all about. Some readers may question the emphasis on the Wojtyla papacy in this book. But I feel it is important to understand what has happened to the church over the past twenty-six years, because this is what Benedict XVI has inherited. The sheer length of the Wojtyla papacy, let alone the idiosyncratic style of John Paul II, means that his successor cannot avoid what happened to Catholicism during that time.

Part One of *God's New Man* examines what happened in the last days of the Wojtyla papacy leading up to the death of John Paul II. It then backtracks to assess the impact of Pope John Paul II's constant travel and the way he tended to project himself as the central focus of the church. In this light, it considers what has happened to bishops and their role in the church. It continues by examining the major theological and ecclesiastical themes of the Wojtyla papacy, and reflects on the consequences of all this for lay people and priests.

Part Two briefly reviews the interregnal period, technically called *sede vacante* ('the seat being empty'), and discusses what probably happened in the conclave. Part Three examines the background and experience of Pope Benedict XVI. It assesses the major issues he faces and discusses how, on the basis of his experience and cultural background, he might begin to react to and deal with them.

Finally, I should declare to readers a personal contact with Benedict XVI. As I explained in my contribution to the book I edited, *From Inquisition to Freedom* (2001), I was subject to an investigation by the Congregation for the Doctrine of the Faith (CDF) between 1997 and 2001. I thus have personal experience of the way in which the Congregation operated under this pope as Cardinal Ratzinger. Although I remain highly critical of the Congregation's methods and the standards of its theological assessments—I was quoted correctly in the London *Tablet* saying the CDF's theological consulters were 'fourth rate'—I have become increasingly fascinated by Benedict XVI. He brings much baggage to the papacy, but he is nevertheless a highly intelligent man who could become an important pope in a much more positive sense than John Paul II. I have always felt that when genuine conservatives attain the top job, they are able to move towards the centre and act as reconcilers. I have to say that is my hope for Pope Benedict XVI.

Time will tell whether I am right.

Paul Collins
June 2005

Part One

THE WOJTYLA LEGACY

LAST DAYS IN THE PAPAL *APPARTAMENTO*

It's a long way, ecclesiastically speaking, from the city of Milwaukee, Wisconsin, famous for its German immigrants, Pabst beer and heavy industry, to the private papal *appartamento* on the fourth floor of the jumble of buildings that make up the Vatican's apostolic palace. But James Michael Harvey has made that transition. Born in Milwaukee and ordained a priest there in 1975, he trained in church law in Rome, and then entered the Vatican diplomatic service in 1980. He rose rapidly through the ranks, and in February 1998 at the relatively young age of 48, he was appointed the Prefect of the Papal Household. He was ordained a bishop that year and made an archbishop in 2003.

His job of administering the papal *appartamento* was not onerous because the pope lived in an unostentatious and homely area with only a few immediate staff. In theory, Harvey's main job was to run the apostolic palace and to act as John Paul II's gatekeeper. This was because the Household Prefecture supervised the distribution of tickets for the regular Wednesday general audiences in the rather ugly Nervi audience hall besides Saint Peter's. Influence with the Prefecture got you good spots close to the pope, and with groups of 9000 or more attending these events this was important. Harvey also technically controlled access to the pope for smaller groups of people, such as bishops' conferences, those favoured by the Vatican, professional groups, important individuals, cardinals, royalty, presidents, prime ministers and others who wanted to meet the pope. But, as Harvey quickly found, despite the theory, that was not quite how it worked out in practice with the pope from Poland.

When Harvey left the Secretariat of State and arrived in the small, enclosed, world of the *appartamento*, he had not moved far physically. The *appartamento* was a near neighbour of the Secretariat in the same building, and no doubt he was fully aware of what he would encounter in the pope's private world. It was peopled by the 'pope's mafia', a small group of priest secretaries and Polish nuns, who did the domestic work, presided over by Pope Wojtyla's long-term private secretary, Archbishop Stanislaw Dziwisz (pronounced gee-vish). Dziwisz, whose title was Adjunct-Prefect, and who, on paper, was hierarchically lower than Harvey, quietly assured the American that he was 'very good at taking orders'.

In reality, it was the other way round. Dziwisz was in charge—the real power behind the papal throne. Born of a rural family in the hills near Rabka to the south of Cracow in 1939, and ordained priest in 1963, he had been with Wojtyla as his secretary since 1966. He is a modest, taciturn man, short of stature, his black, curly hair now disappearing, with a slightly plump face, a prominent nose and classic Slavic features. Until his appointment as an archbishop he was known in the Vatican simply as 'Don Stanislaw' or to close friends as 'Stas'. When Wojtyla was elected pope in October 1978 he came to Rome with him, and from then onwards Dziwisz dominated the *appartamento* through his constant close contact with John Paul. His bedroom was next to that of the pope and, in many ways, their relationship was that of family; they acted as if they were they were father and son. He was present beside the pope almost all the time to help him in every detail, he went on all the papal travels, was completely devoted to John Paul and, as the pope's health declined, acted more and more as his proxy. By 2003, cynics had dubbed him 'Pope Stan I'.

Even in Cracow, Wojtyla was never one for the boring details of diocesan administration. In Rome he found the endless minutiae that was sent up to him from the Roman curia, the central Vatican bureaucracy, irrelevant to what he felt was his real mission—a kind of globe-trotting papacy engaged in worldwide evangelisation. Because of both security and papal tradition, the *appartamento* was enclosed and claustrophobic, and Pope Wojtyla had always been a man of the mountains and the outdoors. He felt the Vatican was a 'golden cage'. Protecting him meant that this sense of lock-down and imprisonment increased after the assassination attempt on 13 May 1981. Dziwisz was sitting just behind John Paul in the popemobile when the pope was shot in the stomach by the Turkish terrorist Mehmet Ali Agca, as he drove around the crowd in the piazza of Saint Peter's. Dziwisz cradled him in his arms until the pope was put in an ambulance.

Given this relationship, it was Dziwisz, not Harvey, who for most of the last years of the Wojtyla papacy really decided who had access and who did not. While Dziwisz was no fool, his instincts were deeply conservative, and he was not theologically sophisticated. But he knew well who John Paul really wanted to see, and particularly the people he wanted to avoid. Around the Vatican the talk was that this particular person was 'liked by the *appartamento*', and that one was not. Thus some had regular and privileged access, and others could hardly get a hearing. Given that John Paul was a very social person and had always learned more from talking to others than reading reports, those with his ear were the most influential. For instance, Dziwisz certainly made sure that several of the newly founded and very conservative new religious movements (NRMs) such as Opus Dei, the Legionaries of Christ and the Neo-Catechuminate had ample access. At the same time, the representative leaders of the long-established mainstream religious orders with a membership of over a million committed sisters, priests and brothers, the Union of Superiors General, and the International Union of Superiors General, were left out in the cold. In November 2003 the former president of the Union of Superiors General, the Mexican Father Camillo Macisse, reported in *The Tablet* (22 November 2003) that his organisation had not had a meeting with the pope since 1995. This was an extraordinary exclusion of the leadership of some of the most long-established, pastoral and influential organisations in the church.

The same applied to the Roman curia: some officials were preferred over others. Cardinal Giovanni Battista Re, Prefect of the Congregation of Bishops, was much favoured by both the pope (who at one stage seemed to want him as his successor) and Dziwisz, and he was often in the *appartamento* in the declining years of the Wojtyla papacy. The influence of Cardinal Joseph Ratzinger, the Prefect of the Congregation for the Doctrine of the Faith (CDF)—formerly the Roman Inquisition—was profound on doctrinal matters throughout the Wojtyla papacy and continued right through to the end. The position of Cardinal Angelo Sodano was more ambivalent. John Paul certainly wanted him to stay on as Secretary of State, effectively papal prime minister and foreign minister combined. But he was unpopular with Dziwisz and the influential Poles in the curia. There is a story told that when Sodano appeared on Italian TV at a clerical gathering at the Polish Institute in Rome, many called out '*Via, via*'—'Out,

out!' This outburst was symptomatic of a curial bureaucracy in disarray. Deep divisions became increasingly more obvious between John Paul's intimate inner circle of friends led by Dziwisz, and those who felt that they had been left out.

Sodano's link with the *appartamento* was the *Sostituto*, that is Under-Secretary of State, Archbishop Leonardo Sandri, an Argentinian of Italian extraction. He was able to get on with Dziwisz. Also very influential in Wojtyla's last years was Archbishop Stanislaw Rylko, President of the Pontifical Council for the Laity, writer of many of the pope's speeches.

But as Parkinson's disease increasingly took over John Paul's body from about the 2000 Jubilee year onwards, fewer and fewer people had regular access to him. Throughout 2003 it became obvious that the pope was a very sick man. Slumped over, with his right hand trembling uncontrollably, his movements became ever slower, and his face was almost a mask, although the shrewd, lively eyes still peered out and they seemed to express a feeling of vulnerability. There was an ebb and flow in his strength throughout this period. At times the illness almost seemed to be in remission. This was probably when the doctors got the medication right and the *appartamento* maintained some balance in the pope's activities. He certainly seemed quite strong for most of 2004. But there were still persistent stories about him falling asleep with visiting presidents, and his confusion about the identity of the Anglican delegation led by Archbishop Rowan Williams of Canterbury. What worried many, however, was the fact that the Catholic church has no means of dealing with a mentally incapacitated pope. What would happen if the pope lapsed into prolonged unconsciousness or lost his mental lucidity or the ability to express himself? There is nothing in canon law to deal with this kind of eventuality.

It was also clear that the problem was that the process could drag on for months and years. As the effects of the disease ate away at his ability to concentrate, move, speak and write, and as his energy decreased, Dziwisz assumed more and more responsibility. Even those allowed into the *appartamento* were given only a few minutes before they were ushered out. John Paul quickly became exhausted.

This is a key problem for any absolutist system: once the supreme leader is on the downward spiral toward death, government and administration become increasingly paralysed. Dziwisz became the real gatekeeper. He was the one who filtered the information and the questions that needed decision to the pope. It was he who advised Wojtyla, and even acted for him, and it was he who funnelled back the replies. There was a sense in which Dziwisz became the *de facto* vicar of the pope.

This level of power always leads to resentment and anger among those who feel that they should have access but are excluded, and there is ample evidence that the pope tried to make sure his closest aides would be protected after he died. John Paul did this by getting them into positions of influence while he still had the power to do so. The Italians have a word for this: *sistemazione*, literally meaning 'tidying up' or 'getting things sorted out'. In October 2003, John Paul made Harvey and Dziwisz, and his long-time papal Master of Ceremonies, Piero Marini, archbishops. The tall silver-haired, distinguished-looking Marini from Bobbio in north-central Italy was unpopular among some in Rome, and especially among liturgical conservatives because the worship style used in papal Masses was somewhat less formal than traditionalists wanted. No doubt with the permission of John Paul, Marini had allowed many local customs, for example an Australian Aboriginal smoking ceremony, to be used during Mass when the pope was travelling, and on several occasions he even permitted liturgical dancing at papal Masses in Rome. After the Second Vatican Council, Marini had worked in the Roman curia as a secretary to the important liturgical scholar and reformer Archbishop Annibale Bugnini. Bugnini was hated by liturgical conservatives, and this added to reactionary Catholics' deep suspicions about Marini's approach to papal ceremonies. Clearly, by making them archbishops, John Paul hoped he was giving these three men some protection.

In odd contrast to the more progressive ideas of Marini, it was also during this last period of the Wojtyla papacy that the influence of the reactionary Spanish organisation Opus Dei increased considerably around the Vatican. The Opus had always had a man very close to the pope and much 'liked by the *appartamento*', the medical doctor and former bull-fighter Joaquin Navarro-Valls, who was the papal media spokesman. The Spanish Navarro-Valls is a full, celibate, lay numerary (that is, vowed) member of Opus. No other papal spokesman before Navarro-Valls had played such an important role and had so much influence on the pope's public image. Another friend of Opus Dei was the Camerlengo, or Chamberlain of the Holy Roman Church, the Spanish Cardinal Eduardo Martinez Somalo, whose position gave him considerable authority and influence during the interregnum after the death of the pope.

The Romans, with two thousand years experience of popes, and Roman emperors before them, are quite phlegmatic about the bishops of their city. They loved a few, such as John XXIII, some they have despised and have thrown their dead bodies into the Tiber, and about the death of all they are completely unsentimental. As their blunt saying goes, *Morto un papa, se ne fa un altero* ('When a pope dies they make another one'). But even before a pope dies, the ecclesiastical system begins to prepare for the next papacy. There is a psychological moment in every papacy, often difficult for the outsider to pin down, when subtly things change. The Last Act has begun. Everything is the same outwardly, and the show grinds on. But the historical assessments have begun even before the pope dies. People, including many in Rome, start to talk, quietly and cautiously, about the 'next papacy' and who the next pope might be. For John Paul, the psychological moment probably came sometime after the 2000 Jubilee year.

From 2000 onwards, the pope's ill-health was obvious. By early 2003, Dziwisz's influence on appointments to the College of Cardinals was considerable. An example of this was seen in the failure of the curial Archbishop Luigi de Magistris to get a cardinal's red hat at the October consistory—a meeting in which cardinals are appointed—even though he might have been expected to be a strong candidate because he had been the Major Penitentiary, a job that normally brought that honour. But he had been one of the few Vatican insiders brave enough to be publicly critical of the rushed and suspect process that led to the making of the founder of Opus Dei, Josemaria Escrivá, a saint. Culturally, the Opus is a Latin organisation, and it is very slow to forgive and never forgets. As well, as a liturgical conservative de Magistris was also one of those who attacked Marini over his 'innovations' in papal liturgies. The response was not slow in coming. Dziwisz favoured the Opus, as did John Paul, and Marini was favoured by the *appartamento*. De Magistris missed out on his red hat. This episode also demonstrates that the distinction between 'progressive' and 'conservative' no longer makes sense, although it is often hard to avoid using the words.

Dziwisz's influence was even more manifest when the powerful Cardinal Ratzinger publicly admitted in late September 2003 that 'The pope is very ill. Pray for him.' That this was a fact was clearly shown when a new group of thirty cardinals was suddenly announced in early October 2003. The *appartamento* and the curia wanted to get the consistory in which these cardinals were appointed held in case the pope suddenly died. At around the same time, a number of other senior churchmen made comments similar to those of Ratzinger about the pope's health, including Vienna's influential archbishop, Cardinal Christoph Schönborn. But all this loose talk about a dying pope obviously annoyed Dziwisz, who commented to a group of journalists that he had spoken to Ratzinger and that 'I can tell you that Ratzinger wept, explaining that he had been misunderstood' by the media. In other words, Ratzinger actually did not mean what he clearly said.

Dziwisz also commented to the media that 'Many of the journalists who speculated about [the pope's] health in past years are already in heaven!' Perhaps he had the famous English Vaticanologist, Peter Hebblethwaite, in mind.

On the other hand, Dziwisz's assumption of power may have saved the church from a worse fate, that of unlimited control by the Roman curia. At least there was some guiding hand which was not that of ambitious, curial cardinals looking after their own interests for the next papacy. The Vatican bureaucracy is not numerically large (all up it employs just over three thousand people), but being Italian in inspiration, it tends to work very much on personal relationships, patronage, ambition, saving face, vituperation, and a torrent of gossip. The great English theologian and cardinal John Henry Newman, who himself had serious problems with the curia, commented that there will necessarily always be second-rate people around the pope 'who are not subjects of that supernatural guidance which is his prerogative'. He also commented that 'the Rock of Saint Peter on its summit enjoys a pure and serene atmosphere, but there is a great deal of Roman malaria at the foot of it.' In other words, one can have a clear faith in the church but too much involvement with the curia drags you down into the malarial bog.

The curia also tends to be ruthless with those considered to have too much personal power. Such people are got rid of once their papal patron dies. So there is a sense in which Dziwisz was acting very responsibly and bravely in trying to give some direction to the church by representing what he thought the pope wanted, given that he must have known he and other members of the inner circle of friends and colleagues of John Paul II would be swept away as soon as the pope died. There is no one more dead than a dead pope, and no one more dispensable than his immediate assistants.

What also became clear in early 2003 was that the pope wanted to keep the two most senior cardinals in the curia in office as long as he could. Sodano, the Secretary of State (the equivalent of a papal prime minister), turned 75 in November 2002. This is the age at which all curial officials must submit their resignations. Everyone expected that Re from the Congregation of Bishops would replace Sodano. Nevertheless, the pope did nothing and, despite having submitted his resignation, Sodano stayed on beyond retirement age. The same thing happened with Cardinal Ratzinger, who also submitted his resignation when he reached the age of 75 in April 2002. There was a good reason to maintain them in office: it made sure that the new pope did not feel saddled with newly appointed officials from the previous papacy whom he could not replace with his own people without a lot of bad feeling.

Other important posts, however, were filled: Archbishop Leonardo Sandri was appointed Sostituto, the second in charge in the Secretariat of State. A northern Italian who had been Nuncio (ambassador) to Germany, Archbishop Giovanni Lajolo, replaced the Frenchman, Cardinal Jean-Louis Tauran (who became Prefect of the Vatican Library), as Secretary for Relations with States (the equivalent of deputy foreign minister). A Polish friend of Dziwisz, Archbishop Stanislaw Rylko, was appointed President of the Pontifical Council for Laity, a post that normally goes to a cardinal. Two Eastern Europeans, a Slovenian and a Croatian, also replaced two retiring curial cardinals, a Belgian and a Spaniard.

Thus even though the pope was increasingly incapacitated administration more or less continued. While there was no love lost between Sodano on the one hand and Dziwisz and Re on the other, the Vatican continued to function largely because Sodano focused his attention on Italian politics and international relations and left much of the internal business of church administration to Sandri, who did get on well with the *apparta-mento* and kept the curia running.

By 2003 it was clear that John Paul II was a very sick man. The complications that slowly began to accompany Parkinson's disease were becoming more obvious. It was almost as though Pope Wojtyla had made a decision to die, as he had lived, in public. His spirituality centred very much around the crucifixion of Jesus and, just as he had died publicly nailed to a cross, so Wojtyla sought to follow his example. Suffering was always very close to him. His mother and brother died when he was young, and after his father's death he had no close living relatives. He was born in the town of Wadowice, just thirty kilometres by road from the concentration and extermination camps at Auschwitz-Birkenau. This 'Golgotha of the modern world', as he called it, is the most potent symbol of the slaughter of the Jewish and other peoples. As a young man, Wojtyla had a devotion to St John of the Cross, the great sixteenth-century Spanish mystic whose own life was characterised by much physical and spiritual suffering. So it was entirely in tune with John Paul's spirituality that he set out to die a Christian death in public.

The turning point seems to have come in mid-August 2004 during his painful trip to Lourdes. The US *National Catholic Reporter*'s Vatican correspondent, John Allen, who was there, calls it the pope's 'apotheosis', his transformation from supreme head of Catholicism to 'a living symbol of human suffering ... an icon of Christ on the cross' ('Word from Rome', 20 August, 2004). At Lourdes it was obvious that the pope was weak and struggling mightily with his frailty. Many of the 200 000 people present, who themselves were suffering, identified with him. Allen observed that during Mass

> He could be heard muttering 'Jesus and Mary' under his breath in Polish, and once mumbled 'help me' to no one in particular. Later John Paul seemed confused during the Eucharistic prayer, and had to be reminded to elevate the host at the consecration. At another point he muttered 'I have to finish', almost as if to will himself forward.

He was a sick man among the sick.

This is the key clue to the last eight months of his papacy and even to the period some time before that. Near the end, when he lost his voice, his appearances almost became a mime, the speechless communication of a dying man. In a way the final act was the most powerful of this whole dramatic papacy. From this point onward the most prominent person was his spokesman, Navarro-Valls. The Vatican no longer denied his illness. But more importantly, Wojtyla himself seemed not only to embrace physical suffering and the humiliation of dependence, but to model it as a way of living out a hope-filled and Christian process of dying. For the contemporary death-denying world this was a profoundly important message.

In an extraordinary coincidence, at the very time the pope was dying the case of the severely brain damaged woman, Terri Schiavo, was reaching its culmination in Florida. Ms Schiavo had been kept alive by an inserted feeding tube, and the courts had decided that the tube could be withdrawn and Ms Schiavo allowed to die through lack of nutrition. Every one of the major protagonists involved in this terrible struggle over the right to live and the right to die was Catholic and, although the weight of majority Catholic opinion, including an intervention by the Vatican, was supportive of Ms Schiavo's parents and the obligation to maintain the feeding tube, there is also no doubt that a case could be made from Catholic moral theology that this was using extraordinary means to keep the patient alive, and therefore that removal of the tube could be justified. In this context John Paul's own process of dying was oddly ambivalent. There is no doubt that given Wojtyla's theology of the absoluteness of human life, he would have opted to support maintenance of artificial feeding to keep Ms Schiavo alive, yet he himself ultimately died naturally, really never using machines or technology to maintain life. The parallel is not exact, of course, but there is an extraordinary coincidence between these two events. The particular poignancy of both their deaths was the public nature of their dying.

For the next seven and a half months after the Lourdes' trip, John Paul slowly moved towards death in full public gaze. Occasionally there was a lack of subtlety and what should have been private was public, but these were only minor lapses of taste. He was more and more dependent on the people surrounding him, especially Dziwisz and the other priest secretary, Mieczyslaw Mokrzycki. Most of the official public church matters were handled by Sandri. Harvey seemed invisible.

In early 2005 papal health scares occurred regularly. Two visits to the Gemelli Polyclinic, run by the Catholic Sacred Heart University of Milan, led ultimately to a tracheotomy being performed to assist the pope's breathing. From that point onwards he was a silent presence in the church. It was almost as though he resorted to mime to show what Christian dying meant. He remained a quiet witness to the Holy Week and Easter ceremonies in Rome, all celebrated by senior cardinals. The final collapse came on the Friday of Easter week, and with his vital functions gradually collapsing, he died peacefully at 9.37 p.m., Saturday 2 April 2005.

As well as several doctors and nurses, present with the pope when he died were his secretaries Dziwisz and Mokrzycki, his old and infirm longtime Polish friend, Cardinal Andrzej Deskur, who like Wojtyla was a priest of Crakow archdiocese, Archbishop Stansilaw Rylko, and the five Polish sisters who worked in the *appartamento*. These were the people who were now Wojtyla's family. After his death there was an extraordinary outpouring of grief right across the world, and not only from Catholics.

So where did all this leave Harvey, the Prefect of the Papal Household? He had one official task when the pope died that Saturday evening for which Dziwisz was not responsible. It was his job to inform the Camerlengo of the Holy Roman Church, Martinez Somalo, and the Dean of the College of Cardinals, Ratzinger, that John Paul II was dead. The Camerlengo, assisted by the Papal Master of Ceremonies, Marini, then verified the pope's death and passed on the news officially to the Cardinal Vicar of Rome, Cardinal Camillo Ruini, so that he could inform the priests and people of Rome, the pope's own diocese. Meanwhile the Cardinal Dean officially informed the rest of the college of cardinals, the ambassadors accredited to the Vatican, and heads of governments throughout the world. But they were all too late. The death of John Paul II was a major story for the media and the news flashed around the world in minutes and their official announcements confirmed a fact that everyone already knew. The Camerlengo locked and sealed the private apartment of the pope. Those who served the dead pope and resided in the *appartamento* were allowed to remain until after his burial. This was a sensible decision of Pope Wojtyla himself. He did not want to see his closest collaborators literally thrown onto the street, as papal secretaries have been in the recent past. Stanislaw Dziwisz's power was now at an end, and he was left alone to deal with his private grief.

So what are we to make of the last years of the John Paul papacy? Firstly, they show up the essential weakness in a papal structure that is modelled on absolutism. A weakened or even senile pope who is unable or unwilling to resign could confront the church with a massive constitutional conundrum. Under present rules, no one can sack the pope and the last incumbent to resign was Celestine V in 1294. As informed observers such as Giancarlo Zizola have already said, with modern medicine nowadays keeping people alive much longer, the possibility of an incapacitated pope is increasing and the problem could be disastrous if he suffered from senility or dementia. Secondly, these last years of the Wojtyla papacy reveal the way the church can be forced to mark time with important problems unaddressed as we await the demise of the pope. Everything goes into suspended animation and those trying to move the ministerial and theological agenda of the church along are stymied. Thirdly, there is no doubt that the late pope had slowly lost the ability to either control or even understand the issues confronting him. In other similar situations this could leave the way open for ambitious or scheming individuals or cliques to gain effective control of the papacy. Perhaps the church owes a real debt of gratitude to 'Pope Stan I Dziwisz'!

Finally, the long twilight of John Paul is a warning sign that the church needs to recover its original collegial and consultative structure and leave behind the absolutist, monarchical model. There is a real sense in which John Paul II may well be the last of the pre-modern popes. In other words, his understanding of his role as pope was that he was the final arbiter of everything in Catholicism. Also, assisted by modern communications, he dominated and stood astride the church as no other pope in history. Benedict XVI is an altogether more modest man. Though he will probably retain the doctrinal emphases of the Wojtyla papacy, he is already showing that he has a much more sophisticated understanding of the nature of the church. He has reached out to the Orthodox churches, such as the Russian and the Greek churches, to strengthen the bridges that have been built towards eventual unity with Rome through intercommunion. The Orthodox come to dialogue with Rome with a more decentralised, synodal church structure, and an altogether more constricted notion of the role of the pope. They see him at most as the heart of the communion rather than the dictator and dominator of the church. Certainly John Paul II also reached out to the Orthodox, but the very style of his papacy tended to negate his ecumenical efforts.

So let us now turn to the legacy of the late pope and assess his impact on world Catholicism.

2

THE IMPACT OF THE PAPAL TRAVELS

It was Senior Inspector Aida D. Fariscal's instinct that something might be wrong about an apartment fire in Manila that probably saved John Paul II's life during his visit to the Philippines in 1995. One of the few senior women in the male-dominated Manila police department, she was watch commander at Manila Police Station No. 9 late on the night of Friday, 6 January 1995. Just after 11 p.m. a report came in of a fire in flat 603, a front-facing, 6th-floor room in the nearby Dona Josefa apartment block at 711 President Quirino Boulevard, in the bohemian Malate district of Manila. This is not far north of Manila International Airport, and close to the intersection with Taft Avenue. Flat 603 was not luxurious, but it was well-kept and clean, and the short-term rents were reasonably cheap. This is an area frequented by middle-class Arabs and Middle Eastern business-men on 'rest and recreation' sojourns in the Philippines.

The young patrolman who followed up the call from the Dona Josefa security guard told Inspector Fariscal that the fire brigade had already put out the fire and left, and that it was caused by 'some Pakistanis playing with firecrackers'. But somehow her 'sixth sense' told her it did not add up; she was unconvinced and suspicious. So, taking the patrolman with her, she went around to check. She knew the pope would be staying at the Papal Nuncio's residence just around the corner from the Dona Josefa apart-ments at 2140 Taft Avenue several days later. In January 1995, security was an important issue for the Manila police.

When she arrived, the doorman and security guard told her that a fire had broken out in Flat 603 and that the two Arab occupants had tried to put it out themselves, and that when he arrived at the sixth floor they had attempted to prevent him from entering the apartment. They had left the building hurriedly just before the fire department arrived, pulling on their pants and saying that 'Everything is under control. It was just some fireworks that went off accidentally.' Inspector Fariscal was still curious; the smoke from the fire seemed particularly black and acrid, and the fireworks story seemed implausible. So, even though it was illegal to do so without a search warrant, she decided to inspect the apartment.

What she found was a bomb-maker's workshop. The fire had begun in the kitchen sink where, as it turned out, one of the Arabs had turned on the water which, when mixed with the residue of chemicals in the sink, started the fire. Fariscal noted four new hotplates still in their containers on the floor, bundles of cottonwool scattered everywhere, clear plastic containers of what turned out to be sulphuric, picric and nitric acid, as well as eight other explosive ingredients, circuit breakers, batteries, books in English and Arabic, blue, yellow, green and red loops of electrical wiring, a number of Casio digital watches, a soldering gun, four small pipe bombs, a tobacco pipe, and a laptop computer. In odd contrast there were several bibles, a crucifix, rosaries, a picture of the pope attached to a mirror, and maps of Metro Manila tracing the papal motorcade's route. On the answering machine there was a message from a tailor saying that he had completed the priest's soutane that had been ordered. This is the long black garment that priests often wear in public in Catholic countries. When Fariscal returned downstairs the security guard quietly pointed to a man on the footpath outside. 'That's one of them,' he whispered. The patrolman grabbed the suspect, who struggled free. He began to run, but tripped over and was quickly re-arrested. The other man from the apartment seemed to have disappeared.

As soon as Fariscal's report went in, senior investigators, the scientific squad, the FBI and the CIA from the US embassy, and other experts became involved in the investigation. The man they captured, a Pakistani named Abdul Hakim Murad, refused to talk, so intelligence officers subjected him to sixty-seven days of what in the Philippines they call 'TI'— 'tactical intelligence'—torture in plain English. They broke him in the end when they threatened to hand him over to Israeli Mossad.

As it turned out, Senior Inspector Fariscal had uncovered not just a plot to assassinate the pope but, in a chilling forewarning of the 9/11 attack on the World Trade Center, a plan to destroy eleven American commercial airliners over the Pacific by bombs planted under seats. As a result of the investigation, the US authorities were also eventually able to arrest the Kuwaiti chemical engineer, Razmi Ahmed Yousef, a man closely related to al Qaeda, who was primarily responsible for the first attack on the World Trade Center in 1993. He had slipped away from the apartment crime scene and disappeared from the Philippines, but was eventually detained in Pakistan some months later. Both men are now serving life sentences in the US for the 1993 attack on the World Trade Center.

The pope arrived in Manila four days after the capture of Murad. He remained there for five days, staying at the Nunciature. This last visit to the Philippines seems symbolic of one of the profound themes of the Wojtyla papacy. Single-handedly, he invented what we might call the 'peripatetic papacy'. There was a real sense in which he was no longer just the Bishop of Rome who exercised a primacy of jurisdiction over the church. He was now effectively the 'bishop of the world' and local bishops were increasingly popularly perceived as his local representatives. Not that this was ever spelled out in theory, of course, because it is theologically heretical. Bishops, like the pope, are successors of the apostles. But John Paul was never one to be buried inside the church. He wanted to take his convictions and beliefs about Christ and the meaning of life out into the world.

The Manila visit illustrates this. He was primarily there for the World Youth Day, which culminated with a Mass on 15 January 1995 attended by the biggest gathering of people in human history. Conservatively estimated at five million, and possibly up to seven million, the crowd was so dense that the popemobile could not be used, and John Paul had to be flown to the altar by helicopter. The night before, a million young people had gathered with him for a prayer vigil. These were massive assemblies, even by the standards of John Paul. If Yousef and Murad had managed to assassinate him in Manila it would have indeed been a coup for terrorism.

These youth days, held every two years, became very important in the John Paul papacy. They brought together young people from all over the world to meet the pope, pray, discuss issues of importance to them, attend Mass, and enjoy themselves. It was a chance for them to reconnect with Catholicism. And in Manila, Pope Wojtyla was in his element. He had charmingly engaged those at the prayer vigil by joking about his nickname as a young man, 'Lolek', and his title now as pope. Here he was truly himself, acting as a kind of teacher-catechist, relating to young people, talking to them about Christ and his message, and placing the demanding ideals of belief, fidelity, commitment to the church, premarital chastity and monogamous marriage before them. He was always very much at home with the young who seemed to energise him. For instance, when he visited Australia in 1986 he attended a Youth Rally in Sydney and at the end, during the final folksy hymn, he joined hands with the young people, swayed, danced and sang along with them, and embraced those standing closest to him.

But it was not just the youth who responded. Many people in both developed and developing countries found that attending the papal Masses renewed and deepened their faith and commitment to Catholicism. For many, worship with the pope was a genuine experience of connecting with the church. Here was a spiritual space where they could publicly reaffirm their identity with Catholicism. Of course, it didn't change their approach to what they considered their own moral, marital and sexual business. This is a battle that has already been lost among Catholics, especially in the developed west, not because these people are weak and uncommitted, nor because they have surrendered to what John Paul himself characterises as materialist 'consumerism'. It is simply because they have learned to form their own consciences and feel that the church has lost the plot on sexual ethics. The crisis about clerical sexual abuse of minors has simply reinforced this conviction.

The visit to the Philippines was not only to spend time with the young. While there Pope Wojtyla also wanted to make contact with the government of the People's Republic of China concerning the position of Catholics in the PRC. The then archbishop of Manila, Cardinal Jaime Sin, had already visited China several times in a private capacity and had made good contacts among the members of the government-sponsored Patriotic Catholic Association (PCA) which Rome had excommunicated in the 1950s. The Filipino cardinal felt that these people had really tried to do what they thought was possible and right under Communism, and they genuinely wanted to have closer contact with the Vatican. Their bishops were anxious to get Roman approval for their appointments. As a result, a group of priests, sisters and laity from the PCA were invited to the Manila gathering, and they attended and met the pope. Sin had also visited communities of underground Chinese Catholics who had suffered ferocious persecution for their faith and loyalty to Rome. The Vatican also wanted to try to alleviate their situation. What is interesting is that all the evidence shows that the underground church has grown enormously in numbers since the persecution began with the Communist takeover of China. But in

1995, and subsequently, the Beijing government showed no interest in developing a formal relationship with Rome. The major stumbling block was that the Vatican had diplomatic relations with Taiwan. In 2005 the Vatican was seriously considering severing the link with Taiwan.

In Manila, the pope also met with the Federation of Asian Bishops' Conferences, one of the most thoughtful and progressive groups of bishops in the world. With the exception of the Philippines, which is 86 per cent Catholic, the Asian bishops come from countries and cultures where Catholicism is a minority faith, and, rather than retreat inwards to a kind of sectarian ghetto, the Asian Catholic Bishops' Conference has reached outward ecumenically and they have worked hard at communicating with the other great religious traditions, especially Hinduism and Buddhism.

From Manila the pope travelled on to Port Moresby in Papua New Guinea for a brief visit. Here he beatified a local married catechist, Blessed Peter To Rot, who had been killed near Rabaul for his faith during the Japanese occupation in World War II. It was very much part of John Paul's approach to raise indigenous people to sainthood so that they could serve as models of fidelity for local Catholics.

From Port Moresby he flew on to Sydney for his second visit to Australia for another brief stopover and beatification, this time of Blessed Mary McKillop, the founder of the Sisters of Saint Joseph of the Sacred Heart, popularly known by Catholics throughout the country as the 'Brown Joeys'. John Paul spoke of Mary McKillop going out into the outback deserts to bring the gospel to country people. On the basis of this he talked about modern 'deserts', 'the wastelands of indifference and intolerance, the desolation of racism and contempt for other human beings, the barrenness of selfishness and unfaithfulness'. From Sydney, he went on to Sri Lanka where about 7 per cent of the population are Catholic, but where the church has considerable influence especially through education.

This was his last really long trip, involving more than ten days away from Rome. All up, throughout his papacy he made almost 100 trips outside of Italy and visited in excess of 130 nations. Even in Italy he made 140 trips outside of Rome. And he never forgot that his primary job was to be bishop of Rome. He made almost 730 visits to the city's parishes. There was no doubting his enormous pastoral commitment and prodigious personal energy.

From the pope's perspective, what was the purpose of these trips to countries across the world? John Paul said that they were 'pastoral visits' aimed at strengthening the faith of the local church. They were meant to unite it with the pope as the visible symbol of the unity of the universal church. He also saw himself as catechist and evangelist. His task was to get out and bring Christ's message to the world, which he believed was the only way in which the world could be saved from war and injustice, and peace and stability achieved. As a result, he never hesitated to intervene in world events. From his role in the downfall of the Soviet bloc, and especially the overthrow of Communism in Poland, to his unflinching and unequivocal opposition to the George W. Bush doctrine of pre-emptive warfare and especially the invasion of Iraq, Pope Wojtyla showed that he was a power to be reckoned with in world affairs. He overwhelmingly answered Stalin's sneering question 'How many divisions does the pope have?' by playing a major role in the overthrow of the very Soviet system Stalin had helped to establish. There is no doubt that he successfully used the papacy to influence world affairs considerably.

But it was not just the travel in itself that was significant; it was the way in which his peripateticism has actually brought to a head a new phenomenon in the church, an 'omnipresent papacy'—the perception that somehow the church and the pope are identical. The pope *is* the church. All other Catholics, including the bishops, are just camp followers. This is the problem that is always embedded in the concept of a 'great leader', a *Führer prinzip*: the institution that is led becomes so identified with the leader that the leadership and role of everyone else fades into insignificance. This is what happened with Pope Wojtyla. But unless this phenomenon of an omnipresent papacy is seen in a historical perspective it is difficult to realise how radical this approach is and what a departure it is from the mainstream tradition of the papacy. The omnipresent pope sums up some of the most important features and odd contradictions of the Wojtyla papacy.

There is a sense in which the comment that there is no one more dead than a dead pope is profoundly wrong when it comes to John Paul II. The average length of a papacy in church history is about six and a half years. A papacy which was the second longest in history inevitably has an impact, and this impact is especially significant when you are dealing with a man whom even so careful a scholar as the Cambridge Catholic historian Eamon Duffy has called a 'colossus'. He says that 'No pope for centuries has had so direct … an impact on human destinies, nor set so personal a mark on the church he serves—and governs' ('A giant among popes', *The Tablet*, 18 October 2003).

However, allowing for this, is John Paul single-handedly responsible for creating the omnipresent papacy? The answer is 'no'. Certainly he gave it an extraordinary boost, but it is actually the product of a development that has been going on for one hundred and fifty years.

It is a safe generalisation to say that throughout the first millennium of papal history the pope's real authority and power was largely confined to central Italy and to the area immediately around Rome, which was known as *Patrimonium Petri*, the Patrimony of Saint Peter. Even there the pope governed with the assistance of the Roman Synod which included the Roman clergy and bishops from the surrounding dioceses. Certainly Rome's primacy was recognised throughout the church. But papal 'primacy' in the first millennium meant that Rome was *primus inter pares*, 'first among equals' in the college of bishops, all of whom were seen as successors of the apostles. But while Rome's doctrinal orthodoxy was clearly recognised by the whole church, and its primacy honoured, this did not mean it could order local churches or bishops around, or that it had practical authority throughout the church. Bishops were appointed locally and needed approval from their metropolitan archbishop and their local peers, and often times from the local ruler. Rome really remained at most, a court of last resort.

After the much-needed reform of the papacy at the beginning of the twelfth century, the popes articulated and claimed a universal jurisdiction and pastorate over the whole church in Europe. More and more, their authority was expressed in legal terms and they claimed to have the *plenitudo potestatis*, the fullness of papal power. Some, indeed, such as Innocent III (1198–1216), one of the truly great popes, as well as several of his successors, even asserted a kind of papal overlordship of kings and emperors. One hundred years later, the mentally unstable Boniface VIII (1294–1303) took the meaning of *plenitudo potestatis* to its most absurd extreme. In the Bull *Unam Sanctam* (18 November 1302) he made an extraordinary claim: 'Consequently we declare, state, define and pronounce that it is altogether necessary to salvation for every human creature to be subject to the Roman Pontiff.' This ridiculous statement was not the word of a strong pope but of a weak one, and his successor was forced to take the papacy away from Rome into exile in Avignon, a papal dependency in southern France. However, no matter how extreme the claims of medieval popes, they simply did not have the wherewithal to project their claims outward. Distance, slow travelling times, the power of local metropolitan archbishops and emerging national monarchs, especially in France and England, all limited in practice the real power and authority of the popes. For instance, in England the first of several statutes of *Praemunire* (literally to fortify English law by forbidding appeals from the king's courts to Rome) was passed under Edward III in 1351, limiting the pope's right to interfere even in the clerical affairs of the kingdom.

By the beginning of the fifteenth century there was a Europe-wide schism in the church and there were three claimants to the papacy. The problem was only solved by a general council of the church held in the southern German city of Constance between 1414 and 1418. Given the extraordinary situation they faced, the bishops and theologians of the Council of Constance claimed superiority over the pope, and the theory of conciliarism gained widespread acceptance. For the next four centuries papal authority and influence in the church ebbed and flowed and, no matter what the pope claimed, there were always practical and theoretical limits on papal power. The popes still never really had the ability to project their power and influence outward because the infrastructure for fast travel and swift communications simply did not exist until the early nineteenth century.

The contemporary omnipresent papacy really began with Pius IX (1846–1878), the longest serving pope. He is the also the one who finally lost the Papal States to the mainly anti-clerical forces of Italian unification. The Papal States had straddled central Italy for eleven hundred years. Almost in contrast to the loss of secular power, it was during Pius IX's papacy that the ideology of neo-ultramontanism gained widespread acceptance in the church. The word is literally derived from the Latin *ultra montes* ('beyond the mountains'), and it refers specifically to the tendency of French Catholics to look across the Alps to Rome as the source of power and wisdom in the church. It stands in contrast to Gallicanism, an Erastian theory which saw the Catholic church in France as a state church essentially subject to the French monarchy.

Although ultramontanism was first articulated by Saint Robert Bellermine (1542–1621) and other theologians in the early seventeenth century, from the early nineteenth century onwards a kind of neo-ultramontanism gained increasing credibility throughout the Catholic world. It was spread among middle-class Catholics through the influence of popular newspapers, especially in France. In order to encourage it, Pius IX promoted pilgrimages to Rome and a personality cult soon developed around the pope. He was a populist in much the same sense as John Paul II. There was widespread sympathy for Pius IX in the Catholic world as he gradually lost more and more of the Papal States, with Rome finally capitulating in September 1870. At the same time the Roman curia was increasingly spreading its influence throughout the church. Rome's influence also spread as nuncios or ambassadors were appointed to the governments of all the European Catholic nations, and the power to appoint bishops was increasingly reserved to the Vatican. For virtually the whole of church history before the nineteenth century this power had been exercised locally, usually by the canons or senior priests of the diocese, and often since the medieval period by the king or government.

It was Pius IX who called the First Vatican Council (1869–70) which declared the doctrines of both papal infallibility and primacy. The real problem with Vatican I is the definition of papal primacy, not infallibility. Infallibility can only be exercised under severely limited circumstances. But primacy is a different matter. In Vatican I's definition

> the church is totally handed over to the pope. He exercises the 'absolute fullness' of power without any check other than the law of God and the defined teaching of the church—and, of course, the pope is the final interpreter of both! This definition leads straight to the view that the pope owns the church without any countervailing centres of authority to restore the balance of power. In this legalistic ecclesiology the pope equals the church, and the church equals the pope. (*Papal Power*, p. 57)

Centralised control of all aspects of church life increased from Vatican I onwards, enhanced by subsequent popes casting themselves in the self-imposed role of 'prisoner of the Vatican', thus eliciting sympathy from Catholics across the world as 'persecuted' by secularist, anti-clerical governments in Italy.

The papo-centric mystique reached its apogee in Pius XII (1939–58). The tall, ascetic-looking pope was seen as an almost 'divine' figure who literally pontificated on myriad topics. He also used the unrestricted power of the Holy Office, formerly the Roman Inquisition, and now the Congregation for the Doctrine of the Faith, to control theological or ecclesiastical dissent and suppress any view that did not reflect the contemporary Roman line. He was also quick to realise the importance of media and used it effectively.

But the election of John XXIII (1958–63), and to a lesser extent Paul VI (1963–78), signalled a return to a more humane, transparent and humble papacy. John and Paul were very different men with contrasting experiences, but they had similar backgrounds in the service of the Vatican Secretariat of State, John as a diplomat, Paul as a bureaucrat. Both were imaginative and were willing to take risks, and both were genuinely open with an understanding that they could actually learn something from secular culture and the world outside the church. Under their guidance the Second Vatican Council (1962–65) was brought to a successful conclusion, and the post-conciliar implementation process was completed under Paul VI. This pope also made a number of particularly good curial and episcopal appointments that stand in sharp contrast to some of the disastrous nominations of John Paul II.

However, looking back historically it can now be seen that Vatican II was not as far-sighted as first thought. In a way it was making up for lost time, dragging the Catholic church, part of it resisting vigorously, into the twentieth century, and attempting to correct the power imbalances created by neo-ultramontanism and the primacy and infallibility definitions of Vatican I. But it was also the product of a series of theological compromises. As a result, Vatican II could be and was quickly reinterpreted by many to suit their own theology, and by others to protect their power base. Because ordinary Catholics had been subdued for so long, Catholicism went through a 'wild' period in the decade following the council when some bad mistakes were made. This was also the time when Paul VI's birth control encyclical *Humanae vitae* (1968) was widely rejected by Catholics in the developed world and papal authority was seriously questioned. It is the period described by Peter Hebblethwaite as 'the runaway church' when many, especially conservative Catholics, felt themselves adrift. They longed to return things to the security of the past.

Into this historical context stepped Karol Jósef Wojtyla, a man with a mission to bring his vision of Catholicism to the church.

There was a widespread perception at the time of his election that he was 'progressive' in the western European and Anglo-American sense of that world. How wrong that perception was, even if it was completely understandable because he was non-Italian and he looked very different from the seemingly colourless Paul VI. Even those who put him forward to the other cardinals as an acceptable non-Italian *papabile* (a cardinal who is electable as pope) seem, at least to some extent, to have misread him. The ones who actually proposed his name were themselves anxious to maintain the ongoing pastoral renewal of the church: Cardinal Franz König, then archbishop of Vienna, and the Franciscan Cardinal Aloísio Lorscheider, then archbishop of Fortaleza, Brazil. It is clear that they presumed that he would generally take a more open approach to papal leadership. The mistake was that Wojtyla *sounded* and *looked* 'progressive'.

The fact is that the Wojtyla papacy has transcended the progressive–conservative divide, and his vision was neither progressive nor reactionary. It was idiosyncratic. It emerged from a totalitarian situation where Catholicism found itself engaged in a life-and-death conflict with the ideologies of Nazism and communism. Wojtyla came from a romantic, passionate, absolutist Catholicism, intimately linked to Polish culture; in fact Catholicism provided its underpinning and cement. In this context, western Catholic notions of dialogue with modernity, freedom of expression, individualism, and post-modern relativism seemed self-indulgent and dangerously deceptive. His background led him to a radical critique of all ideologies, including western individualist, consumerist, neo-rational capitalist ideologies. He stood for the values of life, the traditional family, opposition to contraception, abortion and euthanasia, and to what has been called 'a culture of death'. As Pope Wojtyla told the bishops of the Philippines in 1995:

> The culture and religious traditions of your people, who treasure life and freedom, should lead them to oppose measures directed against life: abortion, sterilization, and contraception. The church preaches the gospel of life, a fully positive view of human existence, contrary to the pessimism and selfishness of those who plot against the splendour of human sexuality and human life.

But from a western perspective with its recognition of the enormous population pressures in the Philippines and the terrible poverty which many Filipino women experience, his comments could seem only have been made by a man insensitive to the conditions of life for a poor woman in the Tondo slums or the tenement blocks surrounding the Smoky Mountain garbage tip in Manila.

The fact is John Paul knew all about these conditions of poverty, and throughout his papacy he denounced the systems that create poverty and injustice in the first place. But for him nothing was to be solved by compromising the moral truth that abortion, contraception and all other interferences with the transmission of life are evil. Truth is absolute and he was passionately committed to that absolute. For him reproductive health and birth control programs that were contraceptive in purpose were merely western ploys that maintained the unjust, neo-rationalist, capitalist economic system that created this level of poverty in the first place. Of course, the reality is much more complex, but it would be inaccurate to say that he was unaware of the demands that he was placing on women, especially in third-world countries. He felt that poverty and injustice must be continuously denounced, but that did not mean that you compromised what he felt God intended. In the end, in his kind of absolutist spirituality, everything was in God's hands.

This attitude to truth and belief in the absoluteness of life went right back to the early days of his priesthood, and psychologically, probably back to his childhood when he lost his mother, and then his brother, in tragic circumstances. In the 1950s at the Jagiellonian University in Cracow and a little later at the Catholic University of Lublin, and also as an auxiliary bishop, he had a deep interest in sexual ethics, unusual in clerics of his time, and he often talked frankly with young Polish university students and intellectuals about sexuality. As a youth chaplain he loved to go camping, hiking, skiing and kayaking with young adults where he had a chance to talk to them informally about the issues in which they were interested. No doubt sexuality was an important and regular topic. He was also in touch with a rather 'Catholic' form of European existentialist philosophy which gave him a rhetoric and way of speaking that lent a sense of contemporary awareness to his approach to morality. People felt that he seemed to be in touch with modernity.

But what everyone forgot was that he was first trained in the old, neo-scholastic school of Catholic thinking in 1947–48 at the Angelicum University in Rome under one of the most rigid of its exponents, the French Dominican, Reginald Garrigou-Lagrange. Neo-scholasticism refers to the revival in Catholic theology of the medieval approach characteristic of Saint Thomas Aquinas (c. 1225–74). But, as in most revivals, it was more 'neo' than a genuine return to original sources. The kind of neo-scholasticism taught by Garrigou-Lagrange in the late 1940s was a kind of official 'church philosophy' that was dominent in all seminaries. It had become very rigid, one might almost say 'cocksure' of the rightness of its conclusions. It did not take human experience, history and science into account at all. It was very theoretical and tended to work *a priori*, that is from theory applied to life rather than from human experience. Pre-established beliefs, said to be based on the natural law, determined life how life was to be lived rather than allowing a dynamic interaction between existence and faith.

This approach influenced Wojtyla deeply, and while his language had an existential feel, his conclusions were strictly in accord with traditional, natural law-based morality. In fact he returned to the natural law tradition near the end of his papacy. In February 2004 he told the CDF that he wanted them to study and highlight the centrality of natural law for all humankind. He said:

> The natural law, in itself accessible to every rational creature, indicates the prime and essential norms that regulate moral life. On the basis of this law a platform of shared values can be constructed, around which a dialogue with all people of good will, and more generally with secular society, can be developed.

Pope Wojtyla said he was concerned because what he called 'a crisis of metaphysics' (by which he referred to the unfortunate influence of post-modernism) had led to the fact that the

> truth written in the heart of every human being is no longer recognised in many sectors of opinion. This results on the one hand in the diffusion among believers of a morality with a fideistic character, and on the other, legislation comes to lack an objective reference so that it is based solely on social consensus, making it more difficult to reach a common ethical foundation for all humanity. (6 February 2004 to the Plenary Assembly of the CDF)

By 'fideism' he refers to the tendency of many modern people to relativise moral norms so that their morality is based on personal experience rather than on universal truths about humankind and the moral life.

John Paul was not a theoretical conservative, but he believed passionately that nature not nurture determined how we should act, and that nature was the product of God's design. This is why contraception is wrong; it contravenes nature. Men and women have specific roles that nature itself has predetermined. This cannot be changed without doing violence to our essential humanity. Like many European intellectuals of his generation, Wojtyla was also much given to discussing the role and 'particular vocation' of 'woman'. He seemed to be speaking about a kind of abstract ideal. But that is misleading because he certainly had several close women friends throughout his life, and two of them particularly influenced his views. Nevertheless, for John Paul 'woman' is biologically bound by her natural role to be either a virgin like Mary, or a married mother. All genuine personal relationships are governed by what he called 'the personalistic norm'. He set this up in opposition to what he called the 'utilitarian ethic' by which he meant a moral approach whereby we 'use' others. True personalism involves permanent committed relationship, that is marriage. All other forms of sexual expression are utilitarian, that is we use others for our own ends without commitment. Freedom of religion meant the liberty to explore divinely revealed truth, not the freedom to believe whatever seemed 'good for you'. In this context he considered the call for the ordination of women as merely an expression of a secular form of liberation.

In the Wojtyla lexicon the word 'utilitarian' was parallelled in practical life by the word 'consumerism'. To consume means to eat up, to destroy. For him it was a particularly pejorative word. You consumed not just the endless accumulation of unnecessary material goods—the 'live to shop' syndrome—but he also spoke of sex outside marriage as a form of consumerism, that is the 'eating-up' of another person without commitment. From an English-speaking perspective this is an unusual use of the word, to say the least.

The personalistic ethic was also important as a form of guidance for church–state relations. Vatican II made a decisive break with the past, especially in its *Declaration on Religious Liberty* (1965) when Catholicism broke away from the notion of the state supporting and enforcing an 'established church' to declare that coercion in religious choices be abandoned and people be free to choose their own religion. Certainly Pope Wojtyla believed in freedom and democracy, but he thought that liberty was essentially a freedom to do what the church and the natural law itself laid down as right. This is not quite the same as the emphasis that is found in the *Declaration on Religious Liberty*.

Ultimately Pope Wojtyla was deeply concerned that contemporary democracy had become intrinsically intertwined with what he called 'moral relativism' in its search for minimally divisive ethical positions. Perhaps the best clue to his view on this is his encyclical letter *Veritatis Splendor* ('The Splendour of Truth') of 6 August 1993. In it he argued that truth, freedom and democracy are all intrinsically interconnected. He admitted that insisting on 'difficult' issues can make the church unpopular.

> The church's teaching, and in particular her firmness in defending the universal and permanent validity of the precepts prohibiting intrinsically evil acts, is not infrequently seen as a sign of intolerable intransigence, particularly with regard to the enormously complex and conflict-filled situations present in the moral life of individuals and society today ... [But] the church's firmness in defending the universal

and unchanging moral norms is not demeaning at all. Because there can be no freedom apart from or in opposition to the truth, the categorical —unyielding and uncompromising—defence of the absolutely essential demands of man's personal dignity must be considered the way and the condition for the very existence of freedom. (paragraphs 95–6)

The English translation may be a little convoluted, reflecting the underlying Latin in which the letter was written, but this is pure and unadulterated Wojtyla: personal freedom and democratic political structures need the guidance of the unchangeable moral law which will determine what is acceptable civil law and what is not. Civil laws, such as freedom to choose euthanasia, contraception or abortion, actions which are contrary to the intrinsic moral makeup of humankind, are symptoms of ethical relativism and must be rejected. While he certainly did not want to return to the concept of an established Catholic state, John Paul believed that the pope and the bishops were the trustees and guardians of the universal moral law which applied to everybody, and he was determined to do his best to persuade even democratic regimes to conform to his conception of that universal moral law. This tendency to want to 'guide' democracy along the right path is also reflected in the attitudes of a number of bishops, especially in the United States, who say they will excommunicate politicians and candidates for political office who do not fully support the church on abortion and vote against abortion rights. Some bishops have even threatened lay Catholics who vote for pro-choice candidates.

Wojtyla also passionately believed in 'culture'. But again this word is easily misunderstood by English speakers. In western democracies we believe more in 'multi-culture' rather than in 'culture'. For us culture is expressed when we express ourselves, when we have the freedom to be ourselves, when we are liberated from constricting traditions and inhibiting restrictions. Our approach to culture is pluralist and post-modern. Taken to its extremes, everything goes. A casual meander through a modern art gallery tells you everything: contemporary western culture is subjectivist, irreverent, content-less, often disturbing and disconcerting, and seemingly without discipline, shape or form. Whereas for Wojtyla culture is 'a lively awareness that man does not create truth; rather, truth discloses itself to man when he perseveringly seeks it'. In other words, culture is the revelation of eternal truth in a particular form. The role of the artist is to penetrate into the real meaning of the truth of existence and give it expression. Culture is the inheritance of language, art, literature and music that is handed down by a particular group. It is also the tradition and faith that gives coherence and a sense of meaning to a civilisation. The church is right at the heart of culture, especially European culture. It is the ethos that holds the community together and gives it identity. But while it is communal, it is not to be identified with the state, and particularly not with any specific ideology, such as Communism. States, rulers, politics and ideologies come and go. It is culture that remains.

With an experience and views such as these it was inevitable that Pope John Paul had little sympathy with a western notion of a 'runaway church' which is caricatured as a community in which 'everything goes'. He believed that God had called him to the papacy at the particular moment of 1978 for a reason. And he remained pope under the protection of Mary, despite an attempted assassination and the ravages of Parkinson's disease. What he wanted to do was to restore to the church discipline, orthodoxy and a radical commitment to the truth of the gospel. In the way of a European-trained intellectual, formed in philosophy and abstract ethics rather than in the historical and social sciences, his approach seemed very dogmatic and abstract to Catholics and others from the pragmatic, English-speaking, Anglo-American, sociologically dominated world in which we live. He had very little appreciation of what it is like to survive as a believer in a pluralist society where Catholicism must take its place in a democratic marketplace of ideas and ways of life.

It is important that the Wojtyla philosophy is described because there are an increasing number of conservative Catholics and other thinkers in the Anglo-American world who think that John Paul's approach is the way for the church to go. They say that Catholicism must increasingly stand against the prevailing post-modern culture. They see Wojtyla's thought as a clear challenge not only to the contemporary culture, but also to the church and its bishops, clergy and laity. They feel that many Catholics are all too ready to compromise with what they see as pluralism, individualism, selfishness, 'pan-sexualism', fake liberalism and the post-modern relativisation of truth. However, because almost all these critics are themselves conservative politically as well as ecclesiastically, they tend on the whole to be supporters of neo-rationalist economics and governments like the Bush regime in the United States. Most of them are American, and as a result they are far less sympathetic to Pope Wojtyla's radical critique of the contemporary US doctrine of pre-emptive and unilateral militarism, as exemplified in the invasion of Iraq, and the capitalist addiction to consumerism. While neglecting his social teaching, they tend to see John Paul above all as the one who stood for the values of life, the traditional family, opposition to abortion, discipline in church life, and what they call 'a culture of death'. This is the kind of view put forward by the pope's 'semi-official' biographer, George Weigel in his book *Witness to Hope* (1999).

What these Catholic supporters of the Wojtyla vision tend to forget is that most of us in the west do not live in monolithic cultures. The United States, Canada, Australia and similar countries are essentially multicultural migrant communities in which we all work hard to make cultural pluralism succeed. Even in 'old' Europe, countries such as Germany, France, Italy and the United Kingdom are struggling with large numbers of immigrants, and have increasingly multicultural populations. The pristine notion of 'culture' which John Paul promoted now exists in very few places. Even Poland and Ireland, the last outposts of 'Catholic culture', are increasingly challenged by immigration and multiculturalism, as well as capitalism, consumerism and individualism. What John Paul never seemed to realise was that it is precisely consumerism and personal freedom that are attractive to the poor and the 'have nots'.

As a result, even his home country has not subsequently turned out quite the way he expected. After the fall of communism, Pope Wojtyla looked forward to seeing Poland as an ideal 'Catholic commonwealth' in which church, culture and state worked together, justly and equitably, for the social and spiritual good of the Polish people. But near the end of his life John Paul was deeply disappointed by what he conceived as the failure of democracy in Eastern Europe, especially in his beloved Poland. What he really wanted in his own country was an ecclesiastically guided and protected democracy whereby the church's teaching, especially in the areas of bioethics, euthanasia, sexuality, divorce and abortion, would become part of the nation's civil law. In other words, he did not believe in the total separation of church and state that we tend to have in the English-speaking democracies. What in fact happened was that there has been a secularist and consumerist backlash in Poland, and the enactment of what the pope considered 'permissive legislation' in ethically sensitive areas. As well, the Poles took to western-style consumerism, with its concomitant crassness, with a vengeance. Many people wanted the rough and tumble and give and take of the complex world of democratic politics because at least it gave them a voice. They were sick of authoritarian clergy and the church interfering in politics and issues of reproductive health. A kind of latent anti-clericalism started to surface in the 1990s. A clear sign of the failure of Wojtyla's vision of a Catholic commonwealth in his own country was the almost desperate fury of his condemnation of abortion, 'false freedom', adultery, the 'lies of the media', and the separation of politics from faith during his 1991 trip to Poland.

Right from the beginning of his papacy, John Paul strove to bring his particular vision of Catholicism to the church and to the world. This was certainly not a 'modern' vision of Catholicism in the usually understood meaning of that word. Essentially he was a 'Polish romantic' who saw the suffering churches of eastern Europe, persecuted by the Nazis and the Soviets, as a model for the world church of the future. Led by local bishops in close union with Rome, the Polish church's solidarity in the face of often vicious oppression was a genuine identification with the crucifixion and death of Jesus, and a preparation and paradigm for a radically committed world Catholicism of the future. Pope Wojtyla felt that unlike the secularised and consumerist masses, and compromised and worldly churches of Western Europe and the Anglo-American world, here was a pure church in waiting. That was why he was so bitterly disappointed when the Poles abandoned his vision. Nevertheless, he took the message of his own vision of the church to anyone who would listen wherever he went. To spread this message he travelled all over the world.

But the fact is that there is not a lot of evidence that the majority of Catholics, especially in the west, listened to him. People do not change their essential values as a result of a brief papal visit. Conservative Catholics are quick to condemn progressives as 'cafeteria Catholics' who pick and choose what they accept and reject in Catholicism and who fail to take the papal message seriously. But all the evidence is that this is exactly what conservatives themselves do. For nowadays everyone is selective about what they accept and reject from church authority. This is as it should be, for the pope does not exhaust the church.

When John Paul II died, Catholicism was left with a conundrum. What was his legacy to the church?

This is not an easy question to answer. What is clear is that the way different people see him depends very much on their point of view. For some, like his biographer, George Weigel, this papacy 'has been the most consequential since the sixteenth century Reformation'. He says that John Paul's determination 'to live without fear, to live beyond fear, so transparently evident in the life of Karol Wojtyla, changed innumerable individual lives. By doing so, John Paul changed the course of history' (*Witness to Hope*, p. 849). He was 'John Paul the Great'. However, while he was without doubt an important figure in the twentienth century, and clearly one of the more important popes since the sixteenth century, he certainly does not rank in terms of historical significance alongside Popes John XXIII (1958–63) who started the Second Vatican Council, or Paul III (1534–49) who, in order to respond to the challenge of Protestantism, launched the Council of Trent. Being pope for a long time does not necessarily make the incumbent historically significant. The ultimate norm of judgement is their contribution to the life of the church.

The fundamental problem in assessing the late pope's legacy is that the Wojtyla papacy was filled with contradictions. Committed to the liberation of Poland and the other countries under the heel of the Soviets, he was willing to use his papal and episcopal office in a most political manner. Yet he was the pope who told priest–politicians in the United States, Nicaragua, Papua New Guinea, Canada and elsewhere to get out of politics, even if their aim was social justice, the spreading of literacy, and the restoration of an ethical system of government. When they refused to do so, as in Nicaragua, he did not hesitate to have them expelled from the priesthood. The pope who wanted to liberate Eastern Europe was the same pope who was profoundly suspicious of the liberation of women in the west. He was also willing to apologise to everyone treated unjustly, offended or hurt by the church, except those who were the victims of his own papacy. This is the pope who said he was on the side of the poor and then destroyed liberation theology. By profession celibate and therefore presumably innocent about sexual matters, he wrote and talked extensively on the topic.

The reality was that Pope John Paul was a mass of contradictions. No one, of course, is consistent. We are all patchwork quilts of often conflicting opinions and emphases, which change and mutate as we get older. But among all the contradictions there were a couple of issues that were consistent throughout his papacy.

Firstly, he was an eastern European, born and bred, and it was the baggage of that culture that he brought with him to the papacy. He never really understood the western democratic tradition nor what it was to live as a committed Catholic in a pluralist society, let alone in a totally non-Christian society. Secondly, he was an absolutist: those who were not with him were against him. He was also convinced that God had called him to restore the church to the path of doctrinal, moral and pastoral righteousness after the silly trivialities and nonsense that had followed Vatican II. There was something messianic about his personality. He was the one appointed by God to bring not only Catholics but people generally back to the true human path. This is why he travelled to virtually every country in the world. They needed to hear the message he had to bring.

Yet there is a profound sense in which an omnipresent papacy creates a very disjunctive situation for the church. Two things happen immediately: the church becomes identified with the pope, and all other authority in the church is totally relativised. It is as though the pope exhausts the church and the rest of Catholicism is merely an addendum. As we saw, this was not all Wojtyla's doing. He simply brought a centralising movement that had begun in the 1840s to its apogee. He and his communications-minders simply used every opportunity to place the pope at centre-stage in every possible circumstance. As a result, never before in history has the church been so centralised. No one actually said this, of course, and if challenged they would deny it. But, in practice, especially during papal visits this is what actually happened. When the pope came to town, even senior cardinals and archbishops were relegated to the role of scarlet and purple-clad altar boys, mere acolytes in supporting roles.

This form of papo-centrism is a serious distortion of the church's long established tradition. The pope is not the managing director with the bishops merely branch managers. He is the president of the college of bishops, *primus inter pares* as the ancient and doctrinally accurate Latin tag has it—the 'first among equals'. The doctrinal distortion that the peripatetic pope introduced was that he never treated the bishops as equals, nor did they ever really assert their dignity, and as his papacy proceeded he increasingly appointed second- and third-rate people to the episcopacy, men who would never challenge his dominant hold on the church. As a result there is a real sense in which the Catholic church now faces a fundamental doctrinal crisis about the very nature of its own government.

3

A CRISIS OF LEADERSHIP

For the past forty years the church has been in crisis. Some people in the church such as the former Cardinal Joseph Ratzinger, now Pope Benedict XVI, say that the crisis has been created by dissenters from orthodox belief and a failure of Catholics generally to commit themselves to strict traditional moral norms. These people argue that there is a real danger that many Catholics, including priests and theologians, will become completely compromised by secularism and relativism. There is only one solution: absolute commitment to what they conceive as 'traditional' Catholicism especially as taught by the papacy. For these Catholics the crisis is one of orthodoxy.

However, for many thinking Catholics this does not really get to the heart of the matter. They feel that at the core of the problems facing the contemporary church is a complex of issues focusing on authority, leadership and the credibility of the hierarchy. It is said of Jesus in the gospels, even by his critics, that unlike the scribes 'his teaching made a deep impression on them because he spoke with authority' (Mark 1:21), by which they meant that there was a real integrity between who he was, what he said, and what he did. People realised that he was believable not because he used titles or was a member of the religious establishment, but because of the goodness and consistency that so patently flowed from his personality. Part of the reason why many people today distrust church leaders is because authority, in the sense in which the word is used of Jesus, is often confused by contemporary churchmen with the exercise of power, and leadership is construed as a kind of bullying of people and a stridency of utterance. This is most vividly illustrated by those American bishops who are threatening to excommunicate Catholic politicians who do not completely oppose abortion and vote consistently to strike it off the statute books. These bishops refuse to recognise the complexity of the issues confronting politicians in pluralist democracies and they reduce the question to a simplistic choice between good and evil, sin and virtue. So they try to bully politicians by stridently threatening them with ecclesiastical penalties.

This has happened because the types of bishops who understood what it is to live a full commitment to Catholic faith within the complexities of pluralist societies have been gradually replaced over the last twenty years by many who are seemingly incapable of offering any form of leadership to a church undergoing major change and to a society dominated by the relativities of post-modernism.

This is well illustrated by what happened since 1986 in the archdiocese of Vienna. This story involves one of the twentieth century's greatest and most long-lived cardinals, the man who was principally responsible for the election of Carol Wojtyla as pope. Cardinal Franz König, archbishop of Vienna from 1956 to 1986, was a pastorally sensitive bishop who engaged with secular society through his patience and courtesy to non-Christians and to those alienated from the church. He was a leader of the progressive majority of bishops at Vatican II and, after the council, came to symbolise reconciliation within the church and an openness to the world. Despite the role he played in the Wojtyla election, König adopted a very different approach to that of John Paul II. He stood for a broad, all-embracing vision of Catholicism.

This is also the story of one of the worst episcopal appointments made by Pope John Paul. Cardinal König was a month over 81, long past the mandatory retirement age of 75, when in September 1986, John Paul suddenly chose a completely obscure 67-year-old Benedictine monk, Hans Hermann Gröer, as König's successor as archbishop of Vienna. Two years later, the hardline, uncompromising traditionalist Gröer was made a cardinal. Almost exactly seven years later he resigned amid accusations of sexual abuse arising from his days as a priest. The circumstances of Gröer's appointment to Vienna were distressing, especially for König. As is customary for a senior archbishop, the cardinal had presented a *terna* to the papal nuncio, who would usually forward it to Rome. A *terna* is a list of three names, suggested by the local church, from which Rome would usually choose the first person on the list. At the top of König's list was

Bishop Helmut Krätzl, a deeply pastoral priest who had worked closely with the cardinal, and who had been appointed Vienna's auxiliary bishop in 1977. However, the cardinal was politely told by the nuncio that he had been instructed 'from up above'—in other words Rome—to add the name of Hans Hermann Gröer to the terna. The unknown Gröer was then rector of the Marian shrine of Our Lady of Roggendorf outside Vienna.

Gröer was born in Vienna in 1919, and had grown up partly in Czechoslovakia. Educated in the Vienna seminary, he was ordained priest for Vienna archdiocese in 1942. Always deeply conservative and apparently pious, he had spent most of his priestly ministry teaching in the minor seminary of Hollabrunn, a secondary boarding school for boys seriously thinking of joining the priesthood. He had also been involved in traditionalist pilgrimages to the shrine of Roggendorf. In 1974 he joined the Benedictine order at the Abbey of Güttweig, near Sankt Pölten. As a monk, he worked at the shrine of Roggendorf. So it was a complete surprise to everyone when Gröer was appointed archbishop of Vienna on 15 July 1986. This was a particularly humiliating appointment for the long-serving König, who had made it quite clear to Rome that he thought the priest-turned-monk was completely unsuitable and pastorally unprepared for ministry as archbishop in one of the most important Catholic dioceses in the church.

The background to this extraordinary appointment seems to have been that Gröer's name had been put forward in Rome by an Austrian priest who had worked for years in the Roman curia, Cardinal Alfons Maria Stickler, the then Prefect of the Vatican Library. A legalistic reactionary, Stickler did not approve of König's and Krätzl's pastoral approach in Vienna, and he was particularly critical of their policies of openness and dialogue with those outside the church. He felt this was leading to wide-spread loss of faith among Catholics in the Austrian capital. This was an extraordinary judgement for someone who had not lived in Vienna since 1937.

Pope Wojtyla himself also probably played a considerable role in the humiliation of König. It was a particularly nasty action because they had known each other for many years. König was the first senior western European churchman to go into the Soviet bloc in the late 1950s to try to support Catholics there. He first met Wojtyla when he was auxiliary bishop of Cracow, and König had done much to help him when he became arch-bishop. Wojtyla normally stayed with him in Vienna on his many visits to Rome. They were certainly on friendly terms. When the opportunity came after the death of John Paul I in September 1978 to elect a non-Italian, it was König who canvassed votes among the other cardinals for Wojtyla, although he admitted in a 1999 interview with the *National Catholic Reporter*'s John Allen that, at the time, the cardinals really had no idea which way the John Paul II papacy might go. 'We did not really did not know what we had done,' he told Allen.

Given this background, the appointment of Gröer over the head of König was particularly inappropriate. It turned out to be a complete disaster. Perhaps John Paul wanted him because Gröer had a strong devotion to the Virgin Mary that parallelled the pope's own.

But Gröer was not the only bad episcopal appointment made recently in Austria. In the early 1980s a perception developed in Rome that the Austrian bishops were 'out of control' and that König was largely responsible for this. In fact most of the Austrian bishops at the time were pastorally and theologically moderate. The only real progressive among them was Bishop Reinhold Stecher of Innsbruck. To bring the episcopate to heel, a series of new appointments of bishops were made by the Vatican, completely ignoring local recommendations. Three of the new appointees stand out as particularly inappropriate: Klaus Küng, the local head of Opus Dei (and no relation of the world-famous Catholic theologian, Hans Küng), was made bishop of Feldkirch near the Swiss border in northwestern Austria in January 1989. At the same time, Georg Eder, a priest with a reputation for publicly expressing extreme views, was made archbishop of Salzburg over the strong protests of the cathedral chapter which was made up of all the senior priests of the archdiocese. Kurt Krenn, an arch-conservative extremist, was made auxiliary bishop of Vienna in 1987, and in 1991 he was appointed bishop of Sankt Pölten. Krenn was eventually forced by the Vatican to resign in disgrace in 2004, after a series of sexual scandals in the seminary he had established to train so-called 'orthodox' priests.

This was not the first time the Vatican had changed the whole approach of a small national bench of bishops. The same change of episcopal ethos had been achieved in the Netherlands with seven dioceses in the 1970s, although the new Roman-oriented conservative bishops had done nothing except create polarisation. There, a church that had once been flourishing and which had contributed an enormous number of foreign missionaries to Catholicism was left frustrated and the number of practising Catholics decimated. So the Vatican already knew that in smaller countries like

Austria, with only nine dioceses, a change in the attitude of the episcopal bench was easy to achieve. What Rome never considered was the pastoral cost to local Catholics. Submission to the latest papal or Vatican decree, rather than care and sensitivity to local spiritual needs, was what counted in Rome.

After his appointment, Gröer's authoritarian and conservative approach alienated many in Vienna Catholicism. As president of the Austrian Bishops' Conference he did nothing to heal the deep rifts that now divided the bishops. However, it seemed that relief was in sight when he approached the mandatory retirement age for diocesan bishops in early 1995. But just before he submitted his resignation, a sexual abuse scandal involving him broke out. The case rocked Austria, and became headline news across the world. In the respected weekly magazine *Profil* accusations were made that Gröer had sexually abused several underage boys in the minor seminary at Hollabrunn some twenty years before. One went public, but the rest did not want their names mentioned because they were still in church employment and feared for their jobs. Eventually more than thirteen claimed that they had been his victims. The police never brought charges against Gröer: there was a legal statute of limitations in Austria on such accusations. Gröer's response to all of this was silence and evasion of the issue. Rome thought it had a way out by accepting the resignation he had tendered because he had reached 75, although John Paul was profoundly annoyed about the public attacks on Gröer, making the astonishing comment that Christ had also been confronted 'with unjust accusations' like the Vienna cardinal. To many people in Austria it seemed as if the pope was condoning him and that the curia and the bishops were going to sweep the issue under the carpet. And at first, this is what actually happened.

Again passing over Krätzl, Rome eventually replaced Gröer in September 1995 with a 51-year-old Dominican, Christoph Schönborn, who was already an auxiliary bishop in Vienna. Trained as a professional theologian, he had worked in Ratzinger's CDF before being appointed to edit *The Catechism of the Catholic Church* in 1987. For much of the latter part of the Wojtyla papacy many saw Schönborn as a possible papal successor to John Paul.

Gröer, still refusing to respond to the abuse claims, stayed on for another term as president of the Bishops' Conference after his retirement as archbishop. Because they claimed that he was innocent, the conservative Austrian bishops were able to force through his re-election. It seemed that only the older, more progressive bishops were taking the accusations seriously. The whole affair and the response of Rome created absolute outrage in Austria. It led to the formation of the 'We Are Church' movement in Easter 1995, followed by the 'International Movement We Are Church' (IMWAC) in November 1996 as the movement spread across Europe. It also led to the 'Petition of the People of the Church', a collection of a million and a half signatures in Austria and Germany calling for change and reform in Catholicism and free election of bishops by the church community. This petition spread to France, Italy, Belgium, the Netherlands, the United Kingdom and the United States. A 'Dialogue for Austria' was set up in 1998 which discussed issues such as married priests, a more democratic way of electing bishops, and more lay participation in church decision-making. If nothing else, the Gröer affair had energised many people, at least in the short term. Sadly, on the negative side, it had also led to large numbers of Austrian Catholics leaving the church by cancelling their civil registration as Catholics. Some estimates have placed these numbers as high as forty-thousand a year in the mid-1990s

The whole affair blew up again in 1997–98 when it was discovered that Gröer, with the approval of the pope, had been quietly appointed prior of a Benedictine Abbey in Lower Austria. That discovery was quickly followed by a entirely new round of sexual abuse claims surrounding the retired cardinal. What emerged was that when he joined the Benedictine monks at Güttweig in 1974 Gröer had taken with him a group of young male 'disciples', all apparently over the age of consent. Some of these men, now monks, claimed that they had been molested by Gröer, but that they were not under age. Some of the stories they told about what had happened to them pointed to the fact that Gröer was profoundly disturbed and sexually perverse. Even Archbishop Eder in Salzburg was horrified.

Rome was at last reluctantly forced to act. They appointed Abbot Marcel Rooney, the Abbot-General of the Benedictines, to investigate. His report was never published, but the Austrian bishops knew they also had to confront the Gröer scandal. Archbishop Schönborn, Bishop Johann Weber of Graz, now president of the Bishops' Conference, Bishop Egon Kapellari of Gurk (Klagenfurt), and even Eder of Salzburg, made a statement that 'to the best of their knowledge' Gröer was guilty of sexual abuse as the groups of monks and laymen claimed. The nearest thing to an apology that they could get out of Gröer was this comment: 'In the past three years there have been many often incorrect statements concerning me. I ask God and the people for forgiveness if I have brought guilt upon myself.' This was hardly eating humble pie, but it was all that Austrian Catholics were ever to hear. The disgraced cardinal died in April 2003.

Gröer was just the worst of a number of very bad episcopal appointments made by Pope Wojtyla. Most of these disastrous appointments were made in an attempt to replace moderately progressive bishops with more hardline priests who were acceptable to Rome. What is significant is that no account was taken of the needs of the diocese, and the consequence was often that many of these bishops showed little or no pastoral sensitivity to their priests and people. They were too busy looking over their shoulders making sure they were pleasing the Vatican. A number of them were literally sent from 'head office' in Rome. Several former long-term Vatican bureaucrats with little or no pastoral experience, such as Cardinals Edward Egan and Justin Rigali returned to the US, eventually to prestigious dioceses like New York and Philadelphia. Rigali was archbishop of Saint Louis before he went to Philadelphia in 2003. In late 2003 he was replaced in St Louis by the very conservative archbishop Raymond Burke. Burke is one of those who has demanded that Catholic politicians and candidates for public office that do not publicly and openly oppose abortion be denied communion. This created a profoundly fraught and difficult issue to deal with, especially for more socially progressive Catholics.

Another example of a disastrous appointment by Pope Wojtyla was in the Swiss diocese of Chur, which geographically covered all of the Graubünden (eastern Switzerland), the central Swiss cantons, and the city of Zurich. Until 1997 it also included the independent tax haven, the Principality of Liechtenstein. In this case as problems with the bishop's behaviour became more obvious and public, the Vatican tried to resolve the issue by making half-baked compromises. But they constantly refused to recognise that they made a bad mistake in the first place by choosing the wrong man.

In March 1988, John Paul overruled the now very rare right still held by the cathedral chapter of Chur to elect its own bishop from a *terna* already approved by Rome, to impose on the diocese an inexperienced 39-year-old priest, Wolfgang Haas, as coadjutor bishop with right of succession. In May 1990, at the age of 41, he succeeded to the diocese when the previous bishop reached retiring age. Local Catholics were so angry that, for his installation, Haas had to enter the cathedral through a side door because people were lying on the ground outside the front door. As a result of this appointment, everyone in the diocese became immured in seven years of vitriolic dispute with a rigid bishop without any pastoral sensitivity. The head of the council of priests said bluntly in 1997: 'We have a madman at the head of the diocese. And he's wrecking it.' Haas brought far-right-wing groups into parishes and the seminary, and antagonised the vast majority of Catholics to such an extent that the auxiliary bishop, Paul Vollmar, said that 'No new beginning is possibly until we have a change in bishop'. His comments were later supported by the Swiss Bishops' Conference. Eventually the Swiss government asked the Vatican to intervene, but throughout this whole dispute Rome tried to prop up Haas, and then find inappropriate compromises to save face for appointing so incompetent a person in the first place.

In the end, the problem was solved in December 1997 when the scandal was compounded. A new bishop, Bishop Amédée Grab from Lausanne, was appointed to Chur and peace eventually returned there. But Haas, at the still-young age of 49, was promoted to archbishop and, after 1500 years as part of Chur diocese, Verduz, the capital of Liechtenstein, was suddenly split off by the Vatican and made into an archbishopric covering the tiny principality. This led to deep divisions being created in Liechtenstein. The local prince, Hans-Adam II, accepted Haas's appointment, but the democratically elected government did not. A letter signed by 8000 of the 25 000 Catholics of Liechtenstein wanted Haas to remain in Switzerland. A Catholic reform group, 'Union for an Open Church', was soon set up in Liechtenstein along the lines of 'International We Are Church' with which it quickly became associated. Because the Catholic church is the state church, it has a quasi-democratic system of government which Haas vigorously opposed.

These are just some of the worst and most divisive appointments made by Pope Wojtyla to the episcopate. One might justifiably argue that a few poor decisions are inevitable in a church as large as Catholicism during such a long papacy. After all, the argument goes, the vast majority of the world's current bishops were appointed during the John Paul period, and most of these would certainly pass muster. So what about the good bishops he has appointed?

Certainly, early in the John Paul papacy some very good men were promoted to bishop. In 1979 for instance the Jesuit biblical scholar Carlo Maria Martini was taken from the rectorship of the Gregorian University in Rome and appointed to the archdiocese of Milan by John Paul and made a cardinal in 1983. He became one of the great Italian bishops of the century, pastorally sensitive, and as a great preacher and popular writer he drew many people to the church. Although he was appointed archbishop of

Cincinnati in the time of Pope Paul VI, one of the greatest of American church leaders of the last five decades, Cardinal Joseph Bernardin, was also an early appointment of the Wojtyla papacy to the important archdiocese of Chicago. Even some of the more conservative nominations of John Paul, such as Cardinal John O'Connor in New York and Cardinal Thomas Winning in Glasgow, turned out to be men of pastoral compassion who certainly earned the respect of their priests and people. So without doubt there have been good episcopal appointments by John Paul. A number of the Australian bishops are examples of this, such as Bishops Michael Malone of Maitland-Newcastle, Brian Heenan of Rockhampton and Patrick Power, the Auxiliary of Canberra-Goulburn. Cardinal Keith O'Brien of Saint Andrews and Edinburgh is another example.

But the problem is that Gröer and Haas were by no means the only bad appointments made during the latter part of the Wojtyla papacy. There have there been a number of other bishops appointed in the last decade who, like Gröer, have been credibly accused of sexual molestation of minors before they were appointed bishops, and were subsequently forced to resign. In the United States, for instance, one diocese, that of Palm Beach, Florida, had two successive bishops accused of abuse in the period 1998 to 2002. Both were forced to resign. The bishop of Springfield, Massachusetts, also had to resign over sexual abuse allegations in 2004. There have also been a considerable number of hardline, ideologically driven bishops appointed whose approach to pastoral care in their dioceses has been very divisive. But the biggest problem was the appointment of a large number of mediocre bishops who lacked any real leadership skill or genuine pastoral sensitivity. It is not a bishop's theological stance that is really important, but much more their concern to act as sensitive and thoughtful spiritual leaders in their dioceses.

Part of the reason for the election of mediocrities was that many priests with leadership qualities who would have naturally become bishops left the priestly ministry for marriage and other careers. But more important was that the general intellectual, pastoral and leadership ability of the priests appointed to the episcopate fell considerably. The core reason for this was that the process of selection under John Paul has tended to exclude priests of independent mind, leadership skills and creative pastoral ability. During the latter part of the Wojtyla papacy, no one who had spoken out on contentious church issues or publicly disagreed with the official line from Rome had a hope of being appointed bishop. As a result, many national bishops' conferences have an increasing number of 'yes men', or perhaps worse, ambitious priests for whom a promotion to the episcopate has been a key aim in life.

It is not generally known that Rome only gained complete control of the appointment of bishops in the western Roman church in the mid-to-late nineteenth century as part of the centralising tendency rampant at the time. In the early church, for the first four centuries bishops were chosen freely by all the members of the church community by direct election. This was because the community was small and everyone knew each other.

As soon as the church became part of official processes of the late Roman Empire in the early fourth century episcopal elections, including those of the bishop of Rome, became much bigger affairs involving many more people. As a result, episcopal elections were sometimes fraught affairs, with factions, politics, and even hired thugs trying to force people to vote for particular candidates. So, gradually, the actual episcopal election was entrusted to the local clergy, with the people approving, and the other nearby bishops and the metropolitan archbishop accepting and ordaining the chosen man. It did not always work out perfectly, but nevertheless the church of the first millennium firmly believed the traditional theological doctrine that *Qui praesidet super omnes ab omnibus eligatur*—'Whoever presides over all must be chosen by all'. In other words, the church of the first seven or eight centuries got their bishops by a process that was basically democratic. Rome sometimes became involved when there were disputes that could not be solved at the regional level. Later in the medieval and post-Reformation periods, the influence of emperors, kings and civil rulers became very important in the nomination and selection of bishops, but the idea of election by at least the senior priests of the diocese survived right through until the present day. In some dioceses (Chur is an example) in Switzerland and Austria the canons of the cathedral, that is the senior priests, can choose a candidate from a *terna* already approved by Rome. The *terna* will have originated in the diocese itself. Still today Eastern rite churches in union with Rome, such as the Melkite (Syria and Lebanon), Chaldean (Iraq), or Ukrainian churches, usually elect their bishops at synods with the pope afterwards approving. But in the vast majority of dioceses in the present-day church, new bishops are appointed directly by Rome.

There are real problems in the way a *terna* is drawn up and submitted. What happens is that most of the time the bishops of a particular province (for example, in Australia, the bishops of New South Wales or Queensland) discuss and then recommend the names of priests they think might be suitable for the episcopate. These names are forwarded to the papal nuncio who then 'vets' these men thoroughly. This is done through secret consultations with about twenty or so carefully chosen individuals, mainly bishops and other priests, and some times lay people, who are thought to know the priest involved. They are usually sent a set-piece questionnaire. They are sworn to secrecy, and asked about the priest's moral, spiritual, priestly and intellectual qualities, and their ability to work with others in a 'fatherly spirit'. Some of those consulted might actually dislike or be quietly biased against the person on whom they are commenting. In other cases they might be friends who are blind to the proposed candidate's limitations and faults. Thus the question of who is consulted is a key one, but since it is all done in secret no one knows who these people are or what they said. As a result the Catholic community is unable to judge the assessors' own biases and blind spots. This is the first indication that the church needs a much more open and transparent process. Catholicism could learn much from the other Christian churches who elect their bishops and leaders in open synodal gatherings.

Most important, from Rome's perspective, is that the nuncio follows a set of norms (which were only clearly articulated in the John Paul papacy) and tries to find out about the individual's attitude to 'the priestly ordination of women, the sacrament of matrimony ... [and his views] ... on sexual ethics and on social justice', as well as his 'loyalty and docility to the Holy Father, the Apostolic See, and the hierarchy; [and] esteem for and acceptance of priestly celibacy' (quoted in Thomas J. Reese, *A Flock of Shepherds*, p. 6). The investigations will also be looking for any moral flaws in the priest's character. Has he been or is he presently involved in a sexual liaison, or is he a gambler, or an alcoholic? Above all, the nuncio will be trying to ascertain whether the priest is a 'party man' and 'orthodox'. The key question is, does he follow the Roman line on all the key theological and moral issues that the Vatican and the pope thinks are important? The nuncio must make sure that the priest is absolutely loyal and docile to Rome, and that he has never been heard contradicting any of the pope's teachings, even if these are not infallibly defined. Any dissention would immediately exclude him. Thus, unless someone somehow slips through the net, its only conformist 'yes men' utterly loyal to Rome rather than to their dioceses who are appointed. This is the second reason why the church needs a more open process.

In other words, all troublemakers, or those with their own opinions, or 'spunky' priests, or those who have an ability to articulate the concerns of contemporary Catholics, or anyone publicly critical of the pope or the Vatican, are simply eliminated right from the beginning. Out of this process the nuncio further 'refines' the *terna* and draws up an accompanying dossier describing each candidate. All this investigation is usually going on without the knowledge or permission of the person being investigated. The nuncio's *terna* and dossier is then sent to the Congregation of Bishops in Rome, where a whole new process of vetting occurs. A staff member in this Vatican department checks the whole thing again, and also double checks with other curial departments to make sure they also have nothing unfavourable on their records about the candidates. Moving slowly through this process of bureaucratic checking, eventually three names emerge that are suggested to the pope. Trusting the process, he will usually, but not always, choose the name on the top of the list to be appointed bishop. Of course, from about 2002 onwards as the pope's health declined, the power of Cardinal Re and the Congregation of Bishops increased. Given his weakness, John Paul simply had to trust Re's recommendations.

Rome does not have to follow its own process. This is most likely to happen when the Vatican is determined to bring an episcopate to heel because it is considered too 'progressive' or 'democratic'. The Vatican then intervenes directly to appoint its own man, usually to an important diocese. After that it largely tends to trust this man's recommendations on who should become bishops. This is what most probably happened when Cardinal George Pell was first appointed archbishop of Melbourne in 1996. It was clear that by then Rome was concerned about what was happening in Australia, mainly as a result of a campaign of complaints to specifically targeted Roman prelates by a tiny minority of reactionary lay Catholics, possibly quietly encouraged by a couple of the bishops. These laity constantly complained about the Australian bishops being 'too easy going'. They told Rome that the church generally, and some of the priests particularly, were 'out of control'. This assessment of the Australian church was believed in Rome. What subsequently became clear was that after his appointment as archbishop, Pell was increasingly influential in the selection of many of the bishops. Something similar had happened in the United States, although no one archbishop there was the dominant influence.

Pope Wojtyla did not invent the process to select bishops. It had evolved throughout the late nineteenth and twentieth centuries, but it was used during his papacy to make sure that only those who followed his line were chosen. This process led to the appointment of an increasing number of priests who have made sure that they always obeyed Rome, and who have not stood out or made waves. Some commentators, such as the American priest–sociologist Father Andrew Greeley, maintained that in the US the Vatican has largely appointed 'mean-spirited careerists—inept, incompetent, insensitive bureaucrats, who are utterly indifferent to their clergy and laity.' I heard a slightly kinder but equally devastating comment about the US bishops in 2003 from a well-informed Catholic woman who had just attended the US Bishops' Conference as a lay observer. She told me that as she looked at the bishops as a group she was struck by the fact that most of them were 'slovenly, unenthusiastic, joyless, grey and dull'. This also describes the bishops of most western countries. My friend contrasted the majority with a small minority of truly pastoral bishops, one of whom she described as 'beatifically happy and saintly'. Significantly, this particular man was appointed by Paul VI.

What is striking about the personality of some bishops is a significant lack of passion about faith and spirituality. Also they seem to lack any deep desire to communicate Christ's message. Some of them seem unsophisticated morally, judging things in absolute terms where everything is seen in terms of black or white, right or wrong. The reality is that many of those appointed in the later Wojtyla papacy were really institutional men of very limited ability who would be good in second or third tiers of administration, but who were not really capable of creative leadership in any type of organisation, let alone one whose essential task is sensitive pastoral care and moral and spiritual guidance.

This not to say that all the bishops appointed by John Paul are like this. Many of them are good, spiritual men, concerned about their people and dioceses, but they feel caught in a terrible bind between Rome on the one hand, and their own pastoral inclinations and sense of responsibility to the local church on the other. But most are simply not strong enough to make the kind of stand that is needed by telling Rome where their real loyalties lie. Thomas J. Reese correctly sums up the consequences of this type of process of appointment. 'By stressing fidelity to the pope over sensitivity to local concerns, the Vatican's choices of bishops have in many cases alienated the local church from Rome rather than fostered unity … Under the current system the pope is getting bishops who support his policies, but he is not getting bishops capable of winning over their people' (*Inside the Vatican*, pp. 241–2). In fact, if anything, most Catholics simply find their bishops completely irrelevant to their spiritual lives.

For any bishop to make a stand under John Paul II required real courage. Yet the traditional theology of the church is completely on the side of those bishops who stand up for what they believe. As bishops they, too, are successors of the apostles, equal members of the college of bishops and, as John Paul himself said in the encyclical letter *Ut Unum Sint* (1995) they are just as much 'vicars and ambassadors of Christ' as he is. While their primary pastoral and spiritual responsibility is to their own dioceses they also have a responsibility to share in the government of the universal church. Despite the ancient and traditional doctrine that all bishops are equal to each other, during the Wojtyla papacy the bishops were effectively reduced to impotence. When they disagreed with their local bishops, re-actionaries, who represent only a tiny percentage of Catholics, simply went over the bishops' heads to Rome and there they found they were taken very seriously. Only very strong bishops had the strength to stand up to this type of treatment.

It is interesting to compare what is happening in the church with the crisis of leadership that many western democracies are also facing. Most national and world leaders today reflect the same triumph of mediocrity over conviction and substance. Our democratic leaders mouth clichés but ultimately stand for nothing except meaningless economic dogmas. Perhaps the dearth of inspirational leadership in the world generally is why Pope Wojtyla stood out so much. He at least had the courage of his convictions and stood firmly for what he believed Catholicism represented.

But while many Catholics respected his views on world peace, justice, the need for equity in relations between the developed and developing world, and even on environmental issues, they had real problems with his moral, doctrinal, reproductive and intra-mural church stances. As Catholics became more and more disillusioned with the approach taken by John Paul, they had no where else to turn for leadership because most of the bishops were papal 'yes men'. There is a common Catholic joke that when the bishop lies prostrate on the floor during his episcopal ordination while the choir sings the litany of the saints, his consecrators are actually removing his backbone. It is tempting to think that, at least in some cases, they are also removing his brain. Given that they had very little sensible episcopal guidance, many Catholics have ended up with a profound sense of a rudderless church lacking any form of credible leadership, so they have simply withdrawn and sought their spiritual guidance elsewhere. A more inclusive papacy may have prevented this level of alienation.

The flip side of mediocre local leadership is that the power, influence and prestige of the central leadership is enhanced considerably. If there are no bishops at a national level of the calibre of Cardinals König, Martini or Bernardin, or local bishops with real stature in the community, people inevitably look elsewhere for leadership. And here I stress that confront-ational episcopal behaviour should not be confused with Christian leader-ship. Some bishops apparently think that righteousness and confrontation go together. These are the kinds of bishops, like Cardinal George Pell of Sydney, who present a hard-edged, boots-and-all image of Catholicism. Pell says that 'Catholics need a style a mite more confrontational and cer-tainly much less conciliatory towards secular values. The cross is a sign of contradiction.' It is much more a sign of redemption, of the vulnerability of God, of a man whose extended and crucified arms reach outward in a sign of welcome and embrace.

The dominance of the papacy was vividly illustrated when Pope Wojtyla visited any country. He was the complete focus of attention. The local bishops simply faded into insignificance. The tragedy is that this is a complete distortion of the traditional nature of leadership in the church. Bishops are successors of the apostles and they represent Christ in their dioceses. In his own diocese the bishop should be a more significant person than the pope. Meeting in synod and local conferences, bishops have always traditionally had power to pass laws for and interpret the faith in their own local areas. In an ecumenical council they defined the faith and legislated for the whole church. The idea of a synod or bishops' conference is historically at least 1500 years older than the Roman curia as at present constituted. In the first millennium it was bishops meeting together in synod and ecumenical council who decided what the church believed. Certainly, especially in the west, there was usually some reference to the see of Rome in disputed matters. But the original structure of the church was synodal and conciliar where bishops, representing their local churches and regions, debated and discussed all the important issues that affected the church, from merely disciplinary matters such as the behaviour of the clergy, to absolutely central doctrinal issues like the nature of the personality of Christ and the Trinitarian Godhead. In the first millennium the bishop of Rome participated as *primus inter pares*, first among equals, not as a kind of solo, Delphic oracle, handing down infallible truths from above. While the pope or his representative sometimes presided at conciliar gatherings, they often did not. In other words, there are many precedents from church history to justify a shift away from a highly centralised papacy to a much more decentralised model of church where decisions are much more taken at a local level.

Vatican II attempted to restore this more synodal approach to church government. But this was, in both theoretical and practical terms, stamped out during the Wojtyla papacy. Three things contributed to this: firstly, the way in which John Paul cast himself in the role of 'world bishop'. Wherever he went it was the pope alone that mattered; everyone else was an acolyte. What he said, thought and did was determinative. The bishops and other local church leadership faded into insignificance. Secondly, the sheer weight of mediocrity among those appointed in the John Paul papacy has created an ongoing problem. In 1997 in *Papal Power* (pp. 197–218) I suggested that a general council of the bishops might be a way forward for the church in the near future. But I would question that now. At present there are so many bishops totally lacking leadership skills, and an increasing number of fundamentalists and even a few fanatics among them, that it might be a real risk to have a council too soon. Thirdly, a dominant Roman curia and a campaign by Cardinal Ratzinger moved vigorously to stamp out any genuine episcopal initiative. It is now part of canon law that bishops' conferences can only issue statements if they have passed unanimously, or the Vatican has approved them. Previously only a two-thirds majority was needed to pass a statement in the name of the whole conference. This demand for a unanimous vote has no precedent in the church's tradition or history, and is almost humanly impossible to achieve, especially in a numerically large or divided conference.

It is important to understand the context here. The document on the *Pastoral Office of Bishops*, as well as the *Constitution on the Church* at Vatican II, constantly talk about the *collegium*, the college of bishops, and the fact that the bishops share in the government of the church in a 'collegial' manner. The role of the bishops is to offer leadership in the *communio*, the communion which is the church made up of the whole people of God.

The purpose of this approach at Vatican II was to try to correct and rebalance a situation that was completely skewed towards papal centralism. The theological term used to describe the interrelationship of bishops among themselves was 'collegiality'. After the council, Paul VI set up the world Synod of Bishops and encouraged the development of national and regional episcopal conferences to give expression to collegiality. Bishops' conferences could issue decrees on behalf of local churches, and dissenting bishops were encouraged by the Vatican-issued *Directory on the Pastoral*

Ministry of Bishops 'to accept with loyal submission' decisions taken by the conference and to implement them in their dioceses. Conferences were supported in their work by lay people and priest specialists. As a result, a number of national bishops' conferences really came into their own in the late 1970s, especially the US Bishops' Conference. The Americans issued two splendid pastoral letters, the first on war and peace in 1983, and another on the economy in 1986, which were the product of wide consultation across the US church. Both caused a considerable stir among supporters of the Reagan government and right-wing Catholics. These pastorals also caused concern in the Wojtyla Vatican which was already moving away from the more participative approach taken by the curia under Paul VI. When the US bishops attempted a pastoral on women they ran into trouble. After a decade of consultative work around the country, the bishops abandoned the letter because of right-wing opposition at home, and constant stalling by the Vatican. The document was too close to reproductive issues for comfort in Rome, and rather than issue a compromised document, the US bishops abandoned the whole process.

The real attitude toward collegiality in the Wojtyla papacy was revealed in the 1998 Apostolic Letter of John Paul II, *Apostolos suos*, on the judicial and theological nature of episcopal conferences. This letter is the end-point of a long-haul attempt by the Vatican, orchestrated largely by Ratzinger, to regain complete control over episcopal conferences. The CDF cardinal had begun in the 1960s as a great supporter of episcopal conferences. But by the mid-1980s, after he had come to Rome, he was already saying that national conferences had no *mandatum docendi*—mandate to teach. Only an individual bishop or the pope had that. Most likely the reason for the change was that Ratzinger was confronted by strong episcopal conferences who were not prepared to take his *fiat* at face value and knuckle under. Individual bishops were much more easily cowed and managed, but a big conference could stand up to Rome. The long-term result was *Apostolos suos*. Effectively, this letter emasculates episcopal conferences so that now they can only issue a binding document if there is unanimity with no dissenting bishops—and anyone who knows bishops will know that that is a complete impossibility. Or, they can issue a document if it is passed by a two-thirds majority and then obtains approval by the Vatican. So effectively the conference can be stymied and controlled by Rome.

Finally, the world Synod of Bishops: this was another institution set up by Paul VI in an attempt to give expression to episcopal collegiality. This body really never got off the ground and recently it has become nothing

more than a papal rubber stamp. Two statements of Ratzinger, quoted by
John Allen, tell the whole story. In 1965 the young theologian Ratzinger
said 'The synod is a permanent council in miniature ... [it] guarantees that
the council will continue after its official end; it will from now on be part
of the everyday life of the church.' By 1987, CDF Prefect Ratzinger had
changed his mind: 'It [the synod] advises the pope; it is not a small-scale
council, and it is not a collegial organ of leadership for the universal
church.' (John L. Allen, *Cardinal Ratzinger: The Vatican's Enforcer of the
Faith* (2002) pp. 61–4) That is what you call a 180-degree turn. The Synod
of Bishops was completely nobbled by the Wojtyla Vatican and no one
with any knowledge of the way Catholicism works takes it seriously.

But it does still exist and could be reinvigorated. This would happen if
the bishops had the courage to reassert their right to participate in the
government of the church, in union with the pope and respectful of his
authority. The saddest thing is that while this is the kind of leadership that
the church so badly needs, it has been marginalised by a pope who had no
conception of how to encourage a collegial leadership to emerge.

So Catholicism comes to the end of the John Paul papacy confronted
with a profound crisis of authority and, at a deeper level, of constitutional
structure. Many Catholics, including many of the more intelligent bishops,
feel that we are now facing a distorted situation in which the church is
completely over-centralised, with Rome attempting to micro-manage every
level of the structure from national episcopal conferences down to the lay-
person in the pew. Those who view this situation from a historical perspective see the Wojtyla papacy as the tag-end of an absolute monarchy
model of papacy and church. Most informed observers feel that the church
cannot get any more centralised. Already the pastoral damage done by this
way of operating is considerable and many Catholics had already lost con-
fidence in church leadership before the handling of the sexual abuse crisis
confirmed them in their view of the episcopate. Also, the fact that there is
considerable anger and resentment among bishops, priests and laity with
the curia and its power indicates clearly that the relationship between
Rome and the local churches is in crisis.

So there has to be a change of direction. It has to be centrifugal—a
movement away from the dominance of the centre. Otherwise local pastoral care and spiritual leadership will suffer even more than it already has.
Certainly the papacy will remain as the symbolic centre of the church. But
the real work of the church occurs at the national and local level and it is
there that effective leadership is needed. So the centre of attention has to

shift to the diocesan and parish level where people are cared for and effect-ive action taken to work towards a more just community and more caring relationships. The primary issue that has to be dealt with is theological: Catholics have to recover the church's early tradition whereby bishops, both as individuals and as a 'college' were responsible for the local and uni-versal church. They offered leadership to people and priests and both singly and in synod made important doctrinal, liturgical and pastoral deci-sions for their churches.

The early church did not shift bishops around. Once elected, they were 'married' to their church and could not transfer to a 'better' diocese. Also, in order to make sure they were in touch with their people and clergy, they needed either to be closely related to the local area or actually come from it. Ever so occasionally someone was brought in from outside, but this was the exception rather than the rule. In order to revive this Catholicism needs a new process to select bishops. It must be open and transparent with inputs from local laity and priests. Above all, it needs to be geared to the selection of a person who is in tune with the local church and whose pas-toral care and focus of interest is primarily directed toward leadership of their community. The concerns of Rome are only of secondary importance.

But the divisions within contemporary Catholicism are not just over leadership. They are also over approaches to belief, spirituality, pastoral care and the kind of attitude that the church needs to take in the post-modern world, and to the other great religious traditions such as Buddhism and Islam. Even the worship of the church itself is still some-thing of a battleground. In the Wojtyla papacy all of these issues came to head. They have yet to be resolved.

4

LINES OF DIVISION

With the death of John Paul II the church is undoubtedly a deeply divided institution. There is no suggestion that he is entirely to blame for this. The whole history of Catholicism since the 1960s has been characterised by a struggle to delineate the essential elements of what it is to be Catholic and this has been a passionately debated issue. Nor is it to suggest that there are not still many good, generous priests and people carrying out the church's essential missions of pastoral care, spirituality, worship, prayer, service to others and evangelisation, and that at the parish, school, hospital, or social service level many good things are not being achieved. But there are also many Catholics who would like to be part of the church who feel deeply alienated. On many issues, such as sexuality, they find the church literally out of touch with their experience and therefore unbelievable. There is a kind of wound at the heart of Catholicism which refuses to heal. Part of the problem for the ordinary believer in expressing the nature of this illness is that it actually lies deep in theological attitudes about the nature of Catholicism itself and about how it relates to the world. Teasing out these issues that divide Catholics as the church faces a new papacy will help us to understand the challenges facing the new pope.

The clearest line of division that Catholics have inherited is really not between 'dyed-in-the-wool conservatives' and 'laid-back liberals', between those who don't believe in Vatican II and those who do. Most hardline reactionaries broke off from Catholicism years ago and went into schism. They are actually very small in number, probably fewer than a quarter of a million out of a total Catholic population of over a billion worldwide. The best known group are those who follow the late Archbishop Marcel Lefebvre.

The real fault line in modern Catholicism is between two groupings of Catholics who all still believe in Vatican II but who differ considerably on its interpretation. This division was exacerbated during the Wojtyla papacy leaving a situation in which many who see themselves as more open, pastorally progressive Catholics feel they have been driven to the margins and are alienated from the institutional church. They still maintain strong cultural identity as Catholics, but they have either ceased to attend Mass or only come to church intermittently.

This split began to emerge in the years after the Second Vatican Council, particularly in the 1970s, but was not clearly articulated until well into the John Paul papacy in the mid-1980s. What happened was that after the end of the council in 1965 there was a mad period when Catholics felt that at last they were free from the social and moral constraints of old-style Catholicism. This was felt especially by some of the clergy and members of religious orders. As a result, many silly and some disastrous things occurred. There was an outright rejection by some of everything that reminded them of the pre-Vatican II church. Statues, vestments, church paraphernalia and devotions were thrown out, along with more central things such as old-style catechism-centred religious education, the centrality of the Blessed Virgin and the saints in Catholic life and practice, good music, religious art and para-liturgical celebrations such as Benediction. They all seemed to end up on the scrap heap, like the use of Latin in worship. It was as though some people thought they were reinventing Catholicism. This really alarmed many who had been strong supporters of Vatican II, especially some theologians like the French Jesuits Henri De Lubac and Jean Daniélou, the great lay Catholic philosopher and theorist of the relationship between the democratic state and the church, Jacques Maritain, as well as a maturing German theologian, Joseph Alois Ratzinger.

Ratzinger provides a classic case study of those deeply concerned with the direction of the church after Vatican II. He was born in 1927 in Bavaria, trained as a priest and theologian, and attended Vatican II as a *peritus* (expert advisor) to Cardinal Josef Frings of Cologne. Frings was a leader of those who threw out the agenda of the die-hard curalists who wanted to control the council, and Ratzinger played a pivotal and influential role among those calling for reform. But his attitudes gradually started to change after the Council. The key transition period when he moved from a more open approach to a concern with doctrinal orthodoxy was during the late 1960s and the early 1970s.

The pivotal moment was the 1968 student revolutions in Europe. Inspired by varieties of post-Stalinist Marxism, articulated by the writers of the French left such as Jean-Paul Sartre, the universities of Europe erupted. Even the students in the Catholic and Protestant faculties of theology at Tübingen University, where Ratzinger (together with the great progressive theologian Hans Küng) was teaching, revolted. It is hard to be precise about what they were protesting against, but their violent behaviour appalled many and a shocked Ratzinger gradually came to see this whole period was one in which the fundamentals not only of Vatican II, but of the Catholic faith itself were being undermined and abandoned. This seemed to be reinforced all over the world by the large numbers of priests leaving the ministry, and sisters and brothers departing from the religious life.

Also in 1968, Paul VI's encyclical *Humanae vitae* outlawed all forms of artificial contraception. The encyclical met with widespread condemnation and rejection, especially by Catholics in western countries. This was also the period when traditional Catholic spirituality seemed to be taken over by social and political activism, and theology by the excesses of the so-called 'death of God' and 'secular city' theories, with their embrace of modernity and secularism without much sense of prophetic critique. It was also the time of political theology and the flowering of liberation theology in Latin America. Here the emphasis was on the local indigenous church community geared for social and political action against oppressive governments (often military) and structures that kept people in poverty and ignorance. To thinkers like Ratzinger everything in the church seemed to be up for grabs. In religious education there was considerable chaos when catechetical instruction and faith knowledge was replaced by an emphasis on endless classroom discussion to work out 'your own personal ethics', and solid religious formation was replaced with the psychobabble of 'self-worth' and 'feeling good about yourself'.

Looking back, with the exception of the great creative stream of liberation theology, it was a silly, even tragic period, but it was understandable given its historical context. It was a stage through which the church had to pass. It certainly needed correction, but not the over-reaction that some, like Ratzinger, seemed to think necessary.

Appointed Archbishop of Munich and a cardinal in 1977 by Paul VI, Ratzinger was brought from Germany to Rome to be Prefect of the CDF in November 1981 by John Paul II. He was the one who determined the important theological themes of the papacy and he was by far the most competent and important person brought into the curia by Pope Wojtyla. No one doubts his acuity and intelligence, and there is evidence that he may well have saved the church from terrible and divisive disunity by persuading John Paul not to declare the condemnation of contraception to be an infallible teaching. Ratzinger, now Benedict XVI, was very popular among those who were sceptical about the church's much more open approach to the world. There is even a 'Cardinal Ratzinger Fan Club' on the Internet.

By the mid-1980s, perceptive observers had begun to realise that two quite different interpretations had emerged among those Catholics who had previously supported the reforms of Vatican II. Among European theologians the different sides produced two multilingual quarterly periodicals—*Concilium* and *Communio*—which eventually became symbols of the different understandings of how the church should interpret the Council and react to modern culture.

Concilium, founded in 1964, represented those who were ultimately optimistic about the problems of the post-conciliar period and who were willing to work their way through them. These were the Catholics who felt that the church must maintain its critical openness to the modern world and participate fully in contemporary culture. *Concilium* was founded and supported by theologians such as Hans Küng, Dutchman Edward Schillebeeckx and Austrian Karl Rahner. *Communio*, founded in 1972, took a much more critical approach to modernity and the church's interaction with contemporary culture, and its main supporters were the Swiss theologian Hans Urs von Balthasar, and Ratzinger. The periodical was disapproving of much that happened in late 1960s and 1970s Catholicism, and it wanted to maintain a focus on the pre-conciliar *ressourcement* or 'return to the sources'. It wanted to highlight the great spiritual, liturgical, artistic and theological classics of the Christian past. *Communio* emphasised the need to use this great tradition as a source that was relevant to the contemporary church. At the same time there was a movement to withdraw somewhat from the world and to focus back on the church itself as the real and genuine source of truth and the best way forward for humankind.

The difference between *Concilium* and *Communio* actually highlights the core issues facing Catholicism today, and helps to explain the difference that exists between Catholics of good will. It also takes us to the heart and soul of the Wojtyla papacy. Although many Catholics still use the nomenclature 'conservatives' and 'liberals' to try to place people on an attitude spectrum, the distinction has little or no meaning in contemporary Catholicism.

People like Pope Wojtyla and Ratzinger are not 'conservatives' in the sense that they want to restore the past in a literal sense, like the traditionalists and the schismatic Marcel Lefebvre, who really wanted to return to the *ancien régime* with church and monarchical state in tandem.

The difference between these groups of Catholics revolves around interpretations of three fundamental theological questions. Firstly, how much does the human condition, art, beauty and the natural world reveal God and tell humankind about the divine? Secondly, how central is Christ to understanding and experiencing of God? And thirdly, where does Christianity and specifically the Catholic church fit into one's theological scheme? These were also the central theological and pastoral issues of the Wojtyla papacy. As in all theology, the key question is where you place your emphasis. Two mid-twentieth-century Catholic theologians have articulated different approaches to these questions and, like the periodicals they produced, they have become symbolic figures for the two different interpretations: these theologians are the Jesuit Karl Rahner (1904–84), and the Swiss priest Hans Urs von Balthasar (1905–88).

Rahner gives modern expression to the very traditional Catholic emphasis that God's goodness, grace and generosity pervades the entire cosmos and the whole of human history, and that everyone in their deep, inner core is oriented toward the divine. Thus, in a literal sense, the world and human history become symbols and sacraments of the presence of God, the place where the transcendent is to be discovered. Humans are literally immersed in a universe of grace. Rahner, perhaps more than any other individual, exerted enormous influence on the formulation of the documents of Vatican II. Those Catholics—probably the large majority—who have embraced the Council's vision of reality, mainly unconsciously by a kind of 'osmosis', look outward towards the world not as hostile, evil territory, but as a place permeated by the goodness of God. This is not to pretend that there is no evil, selfishness or destructiveness in the world and that this has to be dealt with by a hard-headed critique. But the emphasis is on the words of Jesus that 'God *so loved the world* that he gave his only son' (John 3:16). Saint Paul picks up a similar theological theme: for him the world is the product of God's creative love in Christ. If it is, it must mirror the splendour of God's affection for every creature.

When asked what role Jesus' life, death and resurrection plays in this process for non-Christians, Rahner replies that fundamentally all good people who have lived spiritual and conscientious lives outside the context of the church have been touched by the grace Christ brought to the world. They are, in a literal sense, implicit or 'anonymous Christians'. Thus Rahner gives expression to a very open interpretation of Catholicism. It is a theology that reaches outward: to the future, to the other great religious faiths, to conscientious unbelievers, to the natural world itself. The church no longer 'possesses' God completely, nor completely controls all access to God's grace. Rahner says that for the first time in Christian history we actually live in a 'world church', and the days of the European dominance of Catholicism are over.

This is not to say that Rahner claimed all of this explicitly. Much of it is a development and explication of his theology. It is an attempt to give a 'feel' for the kind of theological context that most post-conciliar 'progressive' Catholics take toward their faith.

The approach represented by *Communio* is more sceptical about the optimism inherent in Rahner's proposals. Essentially, the Swiss Balthasar feels his Austrian colleague is far too open to the world, and too willing to 'baptise' secular and religious movements outside the church. He feels this leads to the loss of a specific Christian identity and sense of mission. Certainly, Balthasar holds that there is common ground between God and the human world of beauty, music, art, literature, philosophy and poetry. For him, human creativity ultimately opens us out to God, and a major part of the appeal of his theology is that it is essentially an aesthetics of the divine. But Balthasar warns we must always remember that even at the deepest levels of mystical spirituality humans are only at the outer edges of the transcendent depths of God. While sharing being, we must also remember the radical dissimilarity between God and the world.

Balthasar was deeply influenced by the great Protestant theologian Karl Barth. They both lived in Basel for many years. In common with Barth, Balthasar emphasises that Christ is the link and linchpin between our minuscule apprehension of the divine and the reality of God's inner self. While there is common ground between God and the world, it is only in explicit commitment to Christ that this relationship is fully established. He is much more pessimistic about the world and the human condition. It is also significant that Balthasar called the periodical that he co-founded with Ratzinger *Communio* because this is the clue to his ecclesiology, his understanding of the church. Communion is not only what the believers receive in the sacrament at Mass. It also describes their relationships among themselves, as well as their relation to Christ who is the bridge to God. It is the presence of the Spirit of Christ that creates the church. It is upon this that the believer should focus, not the community's sins and failures. In Balthasar's conception the church, like Christ, has descended from heaven above. The pope, as external head of the church on earth, represents Christ in the community.

These sketchy summaries do little justice to the subtlety and complexity of both Balthasar's and Rahner's thought. But they do indicate the two theological paths to the future that have gradually been articulated over the last thirty years within Catholicism. The Rahnerian vision sees a church active in and open to the world. It is a universalist vision, broad, all-embracing, 'catholic' in the very best sense of the word. It has no illusions about sin, destructiveness and evil, and it knows that part of the core of the church's mission is to offer a prophetic critique of the world. In a way it is a theology 'from below', an interpretation of Christian and human life that begins with the human experience of a longing within the self for spiritual transcendence. With Rahner there is the feeling that, despite the almost turgid denseness of his theological writing, he actually lives in and has embraced the real, contemporary world. In contrast, Balthasar's theology is 'from above'. While never denying human spiritual aspirations, it begins with revelation and God's descent into the world in the vulnerability of Jesus' humanity. His theology is attractive in that it is both prayerful and beautiful and shows something of the splendour of God. Nevertheless, there is something naively Eurocentric and Germanic about it. One of the naive things about the theology of Balthasar is the way in which he blithely bestows upon his thought, which arises from his studies of German litera-ture and philosophy, a kind of perennial, universal patina, which is some-how untouched by culture and history. This emerges particularly in his condemnation of liberation theology which he describes as 'particularist and regional' whereas, he says, a genuine Catholic theology must be uni-versal. In fact, Balthasar's theology is particularist in that it represents the 'old world', the world that Rahner looks beyond in his much wider, future-oriented, and more generous vision of the church. In the end perhaps the essential difference between the two approaches of Rahner and Balthasar is that one sees the cup half-full, and the other sees it half-empty.

It is easy to see why Balthasar's theology would have been very attract-ive to Pope John Paul and Ratzinger. In fact, what the Basel theologian achieved was to articulate in theological terms a kind of ready-made under-pinning for the Wojtyla papacy. There is a feeling of pessimism about the world inherent in Balthasar's thought which cautious and melancholic people seem to find attractive. It gives theological expression to the fears inherent in those Catholics whose culture and attitude is rooted in and circumscribed by Europe, and who often show an unconscious but nevertheless annoying disdain for other cultures, particularly for the Anglo-American world. Aidan Nichols, the English Dominican, says that Balthasar's thought was 'exactly the kind of anti-liberal but reforming theologian ... with whom ... [Rome] ... in the later years of Paul VI's pontificate and that of John Paul II, liked to do business.'

Certainly Balthasar's views underpinned the approach that the CDF took to the major theological crises that were dealt with by Ratzinger. The first was liberation theology. Basically, this was an attempt by theologians in Central and South America in the 1960s, 1970s and 1980s to develop a theological methodology from below. It was a radical attempt on the part of the Catholic church in Latin America to rethink the role it played in society and politics. It involved a fundamental shift away from identification with the powerful and wealthy elites, to social activism on behalf of the poor. This shifted the cultural and political landscape of the continent in that the *de facto* established church turned its back on the establishment. The emphasis now was on finding the historical Jesus in the face of the marginalised of the slums, not on a pre-existent Christ who descended into the world from on high symbolically representing the power of God. In liberation theology, God's love was discovered from below, in the communities of the poor and oppressed as they gathered to study the Bible in the light of their experiences of the struggle to exist. The Jesus of the gospel stood against the powerful of his own time and paid with his life. This was, in the most vivid sense, a lived, existential way of doing theology, very divorced from the rarefied heights of Balthasarian thought with its high notions of Christ's role and roots in German philosophy and literature.

But in the early twenty-first century we are seeing the marginalisation and possibly the end of liberation theology. Few theological movements have been more vigorously opposed and attacked. The wealthy Latin American elites, military governments with support from the CIA, the Vatican, and some of the local hierarchy whose power was threatened by a church from below, moved to eliminate this threat. The mid-1980s condemnation by Ratzinger and the CDF, supported by the Pope, certainly contributed to the decline of liberation theology. Closely intertwined with the decline of liberation theology has been the fact that increasing numbers of Latin Americans are turning away from Catholicism to fundamentalist Protestantism. Part of the reason for these conversions is that fundamentalist Protestantism encourages wealth and an upwardly mobile lifestyle as a sign of God's blessing. Also, the days of military juntas in Latin America have passed and most countries on the continent are now viable democracies. There is considerable debate about the actual number who have become *evangelicos* (the word for 'Protestant' in Latin-American Spanish). Guatemala certainly has the largest number (between 25 to 35 per cent of the population). Honduras has 17 per cent, El Salvador, Chile, Brazil, Costa Rica and Panama have 15 per cent and Bolivia 11 per cent. All other countries of the continent are under 10 per cent Protestant.

One can see Balthasar's theological legacy being worked out through a number of other contentious issues which Ratzinger and the CDF tackled. If the questions revolving around liberation theology were the centrepiece of the CDF's investigations in the 1980s, the question of the theology of religious pluralism was what focused the Congregation's attention in the 1990s. The essential question here pivots around the unique role of Christ and Christian revelation, and whether the other great religious traditions—Hinduism, Buddhism, Confucianism, Judaism, Islam, indigenous beliefs—can convey truth about God and salvation as well as insight into the divine.

There is, of course, a larger context for these questions, and it is the way in which in the contemporary world the different religious traditions can be used as weapons of cultural and national identity, and thus as ways of dividing people from each other. Claims to absolute truth can easily be exploited to incite hatred and war. So there is a pressing need for the great faiths to heal antagonisms among themselves, because the question of religious pluralism and dialogue is deeply connected to the task of building the structures of peace. There is no doubt that Pope Wojtyla was convinced about the importance of building peace. He worked particularly hard to make sure that the 'crusade mentality' never infected Catholicism in the so-called 'war against terror'. The determination to build bridges of trust and dialogue with the Muslim faith was at the core of the Vatican's strong opposition to the second invasion of Iraq by the Americans and their allies in 2003.

That is also why he invited the leaders of the other great religious traditions to the Assisi World Days of Prayer for Peace, and sat down among them. The pope was widely criticised by reactionary Catholics over these prayer days because they saw his meeting with other religious leaders as conveying the message that all religions were as good as each other. There is a sense in which there was an element of window-dressing in the Assisi exercise. This is demonstrated by the fact that while John Paul was reaching out to others at Assisi, in 2003 the CDF cardinal was editing his book *Fede, verità, tolleranza* (Faith, Truth, Tolerance). Ratzinger argued that a kind of relativism had permeated Catholicism over the last two decades which declared that all opinions are equally true, even if they are contradictory, and he claimed that this was 'the greatest problem of our time'. He is critical of the fact that 'Tolerance and respect for the other seem to have imposed the idea of the equivalence of all religions', whereas for him 'in Christ we have been given a new gift, the essential gift—the Truth—and, therefore, we have the duty to give it freely to others'. The new secretary of the CDF, Archbishop Angelo Amato, appointed early in 2003, who had a stint in the United States in 1988, has had a considerable interest in the theology of religions. This was a focus of the CDF from about 1997 onwards.

At the core of these debates is the problem of the nature and extent of the uniqueness of Christianity. Central to this discussion is the question of whether more than one religion can communicate truth, salvation and a spiritual experience of the transcendent. Is Christianity the sole source of salvation, the only faith that conveys true knowledge about God, or is it one, albeit the best from the Catholic point of view, among many paths to ultimate reality?

A whole series of issues are embedded in this debate. What does the Christian belief that Christ died for all humankind mean if a person can be saved by being a Muslim or Buddhist, or a follower of an indigenous religion? What are the consequences for the uniqueness of Christianity of saying that since ultimate truth is far beyond human categories of thought and speech, there is every possibility of being able to express the truth in diverse ways through the world's other great religions? Can a Catholic say that other traditions, with their diverse teachings and practices, are authentic paths to God? And what are the consequences of these questions for the missionary outreach of a faith which is instructed to preach to all nations?

It is only in the last two decades that these questions have come to the fore among Catholics. In some ways the opening shot in this attack on religious pluralism was fired when Sri Lanka's Father Tissa Balasuriya heard on the BBC news that the Vatican had excommunicated him on

5 January 1997. An investigation into his theology had been going on since late 1992.

Balasuriya explained the essence of the problem in the book *From Inquisition to Freedom* (2001) and in a way it sums up the kind of questions that all the theologians working in this area face. He says

The origin of my problems with church authority is rooted in the fundamental theological issue of salvation. Many Christians in Asia are increasingly unable to think of salvation exclusively in terms of the [Catholic] church, or as only mediated by Jesus Christ. We have come to realize that such a view would imply that the vast majority of the people of Asia were not saved. The point has slowly dawned on us that this is not acceptable. Vatican II pointed to some openings concerning the salvation of non-Christians, but even in the 1970s the leadership of the Church in Rome was retreating into itself. The more I studied the issue of salvation, the more I was impressed with the serious inadequacy of the Church's doctrinal thinking. It gradually became clear to me that what we have presented for a thousand years as dogma and doctrine is not really from Jesus Christ. Certainly Catholicism and Vatican II have clearly said that the Church is not the sole means of salvation. The real problem is that the Church usually denies this in practice and acts as though you need to be baptized in order to be saved. The whole missionary thrust through sermons and teaching is that, even today, salvation is to be found only in the Church and in Jesus Christ. Thus we are fitting God and people into our own categories and perspectives ...

By 1990 I had realised that the idea of original sin was basic to the concept of salvation, and that once you posit the idea that original sin infects everyone, some form of universal redemption is required. This was interpreted by medieval theologians such as St Anselm (died 1109), and others in the past, to mean that there had to be a divine redeemer. If there is a divine redeemer, the theory of merit and grace follows, with the Church as the medium for this grace. Once you enter into this complex of ideas, you are dealing with the substance of Christian dogma as traditionally presented, and you are dealing with one of the central underpinnings for the justification of missionary work. The Vatican saw this clearly. (pp. 90–1)

Eventually the Vatican was forced by worldwide outrage to lift the excommunication in 1998. But the Sri Lankan was just the first theologian under attack. The Balasuriya case was quickly followed by an investigation of the distinguished scholar, Belgian Jesuit Jacques Dupuis, whose *Towards a Christian Theology of Religious Pluralism* was the subject of an examination by the CDF, and a 19 January 2001 Notification about eight 'ambiguities' in the book. Dupuis' investigation was, in turn, followed by that of the American Jesuit Roger Haight, whose book *Jesus Symbol of God* tries to make room in theology for a pluralist hypothesis. Other writers who have been publicly named by Ratzinger are the Catholic theologian Paul Knitter, and the Anglican John Hick, whose book *God Has Many Names* is critical of Christianity as a 'superior' form of revelation. All these writers are confident that God is active in the world, especially through the other great religious traditions to touch the lives of non-Christian people with grace and salvation.

This creative flurry of thought in the area of world religions and pluralism has stirred Ratzinger. This is understandable, given that he espoused a theology that emphasised the absolute centrality of Christ. The CDF's concern with a more open theology eventually led it to issue the Declaration *Dominus Jesus: On the Unicity and Salvific Universality of Jesus Christ and the Church* [DJ] (5 September 2000). DJ, largely written by the theologian and secretary of the CDF, Archbishop Angelo Amato, is, in parts, extraordinarily inept. This probably results from the narrowness of the consultation that preceded its composition, reflected in the fact that even other Vatican departments were ignored in its composition, as the Australian Cardinal Edward Cassidy, then president of the Pontifical Council for Promoting Christian Unity, made clear when he said that 'neither the timing nor the language of the document were opportune'. Also bishops from across the world criticised the document, including Cardinal Carlo Maria Martini, the then archbishop of Milan. One of the most annoying things about DJ is that it largely ignores all the work that has been achieved in ecumenical dialogue with the other Christian churches and other religious traditions over the past thirty or so years since the end of Vatican II. While DJ is discussed at some length here because of the issues it raises and the light it throws on the Wojtyla and Benedict papacies, the document was quickly forgotten and relegated to obscurity, even though Amato claimed in 2004 that everyone recognised its 'utility, timeliness and justness'.

There are two parts to DJ: the first is concerned with the relationships between Christianity and non-Christian religions, and the second concerns the relationship of the Catholic church to the other Christian churches or, as DJ calls some of them, 'ecclesial communities'. Regarding non-Christian religions, DJ argues that 'Jesus' ... words and deeds manifest the totality and definitiveness of the revelation of the mystery of God, even if the depth of that mystery remains in itself transcendent and inexhaustible'. Further, Jesus' life, death and resurrection is 'the sole and universal source of salvation for all humanity'. The other great world religions can add nothing to Christian revelation which is total and exhaustive. This is because Christ is the sole mediator and the complete fulfilment of God's revelation. DJ also asserts that Christ cannot be separated from 'his church', that is the Catholic church. This is spelled out bluntly in the January 2001 Notification concerning Dupuis' book. It says:

> It must be firmly believed that the [Catholic] church is the sign and instrument of salvation for all people. It is contrary to the Catholic faith to consider the different religions of the world as ways of salvation complementary to the church. According to Catholic doctrine the followers of other religions are oriented to the church and are all called to become part of her. (paragraphs 6–7)

Turning to the other Christian churches, DJ says that the true church of Christ only 'subsists fully' in the Catholic church. This is the view of Vatican II, and the conciliar terminology is open enough to allow that many truths are to be found in the other Christian churches. It is not an assertion that Catholicism is the sole means of salvation. DJ says that whatever 'efficacy' the other churches and 'ecclesial communities' may have is derived 'from the very fullness of grace and truth entrusted to the Catholic church'. DJ also says that to be a 'church' in the full sense you need to have a valid (from the Roman point of view) episcopate, as well as 'the genuine and integral substance of the Eucharistic mystery', that is a valid Eucharist. While at first this sounds like a hard-nosed approach, it must be remembered that the word 'subsists' was used purposely because the Council was trying to express its belief that while the Roman Catholic church had held onto Christ's teaching in its integrity, it was also trying to show that it did not exclude the profound Christian truths to be found in the other churches and communities.

The problem with DJ was that it was an extraordinarily ham-fisted document, couched in an adversarial tone, totally lacking the broad ecumenical sensitivity and generosity manifested at Vatican II. Around the same time as DJ, a 'Note on the Expression "Sister Churches"' was sent to Catholic bishops' conferences. They were told not to call even the Orthodox 'sister churches'. According to the Note 'The one, holy, catholic and apostolic universal church is not sister church but "mother" of all the particular churches'. No wonder a torrent of criticism was stirred up from across the religious spectrum. It is a vivid illustration that the curalists who write this type of thing live in a cosseted world and it shows the insularity of their theological perspective. This is also demonstrated by the fact that DJ constantly harps on terms like 'obedience' and 'authority'. There seems to be an assumption that you can order people to believe.

One of the most acute comments about DJ is that of the expatriate Australian Dominican theologian at Oxford, Philip Kennedy. He points out something that is often forgotten: 'The fullness of the trinity is not incarnate in Christ. Consequently, there is more to God, so to speak, than has been shown in Jesus Christ. God remains a *Deus absconditus* [a hidden God] …' In other words, even the incarnation of Christ is, in itself, limited by the very fact that it is human, and therefore does not and cannot manifest the unlimited and infinite fullness of the Godhead. Therefore, all revelations, because they are expressed in human terms, are limited and ultimately inadequate. This surely applies to the Catholic church? Kennedy also highlights the fact that DJ quotes many texts from Vatican II but neglects to quote an important and more generous passage from Vatican II's document on the church, *Lumen gentium*:

> Those who through no fault of their own, do not know the gospel of Christ or his church, but who nevertheless seek God with a sincere heart, and moved by grace, try in all their actions to do his will as they know it through the dictates of their conscience—these too may attain eternal salvation. (paragraph 16)

One thing that has not been mentioned much by commentators is the tendency towards sectarianism in DJ. It gives voice, both explicitly and implicitly, to a wider movement that is slowly but pervasively turning important elements in the Catholic church inward in an increasingly sectarian and perfectionist direction. Sectarianism is incompatible with genuine catholicity. It is the antithesis of the kind of openness to the world, tolerant acceptance of others and a sense of religious pluralism that most thinking Catholics have embraced over the last three or four decades. But during the Wojtyla papacy, in several parts of the church there has been a movement toward a constriction of the borders of Catholicism.

This has not so much been a retreat to the past when the church thought of itself as a *societas perfecta* (a perfect society), a large and grandly self-sufficient institution, independent of the world, responsible only to itself, its own leadership, and ultimately to God. This pre-Vatican II conception of the church was never sectarian. It was outgoing, missionary, and welcoming of sinners. The new sectarianism is subtly different. It is a constriction of the borders, a narrowing of the common ground on which believers stand. It is expressed by a turning inward, away from the other Christian churches and by an unwillingness to search for a commonality with the other great religious traditions. Thinking Catholics who have been educated and live in pluralist, democratic and tolerant societies often find themselves in conflict with hierarchs who seem to be moving in a sectarian direction. There is an emerging assumption among some very senior church leaders that the contemporary western world is so far gone in individualism, permissiveness and consumerism that it is totally impervious to church teaching. Claiming to assume the broader historical perspective, these churchmen, such as Ratzinger, have virtually abandoned the secularised masses to their fate, to nurture elitist enclaves which will carry the true faith through to future, more 'receptive' generations. This is why the new religious movements (NRMs) received such favour and patronage in the Wojtyla papacy. The NRMs have embraced an essentially sectarian vision of Catholicism, are very hierarchical in structure, closed in on themselves, and theologically reactionary. Examples of NRMs in Catholicism are organisations like Opus Dei, Communion and Liberation, Focolare, the Neo-Catechuminate and the Legionaries of Christ.

There is a sense in which the important theologians who have been targeted by the CDF give a clue to the underlying motif of the Wojtyla papacy. The best known are perhaps the world's most famous theologian, the Swiss-born Hans Küng, and the Dutch Dominican Edward Schillebeeckx. Küng was tackled by the CDF over his views on papal infallibility and the nature of the church and Schillebeeckx over his writings on Jesus and his book on ministry. Both these men were key figures in the *Concilium* group. Moral theologians like the American Charles Curran were also in the firing line for their views on sexuality and contraception.

Underlying all these arguments about doctrine and morality are basic assumptions about the relationship of humankind to life itself and how a person thinks about the world. Is the theological emphasis on reality as primarily 'a vale of tears', alienated from God, and life as a struggle between good and evil? Certainly goodness, beauty and truth sometimes prevail, but it is unlikely that the contemporary world has much to teach those who are already committed to Christ's message and specifically to Catholicism. Generally speaking, the type of person who takes this approach has a more cynical and melancholic view of the world. In contrast, the other theological emphasis sees the world as the creation of God, as a place where the Spirit of Christ can be discerned. Clearly, modern secular society is a deeply compromised place where good and evil co-exist and struggle. But it is not hermetically sealed against the true and the good and it often throws up challenges to which the church needs to respond. This type of person has a more hopeful and sanguine approach to the world.

I have deliberately used the word 'emphasis' here to describe both these attitudes because this is the key to the difference. Theology is largely about what you focus on and accentuate, rather than being about radically opposed points of view. Contemporary divisions within Catholicism are about emphasis, but that does not mean that they are not debated with vigour. There is no doubt that during the Wojtyla papacy the emphasis throughout the curia was on a profound scepticism that the secular world had anything to teach the church. This is paradoxical, given that Pope John Paul was the most travelled pope in history and always seemed to be a man open to the world and interested in it. Yet the fact is, he was profoundly sceptical about what the world had to offer Catholicism. In this he stands in vivid contrast to Pope John XXIII who, when he opened Vatican II in October 1962, outlined an extraordinarily positive vision of the relationship between the world and the church.

I mention this in order to try to penetrate into the mind and *modus operandi* of the Roman curia under Pope Wojtyla. Of course, he did not set up the curia. It was basically established in its present form by Sixtus V in 1588 and has been through a number of reorganisations since then. Following Vatican II there was an attempted radical reorganisation by Paul VI in 1967. But while the structure changed, the old patriarchical Latin cultural attitudes of power, patronage, secrecy and manipulation remained. John Paul's relationship with the curia was always ambivalent. He was uninterested in the minutiae of church government and he assimilated much more information through discussion and verbal communication than through the reading of bureaucratic reports. So there is a sense in which he marginalised the curia to the extent that curial department heads had only limited access to him. Also, in the modern curia since the reforms of Paul VI, an enormous amount of power has devolved on the Secretariat of State which has become, in effect, a kind of cabinet office and foreign affairs department combined. The last two Cardinals Secretary of State, Agostino Casaroli and Angelo Sodano, had good access to Pope Wojtyla and the view of the Secretariat was often more important than that of a particular curial office. John Paul also had a kind of 'kitchen cabinet' made up of his secretary Dziwisz, some members of the papal household and close friends, mainly Poles like Deskur and Rylko, whose advice he usually sought before major decisions.

But this is not to say that, with the exception of the last years of his papacy, Wojtyla did not use the curia or did not know what it was doing. He tended to give curial leaders their head as long as they reflected the policies and emphases that he thought were important. Like all bureaucracies, the departments of the curia tend to act independently under a weak or sick pope. But for most of his papacy John Paul was a strong pope, and he was certainly responsible for curial decisions and for what was issued in his name. There is a tendency among some critics of the papacy to say 'Well, the pope is really a good guy. It is the curia and the Vatican that can't be trusted.' As well as being insulting to an able man like Pope Wojtyla, it also lets him off the hook for decisions that are clearly his responsibility. Certainly the church is far too big to be micro-managed, even by the pope, but ultimately in an absolutist system, responsibility is sheeted back to the ruler. This also operates in a democracy. It is the meaning of the convention in the Westminster system of ministerial responsibility, and what Harry S. Truman meant when he said 'The buck stops here', meaning right at the presidential desk.

In the past, people having trouble dealing with the curia have tended to blame all their problems on 'the Italians'. That cannot be said now because John Paul continued the policy of Paul VI in internationalising the Vatican. Priests of many nationalities have been brought in, and while the system is still basically Italianate in the way it operates, and its *lingua franca* is Italian, no one can claim that a broad cross-section of the world church is not represented. But the problem is that overseas clerics who work in the curia have themselves quickly become 'more Roman than the Romans', in the sense that they have adopted all the ancient tactics used by the Romans to maintain their power and enhance their status. Also, like many bishops appointed in the Wojtyla papacy, those who have come to work in Rome are by no means the cream of the clerical crop. Most are men of very modest ability. Brighter, more committed people tend to want to work at home and use their gifts to help the local church.

Something of the internal thrust of the Wojtyla papacy can be detected in some of the other men besides Ratzinger brought by John Paul to serve in the curia. The first is Cardinal Alfonso López Trujillo, a Colombian-born former archbishop of Medellín and a virulent opponent of liberation theology. He is described by John Allen in his book *Conclave* as 'perhaps the most divisive figure in the College of Cardinals', and by the late Peter Hebblethwaite as 'ambitious and unscrupulous ... a vindictive man with a long memory.' A supporter of the national security state and the dictatorial juntas of the 1970s and 1980s in Latin America, and much given to couching his views in militaristic terminology, he was brought by John Paul to Rome in 1990 to head up the Pontifical Council for the Family. The council, set up in 1981 by Wojtyla himself, represented the Pope's views on the whole range of reproductive questions, and presumably the intention was that López Trujillo take a more aggressive approach to the sexual issues that Wojtyla considered absolutely central for his papacy. The council represented the Vatican on questions of population and reproductive health in the lead-up to and during the UN Population Conference at Cairo in September 1994. While Rome certainly had every right to proclaim its beliefs on abortion and contraception, its use of a very aggressive approach and its last-minute filibustering on the wording of the final Conference statement may well have done more damage to the church's standing as one of the world's influential moral arbiters than a more considered, conciliatory approach would have. It certainly alienated and angered many people who, while not agreeing with the Vatican, were sympathetic to its point of view.

In late 2003, López Trujillo made the assertion that the HIV virus could still be caught by those who use condoms because condoms were permeable, a claim he repeated on a BBC TV documentary *Sex and the Holy City*. He told the BBC: 'This is something which the scientific community accepts, and doctors know what we are saying. You cannot talk about safe sex. One should speak about human values, about the family, and about fidelity.' When the BBC reporter said that the World Health Organization maintained that it was not true that the HIV virus can pass through the latex rubber from which condoms were made, López Trujillo replied: 'Well, they are wrong about that. No dialogue is possible at that level, scientifically speaking, because this is an easily recognisable fact.' It is not immediately evident on what scientific basis the cardinal was making this assertion. He had made the Holy See look foolish.

Another cardinal brought to Rome by Pope John Paul was the Chilean Jorge Arturo Medina Estévez. Also a strong opponent of liberation theology, a social conservative, and a close friend of the former Chilean dictator Augusto Pinochet, Medina Estévez had spent most of his life in Chile as a canon lawyer and official of the Catholic University of Santiago. He was

also said to be something of an expert on worship. He was appointed
bishop of Valparaiso in 1993, and was then moved to Rome as Pro-Prefect
of the Congregation for Divine Worship (the Vatican department supervising worship) in 1996, and Prefect in 1998. He attended the Oceania
Synod later that year, and was reputedly the main conduit into the Vatican
for a tiny group of reactionary Catholics in their successful attempt to paint
the Australian church as out of control, the bishops as weak and the widespread use of general absolution as symptomatic of all the doctrinal and
disciplinary ills afflicting local Catholicism. A highly critical statement
about Australian Catholicism was forced on the bishops at the Synod by
the Vatican.

That same year, Medina Estévez made a fool of himself when he
attempted to interfere in a court process by attempting to put pressure on
the British government to rescue Pinochet while he was being held by the
police in the UK during extradition proceedings to Spain for crimes,
including murder and torture, committed during his dictatorship. Pinochet
was eventually permitted by the British Home Secretary to return to Chile.

Worship is usually meant to bring people together prayerfully in community. But over the years of the Medina Estévez regime in the Congregation for Divine Worship it has become a real battlefield, and is a vivid
example of the way in which elements in the curia try to micro-manage the
church. It has led to the extraordinary situation of this Spanish-speaking
cardinal interfering directly in the work of English translation, and deter-
mining who are best equipped to translate Latin texts into the language of
Shakespeare. This whole affair illustrates how the Vatican operates.

Since Vatican II, the Catholic church has undertaken the gargantuan
task of translating all its liturgy into the many languages of the world.
Because it is so widely spoken, translating worship texts into English has
been an enormously important and often difficult process. The task was
entrusted to the International Committee for English in the Liturgy
(ICEL). Established in October 1963 by bishops from countries where
English is the mother tongue, ICEL's executive secretariat co-ordinated
teams of scholars around the world who prepared the translations. ICEL
had never been under the direct control of the Vatican. It had been
governed and funded by the eleven English-speaking bishops' conferences.

Translation from one language to another is always a tricky business.
Should the result be a literal rendering of the original words, or should the
translated text convey the sense of the original while using the structure and
idioms of the target language? The difficulty is compounded when there

are doctrinal nuances involved, as well as the need to render the translation a good oral text that can be read aloud and used in public worship. Rather than a literal 'word for word' translation, ICEL opted for what it called 'dynamic equivalency', by which it meant taking some liberty with the Latin original to produce a text in contemporary English idiom that is understandable to the ordinary person and readable in public worship.

The Vatican and Catholic groups committed to maintaining what they saw as the 'sacred' rhetoric needed for worship opposed this approach because they said it introduced vulgarities and doctrinal irregularities. For many of these groups ICEL has become a kind of lightening rod for everything in the modern church they oppose. In Australia, the bulk of the criticism of liturgical translation has been channelled through the Melbourne-based magazine *AD2000*. Conservatives argue that the ICEL translators failed to maintain the original doctrinal nuances of the Latin texts by introducing politically correct notions such as the elimination of sexist language. They claim that the translations are ideologically driven and accuse ICEL of desacralising the English texts. By this they mean that English prayers and readings often strip the original Latin down to what they maintain is a kind of shoddy and superficial language that 'domesticates' God. Many have also complained that much of the English used in the translations is banal and simplistic, manifesting an inferior level of literacy.

Liturgical reactionaries have always been politically astute and they have made their feelings about ICEL's work well known in Rome. At Divine Worship they received a sympathetic hearing. This sympathy deepened with the arrival of Medina Estévez. He retired at age 75 in late September 2002, but not before he had engineered a coup against ICEL. Since the late 1990s he increased the pressure on the English-speaking bishops, especially the American bishops, to force ICEL to give in to Roman demands. The core of the problem has been ICEL's preference for gender-neutral language when consistent with the meaning of the text, such as in the use of words like 'people' or 'us' rather than 'man' or 'mankind'.

In May 2001, Medina Estévez issued a set of guidelines for translation entitled *Liturgiam Authenticam* ('Authentic Liturgy') which accused ICEL of excessively free English translations and 'political correctness' in using non-gender specific language. It also praised some of ICEL's most virulent critics. One US bishop who spoke off the record to the US's *National Catholic Reporter* said that 'The issue boils down to who knows best how a liturgical text should sound in English—the English-speaking bishops and their most talented scholarly advisers, or the Vatican?' In March 2002,

Medina Estévez's Congregation rejected a proposed translation of the Sacramentary, a book of prayers used at Mass, saying that it reflected the ethos of 'consumerist societies'. It complained about the use of inclusive language as 'faddish' and 'ill-adapted to the liturgical context'. Medina Estévez emphasised that the word 'man' expressed a collective concept and that by dropping it the translators changed the essential meaning of the prayers. He even insisted that the well-known response to the priest's greeting 'The Lord be with you' should be 'And with your spirit' (a literal translation of the Latin) rather than 'And also with you', as is used and understood throughout the English-speaking Catholic world.

The key to marginalising ICEL and getting around the English-speaking bishops' conferences was the setting-up by Medina Estévez of a new body to monitor the translation of worship texts into English. This committee was called *Vox Clara* ('Clear Voice') and is made up of twelve senior English-speaking bishops, the majority known to be critical of ICEL, chaired by Cardinal George Pell of Sydney. Pell has long disapproved the use of inclusive language. The role of this committee is supervisory; it is not meant to do the actual translations. It will also advise the Vatican in reviewing proposed English texts. The final act of Medina Estévez's prefecture was to bring ICEL directly under Vatican control.

Since his departure the Nigerian Cardinal Francis Arinze has been appointed Prefect at Divine Worship. What became clear was that there will be an emphasis on a more literal translation of the Latin text into English, that the language will be much less gender-inclusive and that the words 'man', 'men' and 'mankind' will be used a lot more in Catholic worship. Also, the English text used will take on a more exalted, sacred feel. Whether this will help or hinder the public prayer of the church is an open question. But for any sensible observer of the English-speaking world the campaign against inclusive language seems like an extraordinarily ill-advised, backward step. And all this primarily orchestrated by someone whose mother-tongue is Spanish. In February 2004 a draft English translation of the Mass was sent to the English-speaking bishops' conferences. The Bishops' Conference of England and Wales highlighted the essential problem with the new text when they said it contained 'lengthy sentences, poor syntax and archaic language'.

Many of the English-speaking bishops' conferences also expressed caution about the new Mass text and most were loathe to change the responses of the congregation too much. What has become clear is that the understated but real resistance by the bishops' conferences has caused *Vox Clara*, and especially the reconstituted ICEL to hesitate and there is some evidence that they might rethink their approach.

Now we turn from the worship of the church to the ecclesiology that dominated the John Paul papacy. The word 'ecclesiology' refers to theories about the nature and function of the church.

One of the elements not mentioned earlier was Balthasar's ecclesiology. There is a Latin word that sums it up: *communio* (communion). This is a very ancient term that has been used since the earliest church and it is still important because it has resonances for Eastern Orthodox Christians who think of the church in this way. Dialogue with the churches of Greece, Russia, Serbia, Rumania and all the other Orthodox churches was one of the important themes of the Wojtyla papacy. This has not been easy because of Orthodox sensitivities and fears about Rome's attempts to rule over the whole church as well as accusations, especially from the Russian church, about Rome's poaching converts from Orthodoxy. So to speak of the church as a communion at least sets up some grounds for dialogue between the churches. This is because it is a word that goes back to the early church before the eastern Orthodox and western Catholic churches were divided. It was actually not until the Middle Ages that a universalist ecclesiology took over in the west, reaching its highest point in the nine-teenth and twentieth centuries. A 'universalist ecclesiology' means a theory of the church that emphasises the importance of a common universality with a strong central authority with all the decisions being taken at the top level. This approach neglects the creativity and initiative of the local churches. The 1917 *Code of Canon Law* and the centralist Roman curia are testimonies to this. Whereas a *communio* ecclesiology tends to emphasise the local church.

Behind the Latin word *communio* is a Greek word, often used in the New Testament, *koinonia* meaning 'to pool' or 'to put or share together'. Both these ideas convey a sense of participating together with others or sharing in or possessing something in common. In the New Testament *koinonia* conveys three related ideas: firstly, sharing in God's gifts given through the Spirit of Christ and a profound relationship between God and humankind. Christians enter the family and become God's daughters and sons. Secondly, the union between God and each believer establishes a deep bond with other believers to form what the creed calls 'the communion of saints'. In other words, faith is never individualistic but is lived out in interaction with those who share the same belief. Thirdly, the community is given its most intimate and profound expression when it shares in the Eucharist. In other words, *koinonia* connotes communion with the Spirit of Christ and membership of the communion of saints, which is most intimately expressed in the celebration and reception of the Eucharistic communion. A theology of communion is fundamentally egalitarian; it is about interlocking fellowships, a communion of communions.

Throughout the Wojtyla papacy, the Latin word *communio* was often officially used to refer to the church, but in a particular way derived from Balthasar. The theory was that the primary relationship with God was 'vertical' and individual, and it was this that provided a basis for a 'horizontal' relationship with other Christians in the church. This is not the way the word was used in the New Testament. Except in the Johannine writings, the New Testament tends not to think of God in vertical terms. The emphasis is much more on a notion of intimacy with God through Christ in a familial sense with the important decisions concerning the family being taken at the local level. This is a strong argument for subsidiarity, that is, allowing local church communities to make as many decisions as possible. But what Pope John Paul, Ratzinger and the Vatican did was to import a later hierarchical and universalist ecclesiology from the Middle Ages into this ancient notion that the church is communal and essentially egalitarian. As a result, there was a kind of corrosive disjunction between rhetoric and reality.

So the use of *communio* language at a time when Catholicism had reached the ultimate development of a hierarchical, universalist ecclesiology is highly misleading and it twists the original meaning of the word 'communion'. The New Testament nicely side-steps the problems inherent in the papalist ecclesiology that has dominated the church for two centuries and which reached its apogee in Pope John Paul. It presents a notion of the church which is essentially horizontal and interconnected. In this conception the church is a universal communion of local communions, and the heart of the church is actually at the local level, not in Rome. It is the church of the parish, neighbourhood and ordinary people.

It certainly became clear during the latter years of the Wojtyla papacy that the modern papacy is too much for any individual to govern and manage, even if this way of doing things were theologically appropriate. Despite modern communications, the church cannot be micro-administered with the Vatican making all the significant decisions. More power has to be devolved to local decision-making bodies, especially synods and national bishops' conferences, and beyond them to parishes and the laity. If this were to happen, the church would not really need the apparatus of the Roman curia. All that would be necessary would be a co-ordinating secretariat that would maintain the bishop of Rome's role as the unifying principle in the communion of the church, and the real heart of the church would be the local community of people and priests.

5

THE HEART OF THE CHURCH

Twenty-five years ago I knew a rather sad and cynical older priest who is now dead. We worked together in a parish in the years after Vatican II and had made real attempts to involve the laity in the ministry. The older priest strongly resisted this and constantly complained about the laity 'invading the territory of the clergy'. He often said that 'he would not have joined the priesthood' if he had thought that the laity could do things like take communion to the sick or help people suffering bereavement or prepare couples for marriage or assist with the formation of converts, or even help with the financial administration of the parish. He constantly maintained that this was 'priest's work'. No amount of evidence of the laity's effectiveness or theological argument would shift him from his position. It was the job of the priest to carry out the ministry and it was the role of the laity to be 'shepherded'. I will never forget one lunchtime when he actually quoted the rather obscure nineteenth-century Anglo-Irish convert to Catholicism who became a powerful figure in the Vatican of Pius IX (1846–1878), Monsignor George Talbot de Malahide. Commenting on the role of the laity Talbot once wrote: 'What is the province of the laity? To hunt, to shoot, to entertain? These matters they understand, but to meddle with ecclesiastical matters they have no right at all.' For my priestly colleague Talbot was right: the laity were meddlers in ecclesiastical matters who should devote themselves to worldly affairs. When his bishop, William Ullathorne, once dismissively asked 'Who are the laity?', the English theologian and later cardinal John Henry Newman responded acidly that the church would look rather silly without them.

As Newman's comment suggests lay people make up more than 99 per cent of the church's membership so their participation in the church is absolutely central. But the fact is that since about the fourth century their role has been increasingly marginalised. The clergy, and later in church history members of religious orders, have monopolised ministry. Looking at the hierarchical church today it is hard to imagine that the earliest church was a much more democratic and flat structure and that there was no real hierarchical distinction between laity and clergy. All Christians were called to ministry and the work of the church was the responsibility of all members of the community. Each one contributed their specific gift. As Saint Paul says, 'there are varieties of gifts, but the same Spirit; and there are varieties of services, but the same Lord … To each is given the manifestation of the Spirit for the common good' (I Cor 12:4–7). Service and equality took precedence over rank and distinction. Everyone was an office-holder and all had a stake in the church. The gift of leadership was simply one important aptitude among many others. The evolution of ecclesiastical distinctions came gradually from the early second century with the emergence of 'monarchical' bishops, that is, leaders of established local communities. This distinction between clergy and laity became increasingly important from the fourth century when the church became part of the official structure of the late-Roman empire. The lay–clergy distinction, which has no basis in the New Testament, also dates from the fourth century as the leadership cadre, what today we would call the 'clergy', adapted themselves to the hierarchical structure of the empire.

The core problem that the church faced in the early period was that the radical equality of all Christians was constantly threatened by the fact that some of the functions carried out in the church became more important than others. The Letter to the Ephesians says that the Holy Spirit's 'gifts were that some should be apostles, some prophets, some pastors and teachers, to equip the saints for the work of ministry, for building up the body of Christ' (Ephesians 4:11–12). It is on the basis of specific gifts that functional diversity emerges. But the constant danger is that equality is swallowed up and functional diversity assumes the dominant role in church life. This is exactly what happened in the fourth and fifth centuries when the ordained and professional clergy cornered more and more the church's ministry. Saint Augustine's warning to his clergy in Hippo was

soon forgotten: 'Let not the priest in you swallow up the Christian.' From
the clerical–lay distinction it was a short step to deny equality between the
two. This inequality was eventually enshrined in medieval canon law.

What Vatican II tried to do was to recover something of the New
Testament vision and the emphasis found in the earliest church. The
Council clearly wanted to restore the dignity of the laity. They were no
longer to be sheep 'shepherded' by omnicompetent clergy, but it was recognised that they had a call, a vocation to work for and within the church.
The foundation for this was laid in *Lumen gentium*, the Vatican II decree
on the church, when it took as its primary image the notion of the 'people
of God'. All members of the church participate in the ministry of Christ
and all are co-responsible for the life and growth of the faith. The laity are
not dependent on the clergy. Vatican II's *Decree on the Apostolate of the
Laity* says unequivocally:

> The laity can engage in their apostolic activity either as individuals or
> together as members of various groups or associations ... [These] are
> established by the free choice of the laity and regulated by their prudent
> judgement ... the laity must not be deprived of the possibility of acting
> on their own accord. (chs 4:15 and 5:24)

The basis of lay ministry is baptism, and all Christians are called to holiness which was no longer to be the preserve of priests and members of
religious orders. The Council was a moment of liberation and challenge
for the laity and there is a real sense in which they were the primary ben-
eficiaries of Vatican II. They had nothing to lose but their chains and they
have not been slow to realise their potential. Monsignor Talbot would have
been completely horrified.

Since Vatican II, lay ministries have grown enormously throughout the
church. In Australia, laity have completely taken over Catholicism's largest
ministry, primary and secondary education. In 1960, 90 per cent of Catholic
teachers were sisters, priests and brothers. In 2003 more than 95 per cent
were laity. Even parish ministry is being taken over by sisters and lay
people, especially where there is no priest, or in rural parishes where the
priest is sick or inadequate. They act as diocesan and local directors or co-
ordinators of religious education and they run most of the social service
and youth ministry of the church. They have leadership roles as spiritual
directors and even sometimes act as officials within the canonical and court
system of the church. There are many more lay ministers than there are
active priests in the United States and 80 per cent of these are women. In

the US there are more than 20 000 laity working professionally on parish staffs alone, let alone other ministries. If religious education teachers in Catholic schools are included, the same kind of statistic would be true of Australia.

The world statistics are quite striking. In December 2002, 17.2 per cent of the world's population was Catholic, which amounts to 1.07 billion people. This figure has been growing steadily for years. According to the *Annuario Pontificio*, the Vatican Year Book, there are 4.2 million people engaged in pastoral work; 405 058 of these are priests. The rest are members of religious orders and laity. This number includes 2.7 million lay catechists and 143 745 lay missionaries. More and more women are active in ministerial roles that are quasi-priestly: hospital and jail chaplains, parish administrators, visitors who bring communion to the sick and aged, educators and counsellors. Increasingly, Catholics do not care about distinctions between ordained and non-ordained. They see Christ as much in a woman as in a priest. The number of priestless parishes is increasing. In the US there are more than 2000 without a resident priest and the number is growing in Australia. Many Catholics in developing countries only have Mass or receive the Eucharist once or twice a year. The laity are stepping into all of these breaches.

The evidence is that thoughtful and active Catholics today see themselves as the people of God. There is a 'horizontalisation' occurring, whether the papacy or hierarchy likes it or not. People feel that they have a right to participate in decision-making about the appointment of their priests and bishops, about what moral rules are binding on them, about what it is that makes someone a Catholic. The Eucharist and the sacraments, spirituality and social justice are still central issues for most Catholics, as well as the morality of reproduction, the role of women and the acceptance of married clergy.

However, Pope Wojtyla was deeply concerned with this more egalitarian approach, especially as the laity became more and more involved in increasing numbers of roles in the church. He felt that this was impinging on the ministry of the priest. Not that he was anti-laity; far from it. He certainly believed that baptism was the basis for an active lay apostolate in the church. In this sense he was no latter-day George Talbot. But when you examine his approach carefully you see that he had shifted the emphasis away from the less hierarchical and more egalitarian style of Vatican II back toward a clearer clerical–lay distinction. This was revealed in his post-synodal response, *Christifideles Laici*, to the World Synod on the Laity in

October 1987. He says that the laity, like the clergy and members of religious orders, are all called to holiness and on the basis of that they go out into the world. But for him the secular world of work, society, culture and politics was the laity's primary place of mission. Their 'secular vocation' was to 'sanctify the world' with the saving message of Christ. They were not called to clericalisation nor to becoming 'junior priests'. This is shown in the words he uses. He never speaks of the 'ministry' of laity for only the ordained have a 'ministry'. The laity have an 'apostolate'. Their primary 'vocation' is to be assertive proclaimers of the gospel of Jesus and the moral message of the church in the world.

There is a sense in which this is a useful corrective, especially when there is a temptation to clericalise the laity. But there is also a more fundamental sense in which John Paul reinforced the old distinction between laity and clergy, and he seemed determined to drive lay people right out of the sanctuary, and even out of exercising any responsibility whatsoever for 'ecclesiastical matters'.

This was made clear in the 13 November 1997 Vatican document 'Instruction on Certain Questions Regarding the Collaboration of the Non-Ordained Faithful in the Sacred Ministry of Priests'. On behalf of John Paul, Cardinal Joseph Ratzinger made it clear that the document was directed to 'problems' in north-central Europe, North America and Australia. He said that there was a danger that some might think that 'the tasks of the laity and of priests as being on a level of substantial equality'. This created, the Instruction said, a 'functionalistic' approach to ministry and broke down the 'ontological difference' between priests and laity. Substantially, what Ratzinger meant is that ministry is not merely a function that can be carried out by anyone with appropriate ability. If the ministry is sacramental, only a priest, one whose essential status in the church has changed through ordination, can carry out that ministry. The key sentence of Ratzinger's comments states: 'The doctrine on the nature of the priestly ministry ... must be underlined with clarity, in order to avoid devaluing the priesthood, clericalisation of the laity and falling into a "Protestantisation" of the concepts of ministry and of the church.' Ratzinger emphasised that 'a loss of the meaning of the sacrament of holy orders' as well as 'the growth of a kind of parallel ministry by so-called "pastoral assistants"' causes 'confusion' among the laity who have lost their sense of the special identity of ordained priests. The practical consequences are that the laity are not permitted to give homilies at Mass, they can only distribute communion when there is a genuine shortage of priests, they must not wear liturgical vestments that resemble those of priests, nor may they join the celebrant in saying the Eucharistic prayer.

Fortunately no one took a great deal of notice of this Instruction, but it does indicate the way in which things were moving in the latter days of the Wojtyla papacy. One of the best aspects of the church is the way in which many lay people generously get on with the job and do not worry too much about the hierarchy unless something directly impinges on them. The shortage of clergy, created by papal insistence on the maintenance of celibacy, means that many laity have had to step in to maintain the church's ministry. Where Pope John Paul and Ratzinger were completely unrealistic was in their failure to comprehend the fact that all over the world local churches were trying to deal with the shortage of priests, and the fact that in the western world so many of those priests available were either approaching or beyond retirement age. If there are no priests then the people have no choice but to carry out ministerial roles. While many of these lack education and formation for the work they carry out, there is a small but important minority who have undergone theological and pastoral training at an advanced level. However, this lack of training should not be ignored if people are to undertake sacramental or strictly pastoral ministries.

The majority of lay people certainly followed John Paul's advice and acted in their various roles in the secular world to build up the Church. But as the Wojtyla papacy reached its last years, a sense of passivity and alienation started to emerge among even the most dedicated laity. The sense of belonging to the Catholic family, with all its dysfunctionalities, was tested to the limits. While committed Catholics did not drop out of the church, a kind of detachment set in which was exacerbated by the clerical sexual abuse crisis. The Wojtyla papacy drove many mainstream Catholics into a kind of wilderness where their faith was in abeyance. As one generous Catholic in his late fifties said to me: 'It is not that we have left the church. We still need the Eucharist and the sacraments, but the institution seems to have withdrawn from us. It simply no longer speaks to us. We are Catholics in suspension.' Women especially feel this. Many have already left Catholicism behind, and many others simply hang on by the skin of their teeth, struggling against the innate sexism and patriarchy that is endemic in present church structures.

Indeed, perhaps the greatest tragedy of the John Paul papacy was that it resulted in the alienation of so many women from the church. This may have been inevitable, but the sad thing is that all the evidence is that Wojtyla

was a man who liked women, valued their company and believed in
genuine equality. Women were his closest friends. But mutual incomprehension and alienation between th e pope and liberated western women
was inevitable because of modern feminist claims and the pope's somewhat
idiosyncratic theology. Feminism insists on the radical equality of women
and men with the corollary that their roles are to a considerable extent
interchangeable. Pope Wojtyla had long-established and strong views on
the role of women. These sprang from his theology of the body which first
found expression in his book *Love and Responsibility*, published in Polish in
1960 just after he became a bishop. Mutual incomprehension was inevitable between modern feminists who insisted on granting basic 'rights' to
women, including leadership roles in the church and the right to priestly
ordination, and Wojtyla who focused on the 'essential role' of women, by
which he meant the functions laid down for women by nature itself and
the natural law.

He believed that the difference in physiology and biology between men
and women connoted fundamentally different psychological and spiritual
approaches to life. He maintained that the physiology and psychology of
women was oriented towards child-bearing and maternity. These differences between men and women were based on God's plan. 'Male and
female [God] created them' (Genesis 1:27). The differences were not merely
cultural or sociological. Thus men and women are specifically different
and have distinct and separate roles based on 'archetypes' that are derived
from nature itself.

Wojtyla argued that the early chapters of Genesis developed a whole
phenomenology of male–female relations. In March 1980, as part of a long
series of talks at general audiences on sexuality that sometimes shocked
pious pilgrims, he said that

> The theology of the body contained in the Book of Genesis is concisely
> and briefly expressed. Yet we find in it fundamental concepts that
> are in some sense primary and definitive … The physical make-up of
> woman differs from that of the male … This is externally manifested
> up to a point in the appearance and form of the body. Maternity reveals
> this constitution from within as the special capacity of the female
> organism which has the creative power to conceive and give birth to a
> human being, with the help of man.

This leads to the idea that women have specific 'feminine characteristics'
and a 'feminine nature'. John Paul agrees with Balthasar that modern fem-

inism has created what the Swiss theologian calls 'monosexism' and the elimination of gender differentiation. Women want to be like men.

This association of woman with child-bearing also conjured up for Wojtyla notions about the 'mystery of woman' and the 'eternal feminine' which you find in writers as diverse as Johann Wolfgang von Goethe, Gertrude von Le Fort and Paul Claudel, as well as late-romantic German, French and English writers. Much of Benedict XVI's early reading was in a similar cultural milieu. Yet nowhere in the Wojtyla corpus will you find a discussion of essential 'male characteristics' and the 'mystery of the male'. While there was something chivalrous, idealistic and 'old-fashioned' about Wojtyla's views, many women found his approach patronising. They saw it as wanting to keep them in a subordinate place with their whole lives oriented towards motherhood. To them it seemed a superficial reading of the meaning of sexual differentiation and reflected little of modern psychology. It was also questionable theologically. It ignored the aspirations of contemporary women in the developed world, and also seemed to con-demn women in the developing world to an endless round of child-bearing and exploitation, especially given that the only method of birth control permitted in the moral theology of Pope Wojtyla was variations on the rhythm method. To many women his views seemed like an exaggerated example of 'biology is destiny'.

Finally, there was the question of the ordination of women. Pope Wojtyla and Ratzinger attempted to close off this question once and for all in the Apostolic Letter *Ordinatio sacerdotalis* ('Priestly Ordination') of 22 May 1994, and the CDF's *Reponsum ad dubium* ('Response to a Doubt') of 28 October 1995. Substantially what was argued was that the ordination of women was incompatible with the 'fundamental constitution' of the church as shown by its constant tradition of not ordaining women. In a John Paul kind of twist, emphasis was laid in the Apostolic Letter on the fact that the Blessed Virgin Mary had never been ordained, so it cannot be argued 'that women are of lesser dignity, nor can it be construed as discrimination against them' (*Ordinatio sacerdotalis*, paragraph 3). Pope Wojtyla solemnly declared that 'the church has no authority whatsoever to confer priestly ordination on women and … this judgement is to be defini-tively held by all the church's faithful' (paragraph 4). This led to a storm of protest. Ratzinger tried to stop this by declaring in his *Responsum* that this teaching had been 'set forth infallibly by the ordinary and universal Magisterium' and that it belonged 'to the deposit of faith'. In other words it was infallible—which it was clearly not. To prevent further controversy, discussion of the topic was forbidden to Catholics. None of this achieved anything. The discussion continues. But what it did achieve was to make many good Catholic women feel even more alienated than ever in the church. In fact, the whole approach to the question of the role of women was one of the most notable failures of the Wojtyla papacy.

Another significant failure of the last papacy was the inability to address the deep-seated issues confronting the Catholic priesthood. This is intimately interconnected with the question of the role of the laity in ministry. However, the tragedy of the failure to deal with the issues embedded in the crisis of the priesthood has had more disastrous results.

If many laity felt themselves in limbo during the John Paul papacy, a great number of priests, especially in the western world, felt they had descended into hell. This was especially so after the child sexual abuse crisis first exploded in the late-1990s and since January 2002 when the scandal broke in the archdiocese of Boston, eventually leading to the resignation of Cardinal Bernard Law. One of the most astute writers on the contemporary priesthood, Donald B. Cozzens, has described the post-Vatican II period as 'a dark night of the soul' for priests.

From the old-style, privileged clerical perspective, priests were the ones who lost most at Vatican II. Bishops had their role as successors of the apostles and members of the episcopal college re-emphasised and reinforced, the laity regained something of their dignity (at least in theory), but Vatican II's document on the ministry and life of priests was particularly disjointed, unhelpful and uninspiring. In one sense this document is radical in that it called priests to a renewed ministry which emphasised involvement in everyday life, openness to non-believers, and service to the poor and outcasts. While it acknowledged the priest's call to the sacramental and preaching ministry of the church, as well as leadership of the community, it actually shifted emphasis across to an external ministry. Priests were told they had to care for those outside the church as much as for those within. So as well as caring for the faithful, they had to become missionaries to the unchurched. This was a radical change in traditional pastoral practice. But the document outlined no corresponding theological shift in its understanding of the priesthood, nor did it suggest any of the adaptations required in the training, discipline and life of priests if they were to carry this out successfully. In other words, it took them right out into the world, but it wanted them to do without adequate preparation and safeguards, and with an outdated spirituality and model of priesthood. In an understatement Cozzens says that as a result most priests for decades now have experienced their lives as 'somehow slightly out of focus'.

In fact what happened in the period after Vatican II was that no longer was the priest to live surrounded by a sacral aura in a Catholic subculture diffused with respect for 'Father' and fully supported by the Catholic community. The days of Bing Crosby, 'Going My Way' and 'The Bells of Saint Mary's' were gone for ever. Shedding his collar, title and direct access to the sacred, the post-Vatican II priest suddenly had to become all things to everybody and servant of all while, at the same time, operate within a hierarchical structure whose stances were often directly at odds with the pastoral concerns of the people to whom he was ministering. Some priests managed to bridge this divide and many of them have acted out this role for decades. Others did not, and retired into a conservative, reactionary stance thus creating a corrosive antagonism among priests with completely different views of ministry. Men with incompatible approaches to the role of the priest have some times had to work in the same parish and live with each other in the same house.

Many priests also felt themselves caught between the pastoral needs and priorities of their communities and the demands of the bishop or the Vatican. This conflict first came to a catastrophic head on 24 July 1968 when the papal birth-control encyclical, *Humanae vitae*, which condemned the use of artificial contraception, was issued. Priests had to negotiate the resulting crisis of conscience with their people and the big majority did it respecting each couple's conscientious decision. Most priests had enough sense to follow the lead of Paul VI himself and never mentioned the contraception issue again in public. But the tension was resurrected during the papacy of John Paul II who made the question of the acceptance of the condemnation of contraception a touchstone of orthodoxy issue again in the church.

As well as conflict over sexuality and reproduction, priests had to deal with an increasingly activist laity. The people understandably wanted a say in the running of their local parish and suddenly priests had to shift from a hierarchical mode of thinking to a consultative one. Parishioners often demanded that the local priest also fulfil an almost impossible range of roles. He was supposed to be an inspiring celebrant of worship and an insightful preacher; a competent parish and school administrator who could also offer counselling in a whole range of areas, while at the same time making sure that the physical fabric of the church and parish school was kept up to scratch.

Having achieved all of this, priests were also expected to be sensitive to the new feminism and to the change in the role and status of women. At the same time, they were also faced with conflicting pastoral situations like the giving of communion to remarried divorced Catholics and to openly gay people, as well as negotiate intercommunion with other Christian churches, and a whole range of other issues that priests now face daily. They also had to offer leadership to the Catholic community through a complex process of change in the church, as well being present to people in their life transitions from birth to death, providing counselling and support for them. Sometimes they found themselves in conflict with conservative bishops who had little comprehension of pastoral reality or who had forgotten what it was like to work in a parish. They also found themselves confronted with a small but highly organised and aggressive cadre of reactionary laity who had never accepted Vatican II and who were determined to make life hell for priests who had. And all of this without any professional preparation whatsoever for such a convoluted and difficult role.

John Paul constantly insisted that priests live out fully the traditional discipline of celibacy. This meant that they also had no immediate emotional support or anyone with whom to share their affections, dreams and aspirations. Having supported everyone else they often came home at night to an empty dwelling. Often the parish house served as both their home and their office, and quite a few priests lost any sense of the essential division between their public role and their personal, private lives. Jane Anderson in her fascinating book *Priests in Love* (2005) brings a whole new perspective to the actual conditions that are part of the lives of some of the most committed priests. She shows how priests have had to struggle with celibacy and the compromises they have made to survive. For men who were often constantly on duty the lack of a private life could be quite disastrous, especially when personal boundaries were crossed. Also in the decades since Vatican II, priests have had to face the fact that many old friends and colleagues have left the ministry to marry. This could be quite psychologically undermining and the danger was that those left behind felt an increasing sense of isolation and siege.

It was a recipe for absolute disaster that was not long in arriving.

At the beginning of the twenty-first century all these problems came to a head. For three and a half decades the leadership of the church had refused to face what was obvious to any informed observer: the church was facing a series of crises of increasing magnitude, and priests were emerging as the epicentre of the problem. This is understandable given that they stand at the ecclesial crossroads between episcopal leadership and the laity. The Vatican and Pope Wojtyla seemed unaware and even uncaring about what was happening to priests in parishes and other ministries, and the most they offered were ineffectual spiritual solutions to what was really a series of problems at the pastoral interface between the church and reality. This is illustrated by the approach Pope John Paul took to the issues confronting the priesthood throughout his papacy. According to him, individualism, hedonism and a lack of a sense of mystery had invaded both church and society, and this made it close to impossible for modern society to understand the real role of the priest. His approach actually heightened the tensions priests were facing because of his constant emphasis on an outdated theology and spirituality, and his apparent lack of understanding of the real priestly situation. This became clear at the beginning of his papacy. On Holy Thursday, 1979, he sent a letter to all priests. It was uncompromising. Using parental imagery, he said that the priesthood was a vocation not a career. That is why it cannot be renounced. 'The priest by renouncing fatherhood ... seeks another fatherhood and, as it were, even another motherhood ... These are the children of his spirit, people entrusted to his solicitude by the Good Shepherd ... [They] are more numerous than an ordinary human family can embrace.' This kind of rhetoric tends to lack persuasiveness with English-speakers, whatever impact it has in the romance languages. The imagery also modulates back to a pre-Vatican II notion of priesthood with 'father' caring for the whole flock who are dependent on him. This is reinforced by the fact that Pope Wojtyla placed the priesthood squarely in the context of the hierarchical church and stated that it was essentially different from the priesthood of all believers. Thus, *de facto*, priests were placed 'outside' their community and it was as though Vatican II had not happened. He made it clear that if you accepted ordination you accepted celibacy and he was certainly not going to let anyone abandon their commitment. A promise had been made and 'Keeping one's word is ... a duty and proof of the priest's inner maturity; it is the expression of his personal dignity.' Even though he denied it, the letter seemed to say that celibacy is essential to the priesthood. He decreed that in Latin-Rite Catholicism non-celibates could not be ordained. So much for the ordination of married men, an idea widely suggested in the period after Vatican II, especially as a solution for the shortage of priests, and as a way of ministry in cultures where celibacy was not valued.

The tradition of Holy Thursday letters to priests continued throughout the papacy. Most emphasised a conventional, almost pre-conciliar view of the priesthood. Pope Wojtyla tended to blame the current priestly malaise on a kind of corrosive secularism that seeped into the church and which was absorbed by those priests who were insufficiently committed to holiness and church discipline

In October 1990 the World Synod of Bishops was devoted to the education and formation of priests in the context of today's world. To make sure that controversial topics were kept off the agenda the Relator of the Synod, Cardinal Lucas Moreira Neves, then archbishop of Sao Salvador de Bahia, Brazil, announced that celibacy, the return of resigned priests to ministry, the ordination of married men and the ordination of women were off the Synod agenda because they had been dealt with 'elsewhere'. This did not stop many bishops at the Synod being very outspoken precisely on these issues. Among them were the Indonesian bishops who have been consistently petitioning Rome for thirty years to allow them to ordain married men, specifically married catechists. Many of the approximately five to six million Catholics in Indonesia, especially those in the outlying islands, only have a priest for Mass once or twice a year. The bishops saw this as a distortion of the nature of church, for Mass and the Eucharist are at the core of the church's life. The Indonesian bishops wanted sufficient priests, whether married or celibate, to carry on the sacramental ministry.

But it was all to no avail. Synods come and go, but the pope and curia are in Rome for the long haul. At the closing session, John Paul told the bishops that the possibility of ordaining married men 'is often invoked within the framework of a systematic propaganda hostile to priestly celibacy'. This was pretty insensitive and unfair to bishops such as the Indonesians, who were primarily concerned about making the Eucharist available to their people. Church and priests had to wait a year and a half for a papal response to the Synod. This came in the form of a very lengthy Apostolic Exhortation, *Pastores dabo vobis* ('I will give you shepherds') of 25 March 1992. The title says everything. Priests are 'shepherds' of the community, and while John Paul placed the ministerial priesthood within the context of the general priesthood of all believers, he emphasised that ordination 'configures' the priest to Christ in a special way. In this Exhortation, the pope stepped right outside the usual New Testament understanding of leadership as one of the gifts given by the Spirit of God to the community and as essentially a form of service to speak about the priesthood in terms of being uniquely 'configured to Christ', actually being 'another Christ'. In other words, the priest uniquely represents the image of Christ in the community. According to John Paul it was precisely for this reason that women cannot be ordained for they cannot represent the male

Christ. This configuration gave the priest a unique sacramental authority and the priest exercised this authority through service to the community.

Most of the Exhortation was quite conventional, but what is interesting is the way in which the pope subtly shifted the focus away from the present generation of priests toward reforming the seminary system, so that a whole new generation of priests, unpolluted by the 'worldliness' of the present generation, would emerge to continue the Wojtyla vision of ministry, and what he called the 'new evangelisation'. In order to achieve this, the Vatican Congregation for Catholic Education in the mid-1980s had carried out a series of 'apostolic visitations' of seminaries throughout the world. It is not clear what these visits actually achieved, if anything.

All this is a long way from the hard pastoral reality that ordinary priests face as they struggle with overwork, loneliness, their own sexual needs, boredom and often burnout. Nowadays priests, especially the more generous and talented ones, are not only faced with exhausting workloads, but their accessibility to the laity means they often bear the brunt of the blame for all the problems of the church. In countries such as Australia, the United States and Britain, Catholicism is also confronting an acute shortage of clergy. The average age of priests is 60 or more, and many are expected to work on almost until they die on the job. After years working in parishes without a break or a change in ministry, let alone a sabbatical or a long holiday, many experience not only burnout but an even more insidious form of *ennui* which saps all their energy. They become so exhausted that there is no time or strength left for study, thought, personal relationship, friendship and aesthetic experience. Their intellectual lives dry up and their emotional experience becomes increasingly shallow. It is often at times like these that they make disastrously wrong judgements about a whole range of issues, but especially in the area of personal and sexual relations.

As if these issues of spiritual and personal exhaustion were not enough, priests now find themselves facing the sexual abuse crisis. While many bishops learned what was happening, the majority of priests were unaware of what was really going on in their ranks because the child abusers were very secretive. So, for many, the revelations have been truly shocking.

Sexual abuse of children has certainly been devastating for those who were its victims. For the Catholic community generally, as well as for priests with decades of commitment, it has come as a shock and humiliation that this was known about by church leadership and was permitted to continue by shifting abusive clergy around. As a result, men who have served their communities generously all their lives now have to confront the fact that the priesthood is often treated as a pariah profession and they are assumed by many people to be sexually maladjusted. Even the best priests are distrusted by some parishioners, especially with children. They are often the butt of jokes about molestation and personal innuendo about their sexual lives, or subjected to outright defamation by the media. They are also vulnerable to false accusation. Of course, no sensible priest is denying that colleagues, some whom they have known for many years, have committed serious crimes and should be punished by the full force of the law, nor are they claiming that the clergy should not be subjected to rigorous professional standards. But they also feel they are in a 'no win' situation, so most are just keeping their heads down and trying to get on with their ministry. But they sometimes find that they have to go out to help people in isolated and unstructured situations without professional support. They also know that it will be increasingly difficult to attract appropriate candidates to replace them, and they are aware that the priesthood is becoming an increasingly gay profession. Nevertheless, gay or straight, most just continue to minister as best they can, trying to be loyal to the communities in which they work. It is a very difficult time to be a priest.

Many priests are also deeply embarrassed by the church and the bishops' totally inadequate response to the child sexual crisis. The storm centre has been the United States: it was events in the archdiocese of Boston in 2001 and 2002 which brought everything to a head. Australia has undergone a similar crisis, but it has been less focused in a specific place and has dragged on over a longer period. The situation in the UK has more or less paralleled Australia. Ireland has had a particularly nasty series of scandals.

Clearly, child abuse has been a problem in the church for many decades, as it has been in society generally. It was first widely reported in the media as a problem for the church in the Kansas City-based *National Catholic Reporter* in the early 1980s, especially by the journalist Jason Berry in his reports on the notorious Gilbert Gauthe abuse case in Louisiana. In 1985 the US Bishops' Conference received a comprehensive report on the problem but nothing was done. In 1992, Berry published a book *Lead Us Not Into Temptation*, the first comprehensive treatment in English of sexual abuse by clergy. In the prologue Berry goes to the heart of the matter. He says: 'The crisis in the Catholic church lies not in the fraction of priests who molest youngsters but in an ecclesiastical power structure that harbours paedophiles, conceals other sexual behaviour patterns among its clerics, and uses strategies of duplicity and counter-attack against the victims'

(p. xx). In all English-speaking countries, the bishops for years stone-walled victims, lawyers and the media over sexual abuse. They pretended there was no problem. But scandals kept cropping up and eventually their obfuscations and denials came home to roost.

In the United States the bishops only really confronted the issue when the *Boston Globe* forced the local archdiocese and Cardinal Bernard Law to surrender the documents that were released to the media and public concerning the John Geoghan and Paul Shanley cases. As a result, the US church is facing payouts to victims of up to one billion dollars. Half a billion has already been paid out. In Australia the bishops had confronted the issue a couple of years earlier. What has angered most people, as Jason Berry points out, is the way bishops in the past refused to do anything about the issue and tried to protect the institution and the offending priests. In a new book *Vows of Silence*, Berry and his colleague Gerard Renner have shown how paedophiles were protected while clergy and sisters who tried to tell the truth or encourage renewal in the church were marginalised or even punished.

The Boston crisis, the bad publicity and the eventual resignation of Law after tremendous pressure from laity and clergy precipitated a frenzy of activity by the US bishops. In an attempt to halt the out-of-control crisis, they decided in mid-June 2002 at their meeting in Dallas to institute a 'zero tolerance' policy for clerical child abusers. In other words, one strike and you're out. What's more, this policy was to be retrospective. The bishops trawled back through their personnel records for five decades, determined to dismiss from the priesthood anyone who could be credibly accused of child sexual abuse. As a result, not only were serious abusers permanently dismissed from ministry, but also priests who were involved in only one incident many years previously. However, significantly the bishops did nothing about their own episcopal colleagues who had colluded in the whole scandal by protecting or moving serial abusers. With the exception of Cardinal Law, not a single United States bishop has resigned or been dismissed over long-term failures to confront this issue.

The focus here has been on the US because the Vatican's reaction was largely framed in response to the American situation. At first Rome tried to isolate sexual abuse as a problem in the English-speaking world resulting largely from secularism and 'pan-sexualism' as one curial cardinal called it. From the American perspective it seemed as though Rome could not understand the issue. While paedophilia was certainly present in Latin cultures it was not talked about, especially in public and through the media. To non-Anglos it seemed as though the US situation was just another example of a degenerate preoccupation with sex with a particularly vicious anti-Catholic prejudice built into it. Typical of the curial reaction was Archbishop (later Cardinal) and Opus Dei member Julian Herranz who told the Italian newspaper *La Repubblica* (25 August 2003) that the whole crisis in the US was far too focused on the church. It seemed as though somebody (the media?) 'wants to sully its image in order to take away its moral force'.

Pope Wojtyla's first response to the crisis came in his regular Holy Thursday 2002 letter to priests. While there was no apology, there was a reference to 'our brothers [in the priesthood] who have betrayed the grace of ordination in succumbing to the most grievous forms of the *mysterium iniquitatis* (mystery of evil).' It was a form of acknowledgement, but it was cold comfort for those hurt by the crisis. The next step was when the eight US cardinal archbishops were ordered to Rome for a two-day meeting which ended on 24 April 2002. In the press statement following this meeting there was an acknowledgement of the problem but no apology was offered, celibacy was defended and it was stressed that no link between it and paedophilia could be established, and there was concern expressed about the slur cast on the reputation of the church and good priests. Following the US bishops' meeting in Dallas, Rome had two concerns: the first centred on the power given to lay boards to supervise the implementation of the bishops' policy. And the second focused on concern about maintaining due canonical process for accused priests. Rome wanted to protect the presumption of innocence. Perhaps lurking below the surface was a concern that the 'zero tolerance' policy was too harsh and unforgiving. It is true that in the past the church was far too forgiving of this crime, but that does not mean that now it is unforgivable. Rome rightly wanted to maintain a balance between punishment and forgiveness.

Yet, at the same time, the Vatican was being somewhat ingenious. What it really wanted to do was to prevent the lay boards getting too much power over bishops. One way of preventing that was to make sure all child sex abuse cases were to be referred to the CDF which could either decide them itself or refer them back to the local diocese for decision. Also, priests who had been permanently stood down by their bishops could appeal to the Congregation for the Clergy in Rome. This happened in several cases in Australia where local bishops were ordered to reinstate priests who had been before the civil courts. However, the bishops stood their ground.

It quickly became apparent that no matter how deep the crisis got for local churches, Pope John Paul was not going to shift on the question of celibacy. At the time of his twenty-fifth jubilee as pope he issued an Apostolic Exhortation to all bishops, *Pastores Gregis* ('Pastors of the Flock') on 16 October 2003. He told bishops to

> support and encourage priests who ... have freely assumed the commitment of celibacy ... In the reality of the church and world today, the witness of chaste love is, on the one hand, a form of spiritual therapy for humanity and, on the other, a form of protest against the idiolatry of instinct. (Ch. 2, 21)

His reference to sexual abuse was brief and to the point:

> In cases of grave lapses, and even more of crimes which do damage to the very witness of the gospel, especially when these involve the church's ministers, the bishop must be firm and decisive, just and impartial. He is bound to intervene in a timely manner, according to the established canonical norms, for the correction and spiritual good of the sacred minister, for the reparation of scandal and the restoration of justice, and for all that is required for the protection and assistance of victims. (Ch. 2, 21)

In other words, he was absolutely convinced that celibacy had a real witness value in a world consumed with what he saw as a kind of sexual mania, an 'idiolatry of instinct'. By the phrase 'a form of spiritual therapy' he probably means that celibacy offers an alternative vision of love and passion poured out in the service of others. But as so often happens in this kind of spiritual rhetoric, there is no engagement with the reality that most priests face in the daily grind of parish work and ministry. The feel of *Pastores Gregis* is that somehow the whole matter would be better handled in-house in the church. The Latin approach to these kinds of issues is still dominant.

The image of the priest's 'dark night of the soul'. was also taken up by the popular American spiritual writer Father Ron Rolheiser. He points out that this dark night comes directly from God, who speaks through it to both priests themselves and to the Catholic community. It is purifying experience because it makes the whole church particularly vulnerable and vulnerability, he argues, is a prerequisite for genuine spiritual growth. He says:

Put simply: Right now priests represent less than one per-cent of the overall problem of sexual abuse yet they are on the front pages of the newspapers and the issue is very much focused on the church. While it is painful, it can also be fruitful. The fact that priests and the church are in a way being scapegoated is not necessarily a bad thing. If … [this] helps society bring the issue of sexual abuse and its devastation of the human soul more into the open, then we are precisely offering ourselves as 'food for the life of the world' … If the price tag is humiliation and a drain on our resources, so be it. Crucifixions are never easy.

This is probably the only way in which anyone can make sense of this terrible episode in the life of Catholicism.

The larger irony of this crisis has been that while John Paul offered long-serving and dedicated priests scant comfort in their 'dark night' other than the reinforcement of old disciplines and outdated spiritualities, he provided much great comfort and support for his own favourites, the so-called 'new religious movements' (NRMs) or, as the Vatican preferred to call them, 'new ecclesial movements'.

Pope Wojtyla's saw the NRMs as the 'shock troops' of his 'new evangelisation'. The most well-known and controversial is the oldest of them, Opus Dei (OD), first established in Madrid in 1928. The other NRMs, such as the Legionaries of Christ (LC), founded in Mexico City in 1941, the Neo-Catechuminate (Neo-Cats) begun in Spain in 1964, Communion and Liberation (C+L), founded in Milan in the late 1960s, and the Focolare movement begun in 1942, are less well known but quite pervasive in some parts of the church, especially Italy, Spain and Latin America. All are also present in the English-speaking world but their influence is less obvious than in the Latin world.

There are two other NRMs that are much more open to the wider church and more involved in the mainstream community. They are the L'Arche Community founded by the French-Canadian Jean Vanier, a thoughtful and effective spiritual writer, and the Rome-based Sant'Egidio Community. What I say about NRMs really does not apply to these two latter communities.

The NRMs are sect-like, secretive and elitist. They operate as though there were really two types of Catholics, the committed women and men of an NRM, and the 'also ran' ordinary Catholics who belong to local parishes or who are marginal to the life of the church. The NRMs actually show little respect for local churches and parishes, although they use them for recruiting purposes. The Neo-Cats, for instance, come to a parish with a promise of enlivening practising Catholics and bringing the lapsed back to church. What they actually do is set up a separate and divisive enclave in the parish with their own liturgy. They take people out of the parish and into their own programs that can last for up to ten years. They sometimes force the local priest into the position of having to choose between them and the ordinary parishioners. OD is more elitist and sets itself up as a separate church, legally independent from local bishop, and subject only to its own Prelate in Rome. LC is a separate, pontifically established religious order. All these organisations have a strong feeling of clericalism about them.

The NRMs are also myopically focused on their founders as the source of all wisdom. In OD the founder, Josemaria Escriva (died 1975), is treated within the organisation as though he were the sole font of all wisdom, in practice almost standing in the place of Christ. Three living founders, Chiara Lubich (Focolare), Marcial Maciel (LC) and Kiko Argüello (Neo-Cats) have not yet reached oracle status, but they are certainly more important and decisive for members than anyone else in the church. Their word is final, even down to the music used at Mass for the Neo-Cats. The NRMs claim to be theologically and structurally revolutionary. They say that nothing like them has even been seen in the church before. This is historically wrong. LC is simply a conventional if very closed and conservative religious order of priests. They always stand out in papal ceremonies with their back soutanes and white surplices, short-back-and-side, Mormon-like haircuts, and rigid marine-style posture. The vast majority of OD members (numeraries as they are called) are vowed lay people just like religious sisters and brothers, but the organisation is really run by the 2000 priest members. It actually resembles a conventional religious order with several branches made up of priests and non-ordained men and women. The Neo-Cats are really a secular institute of lay people who make up the vast majority of the membership, but there are some priests, and the relationship between the laity and clergy has not yet been worked out in terms of church law. All of them act like old-style, exempt religious orders, that is they are approved by Rome, they look to a centralised world headquarters, and they are largely independent of local bishops.

OD particularly, and the others to a lesser extent, are said to be like the early Jesuits, revolutionary in structure and pastoral approach. They do resemble the early Jesuits in the sense that they are highly centralised. But the Jesuits were remarkably well adapted to their age, the sixteenth century Counter-Reformation, and the order has evolved over the centuries to meet contemporary needs. In contrast, the NRMs are almost the polar opposites of what Vatican II called for: a church that begins with ordinary Catholics at the local level, not a community that is a highly centralised worldwide movement that promotes an integralist, neo-papal theology. The early Jesuits were incorrectly said to be 'militaristic' in their approach, whereas at the heart of their spirituality was the extraordinary mysticism of the founder, Saint Ignatius Loyola. What is significantly lacking in all the NRMs is any trace of mysticism in their ethos. But they are certainly 'soldiers of Christ', even 'Legionaries'. That is why they appealed to John Paul as the shock-troops of his 'new evangelisation'.

The power and influence of the NRMs was vividly symbolised on Pentecost Sunday 1998. Pope Wojtyla had invited them to come to Rome to celebrate their 'maturity'. He compared the gathering of half a million people around Saint Peter's basilica to the first Pentecost, telling them that 'what happened two thousand years ago in Jerusalem is being repeated … in this square'. He made it clear that he thought that they were the future of the church. Of course, it remains to be seen what the future will bring. As the pope himself told the NRMs 'wherever the Holy Spirit intervenes, he leaves people astonished'. Exactly!

It is always difficult to ascertain the historical significance of any major figure while they are still alive or a short time after their death. Nevertheless, we still have to try to achieve some perspective, especially when the person is as well known and as long lived as John Paul II. His papacy was the second-longest in church history—if we leave out Saint Peter. So what is the late pope's legacy? Is he, as George Weigel suggests, a man of enormous historical importance and the prophet of the twenty-first century? Is he a 'colossus' as Eamon Duffy argues, 'a giant among popes'? Or are his contributions, especially to the inner life of the church, somewhat more modest?

There is no doubt that in some areas external to the church he was someone of political and historical significance, especially in breaking down the Iron Curtain and the divisions between east and west that came with the collapse of Soviet communism. He stood firmly on the side of the poor and offered a coherent and highly critical analysis of rampant capitalism and neo-liberalism. Also, more than any other world leader, he visited Africa often in order to highlight the terrible problems of poverty, depravation and disease that afflicted the people of that continent. He was a tireless campaigner for peace and did not hesitate to speak out on pre-emptive warfare such as the allied invasion of Iraq. He did more than anyone to try to heal the terrible history between Jews and Catholics and single-handedly made it impossible for anyone to remain a Catholic in good standing and be in any way anti-semitic. There is no doubt about his significance as a figure on the world stage in the latter part of the twentieth century.

Bridging religious divides is especially important in our world of fundamentalist religious terrorism, and John Paul has also done much in this area. His 1995 encyclical letter *Ut unum sint* ('That They May be One') signalled an openness to the other Christian churches, especially the Orthodox, although the Vatican often showed scant respect for the Protestant and Anglican churches. It was John Paul's background in eastern Europe that made him conscious of the Orthodox Christian tradition. He said that Europe needed to breathe with both its religious lungs—the Western Catholic and Christian as well as the Eastern represented by the Greek, Russian and other Orthodox churches. To an extent he was successful in this, although relations were severely strained by sometimes clumsy Catholic incursions into post-communist Russia and the appointment of bishops there, as well as by the hypersensitivity of the Orthodox with the justified fear of Roman centralism, and the tensions between Orthodox and Catholic Ukrainians that resulted from the return to the Catholics of churches and property confiscated during the Stalinist period and given to the Russian Orthodox.

But real problems in assessing his contribution come when we review his primary role, that of bishop of Rome and leader of the church. Somewhat kindly, Eamon Duffy says

> John Paul is a prophet, not an administrator: he sees his role as pope as that of travelling evangelist, encouraging, exhorting, rebuking, proclaiming an ancient message he believes can renew the world. He has left the structures of the church largely in the hands of others, sometimes with unhappy results.

This is a reasonable description of his papacy, but the problem is that traditionally and historically, a globe-trotting evangelical ministry is not the primary role of the bishop of Rome. His traditionally understood task is to act as the heart and focus of the Catholic communion. He is the one who draws the multifaceted realities of a world church together.

But what Pope Wojtyla actually did was to modulate that kind of reconciling leadership ministry into something much more pro-active. The most interesting text in the New Testament about Peter as leader of the apostles is where Jesus says that he has prayed for him that 'his faith may not fail', and then building on the basis of that faith he instructs Peter to 'strengthen your brothers' (Luke 22:32). So, as Jesus sees it, the pope's primary task is to have faith and support the ministries of others, particularly the bishops. The problem with the Wojtyla papacy was that what might have been intended as support—visiting every church in the world—quickly modu- lated into a takeover. Papal visits did not strengthen but actually weakened episcopal leadership. The trips made the Wojtyla papacy omnipresent. And meanwhile an interfering Vatican micro-managed the church down to the last detail. While John Paul did not invent this approach, the length of his papacy gave him a chance to develop it to an extent never seen before in church history. In this sense, Pope Wojtyla was a revolutionary, outside the mainstream of the Catholic tradition.

This was also an extraordinarily idiosyncratic papacy in the sense that the Wojtyla vision is, in a literal sense, a peculiar, subjective one. One reason for this was because he emerged from a particular culture—that of Poland—and because he lived out his youth and priesthood in a very extreme period of the culture's history, that of the Nazi and Communist eras. But Wojtyla also came to the papacy with a quite unusual approach to Catholicism that stood outside the mainstream. While he attended all the sessions of Vatican II and often used the rhetoric of the Council, his agenda as pope was not primarily about the debates that have swirled around the church over the last 40 years. What he attempted to do, perhaps unconsciously, was to impose his own perspective on Catholicism. This was absolutist in the sense that he believed that there is an absolute, un- changeable, knowable truth revealed to the world primarily by Christ and the church. He was an ethicist who believed passionately that God had laid down an immutable pattern of behaviour in human nature, and that Catholic moral teaching revealed this. In this sense, Catholicism alone had a full understanding of the meaning of human personhood. In fact at heart Wojtyla was an old-style neo-scholastic whose thought gained a kind of con- temporary patina by the use of personalistic and phenomenological rhetoric.

This is also the reason why so much of his teaching seemed, *a priori*, divorced from reality. He showed little acquaintance with contemporary theology and especially with thinkers such as Karl Rahner. He lacked any real understanding of contemporary biblical studies and church history. There is no sense in his entire corpus that he understood the historical con- ditioning that contextualises all philosophy and theology. He showed no comprehension of the extraordinary historical mutation through which Catholicism has been passing since the papacy of John XXIII the greatest pope since Paul III. Ratzinger, while much more aware of developments in western theology, shared the same kind of historical amnesia and lack of context that characterised the whole Wojtyla papacy.

From the perspective of the internal life of Catholicism the last 25 years have been at best a period of marking time, at worst a phase when a couple of generations of creative, thoughtful Catholics have been marginalised, and many, sadly, driven out of the church. In history, Pope John Paul II must ultimately take responsibility for this.

Part Two

SEDE VACANTE

6

THE EMPTY CHAIR

The funeral of John Paul was probably the largest in human history. Never before in the entire 3000-year experience of Rome had there been so many people in the city. Four million or more visitors, many of them conspicuously young, swelled Rome's usual population of 2.7 million. All roads leading to the city were gridlocked, and people slept in the streets. Many waited up to fifteen hours to file quickly past the pope's body as it lay in state in St Peter's Basilica.

Those world leaders present included four kings, five queens, seven princes and princesses, and some seventy serving and former presidents and prime ministers, among them George W. Bush and his father, George Bush Snr, Tony Blair, Bill Clinton, the UN's Kofi Annan, France's Jacques Chirac, Iran's Mohammad Khatami, and Hamid Karzai from Afghanistan. Prince Charles postponed his wedding to the Duchess of Cornwall in order to be present. The only nation that made itself notable by the absence of representation was the People's Republic of China (PRC), which is still at loggerheads with the Vatican over the appointment of bishops in the PRC. As the media's interest in broadcasting the funeral also showed, the impressive turnout reflected Pope Wojtyla's influence throughout the world.

But why did so many ordinary people come to the funeral? Probably in part because the city of Rome welcomed them. The low-key, non-confrontational approach taken by the Italian authorities and people is a tribute to their urbanity. And this despite the fact that so many heads of state in one place created a nightmare for both Vatican and Italian security. Thousands of extra police were brought in, surveillance planes were constantly in the air above the city, and anti-aircraft missiles and a warship off the coast were ready for action.

Many of the visitors who poured in were from the pope's native country: more than 800 000 Poles are said to have attended. Almost all of this response was spontaneous, and the vast majority of those who came were lay people. They came by car, bus, train, plane—whatever form of transport they could arrange and afford. For instance, for those who came by car it is a 1900-kilometre round trip from Cracow to Rome, so many spent several days driving, just to show their respects.

No doubt the new religious movements, such as the Neo-Catechuminate, Focolare, and Communion and Liberation, made sure their people were present in numbers, ready to give 'witness' to any journalist or TV camera that went past—and there were crews everywhere looking for interviews and 'vox pops'. It is harder to explain the masses of young people who turned out. For some commentators, the reason for their presence was simple. John Paul, they say, had a tremendous impact on the young because of his spirituality and challenging 'orthodox' teaching. According to Cardinal George Pell of Sydney, the pope's appeal was based on 'a reaction against the turmoil and ravages of a radically secular society. In the west there are a lot of dysfunctional and broken families and a great hostility to the idea of fatherhood. But human nature craves father figures. One of Christ's preferred terms for God was the Father. There is a great yearning for authority, for integrity, for fatherhood.' (*Sydney Morning Herald*, 9/4/05) An American Sister, Joan Chittister, observed simply that many young people today lack grandparents, and that the pope 'was the grandfather of their souls'.

Others take a more analytical view. Sociologist Professor Franco Ferrarotti of Rome University said that in Italy especially, and to a lesser extent in the rest of Europe, Catholicism and the papacy are part of the cultural pattern, and while the young cheered John Paul even when he talked of pre-marital chastity, they still made up their own minds about the exercise of their sexuality. They admired the pope as the symbol of Catholicism, but decided for themselves what they do in private. Ferrarotti agreed with Pell that many young people have no meaning structures or moral anchors.

> In liberal minded families and society, young people feel they can do whatever they want. But they don't want to do whatever they want. They want to be oriented. They want to have an ideal in life. That

doesn't mean they will follow it, but they like to be pushed ... Somehow [Pope Wojtyla] filled a vacuum that has been left by liberal education. This pope has been incredibly contradictory. He was an innovator in the mass media but his message was very conservative. Yet I think all the demanding practice and theology was overwhelmed by the media images of the pope as enthusiastic and compassionate. That was what young people loved. (quoted in *Sydney Morning Herald*, 9/4/05)

Clearly there were sincere young people in the crowd who had a genuine commitment to the approach to life that John Paul taught. But they were very much in the minority. And all of them shared a lack of historical perspective on the Wojtyla papacy. He was the only pope that anyone under 30 ever knew. Many of them think that all popes are supposed to be 'super stars' and that Catholicism is essentially about the pope. They don't even know the names of his more colourless predecessors. The attraction of John Paul to the young has much in common with the Princess Diana phenomenon. Both seemed somehow to touch a deep unconscious need in whole groups of people, which was then reinforced by the media turning them into celebrities. The pope probably tapped into the need for guidance and certainty, and for a moral and spiritual sheet anchor.

The media also played an important role in the massive response to the death of the pope. Big stories can build as the networks try to outdo each other, and this story took on a life of its own and quickly gathered momentum. Rhetoric such as 'the biggest in history' and the facile application of words like 'great' and 'saint' to Pope Wojtyla even before he died all helped to build an atmosphere in which people felt they wanted to participate in what seemed like a historical event, no matter in how small a way. The saturation coverage of the pope's death and funeral was symptomatic of the symbiotic relationship between the world media and the papal super star. The media, especially television, thrive on celebrities and big crowds, and John Paul II had the added frisson of the authority and mystique of the papacy. So even when viewers were tired of the saturation coverage and the endless repetition of the same things, and told the media so in emails and calls, this did not stem the flow. The story had 'legs' and it kept running until it was finally played out.

It is hard to comprehend the amount of money and resources that media organisations sank into covering the funeral and papal election. Associated Press and Eurovision had contracted with owners of prime spots—such as the Augustinian friars who had a five-storey building just behind the colonnades of the Piazza of St Peter's, or the grounds of the Pontifical Urban University on the Gianicolo hill above the basilica—to rent space for TV stands and presentation spots. There were two other TV stands, one at the far end of the Via della Conciliazione near the Tiber, and the other right between the Sala Stampa (the Press Office of the Holy See) and the Piazza of St Peter's. These sites were, in turn, split up into multiple presentation spots and sub-let to national and commercial media organisations, such as the BBC or ABC. Very large sums were paid in advance for these sites—AP paid the Augustinian order £280 000 as a deposit for their site plus a daily rental—and understandably media organisations were determined to get their money's worth.

The funeral Mass was celebrated on the morning of Friday, 8 April in front of St Peter's basilica facing out into the magnificent piazza designed in the seventeenth century by Gian Lorenzo Bernini. There were threatening clouds, an overcast sky and a strong wind blowing, but the rain held off until after the ceremony concluded. Heads of state were given a last chance to pay their respects to Pope Wojtyla inside the basilica, and as they emerged to take their places for the Mass they were officially greeted by Archbishop Michael Harvey representing the *appartamento* and carrying out his last function as prefect of the Papal Household. The heads of state fanned out to the right of the altar forming a large group of black-clad men and veiled women, many of them also greeted by the President of Italy, Carlo Azeglio Ciampi, as they arrived.

On the left of the altar were a large group of archbishops and bishops representing the various national hierarchies. Beside them were representatives of the other churches, among them Archbishop Rowan Williams of Canterbury, the Ecumenical Patriarch of the Orthodox Church, Bartholomew I, Metropolitan Kirill of the Russian Orthodox Church, and a now infirm Prior Roger Schutz, founder of the great ecumenical centre of Taize near Cluny in France. There were also representatives of the other great faiths. Looking further down from the basilica into the Piazza there were large crowds of invited guests, and priests from the diocese of Rome, religious orders and other dioceses.

Enclosed by the Bernini colonnades were 6000 more guests, and beyond them a massive crowd right down the Via della Conciliazione as far as the Tiber and the Castel S. Angelo. The vast crowd spilled over into the narrow side streets on either side, making movement in the area around the Vatican almost impossible. The music at the Mass was provided by the Cappella Musicale Pontificia Sistina, the personal choir of the pope and St Peter's, directed by Monsignor Giuseppe Liberto.

After the heads of state had taken their places, Archbishop Piero Marini, papal master of ceremonies, emerged alone from the basilica followed by a little group of archbishops, monsignors, priests, sisters and the pope's Italian valet. The group included Stanislaw Dziwisz, his face reflecting a deep but contained sadness, like a stoic son who had lost his father. These were literally the *famiglia pontificia*, the pope's immediate 'family'. John Paul had no close relatives still alive; the last of his relations, his father, died in 1941. So the small group from the *appartamento* had become the family Pope Wojtyla lost long ago.

The cardinal concelebrants in red vestments then emerged two-by-two from the basilica in a long procession. Bowing in reverence and kissing the altar, they formed two blocks of three rows on either side of the altar. Among them were the Patriarchs of the Eastern Rite Catholic churches in union with Rome in their unique and colourful vestments. Then the plain cypress casket was carried out of the basilica by twelve *Gentiluomini di Sua Santita*, the gentlemen of his holiness, volunteer laymen mainly from the traditional noble families of Rome. The casket was laid on the ground on a beautiful eastern-style carpet. At the head of the coffin stood a magnificent paschal (Easter) candle symbolising the resurrection. The deacon of the Mass solemnly placed an open book of the gospels on the casket, but it soon got caught by the wind and blew shut. The casket was marked with a simple cross and the letter 'M' for Mary, the Mother of Jesus

Then Cardinal Joseph Ratzinger, the Dean of the College of Cardinals, emerged from the basilica to celebrate Mass in Latin with his brother cardinals. Ratzinger, whose 78th birthday was nine days thence, is a shortish man with white hair and a low-key but elegant style. His Latin is clear and fluent, and his Italian laced with a German accent. He was assisted by Monsignor Francesco Camaldo as Master of Ceremonies, one of six MCs from Marini's Office of Pontifical Ceremonies supervising the rites. The Mass was celebrated in a plain, unadorned, almost pedestrian manner. Many who expected something like the Princess Diana funeral in Westminster Abbey with a wonderful choir and a superstar soloist were surprised and disappointed by the understated approach and singing that reflected little of the tremendous wealth of musical tradition in the Roman church. This almost local parish style celebration was deliberately encouraged under Pope Wojtyla, and Marini has been the one who oversaw a less ornate approach to pontifical ceremonies.

Ratzinger took the simple words of Jesus to Peter after the resurrection —'Follow me'—as his text for the homily. The sermon, which was spoken in Italian, was frequently interrupted by applause. It sketched a life in which

Carol Wojtyla lived out the call of Jesus. He was always ready to follow wherever the Lord led him—to the priesthood, the episcopate and eventually to the papacy

> for he heard in the church's call the voice of Christ … He never wanted to make his own life secure, to keep it for himself; he wanted to give of himself unreservedly, to the very last moment for Christ and thus also for us … The Holy Father was a priest to the last, for he offered his life to God for his flock and for the entire human family.

Ratzinger kept repeating 'Follow me' as a kind of mantra throughout the homily. Near the end of the sermon, looking up to the windows of the papal *appartamento*, the Cardinal said:

> None of us can ever forget in that last Easter Sunday of his life, the Holy Father, marked by suffering, came once more to the window of the apostolic palace and one last time gave his blessing *urbi et orbi* (to the city and the world). We can be sure that our beloved pope is standing today at the window of the Father's house, that he sees us and blesses us.

Ratzinger was clearly quite moved, and at the end of the homily there was sustained clapping.

The Mass proceeded quite quickly and, with over 300 priests distributing, even communion for the vast throng was got through with alacrity. But just before the Cardinal Dean began the post-communion prayer of the Mass, many in the crowd started shouting *'Santo subito'* ('sainthood immediately') and *'Santo, santo'* ('saint, saint') over and over. There were many banners around the crowd with these words on them. Some observers said that it was mainly Poles who were responsible for the *Santo subito* calls, but it seemed too well organised. One suspects that the NRMs were behind it—this being just the kind of stunt that they would perpetrate. The calls went on for almost seven minutes. Ratzinger seemed annoyed and impatient with this intrusion into the Mass. It is clear that one of the major problems facing the new papacy is how to deal with these organisations.

After the post-communion prayer, during the final commendation and farewell, the Eastern-rite Catholic bishops prayed—at some length—over the body of Pope Wojtyla. Then, after Ratzinger sprinkled holy water on the casket as a reminder of baptism and incensed it as a sign of respect and, as the bells tolled, the *Gentiluomini di Sua Santita* carried the casket back into the basilica after turning finally out towards the piazza and down towards the Tiber and the city. The cardinals then retreated silently into St Peter's. The pope's body was taken down into the crypt under the high altar and there it was privately placed in the tomb that originally held Pope John XXIII before his body was moved into the basilica itself.

John Paul II was finally gone. The cardinals and the church needed to turn towards the future, but many of us were still trying to gain some perspective on the Wojtyla papacy. There were many different reactions to his death. For some it was deeply tragic; they felt that they had lost a father, friend and Christian guide. Father Richard John Neuhaus wrote eloquently of the emotions he felt as he knelt in St Peter's where the pope's body lay in state:

> There, on the catafalque only a few feet away, was what remained. Kneeling at the prie-dieu, I had only a few minutes, certainly not more than ten, to think what I wanted to think and pray what I wanted to pray in this moment I had so long anticipated and so irrationally hoped would never come. Odd thoughts came to mind. His back was straight again, after all those years of being so pitiably hunched and trembling from Parkinson's disease. He seemed much smaller. Perhaps there was not much that could have been done by those who prepared the body. He was emaciated, beaten and bruised ... Lying there before the altar, under Bernini's magnificent baldachino, his head was tilted just slightly toward the right. Looking north, I though—toward Poland. He had fought the good fight, he had kept the faith. Well done, good and faithful servant. These and other passages came unbidden. Through my tears I tried to see again the years of his vitality, his charm, his challenge, his triumphs; the historic moments when I admired from a distance, and the personal encounters when I was surprised by the gift of an older brother who was the Holy Father. ('Rome Diary', *First Things*, 11 April 2005)

Neuhaus's reactions were very different from my own. I felt a profound sense of relief that John Paul had finally gone to God, and I know that I was not alone in sensing that the burden of a man who had so dominated Catholicism for 26 years was lifted. Although everyone recognises his great achievements, many faithful people concerned for the church and its work were left with the feeling that he had so overshadowed everyone else, had so identified Catholicism with himself, that we found ourselves exhausted, the life and passion drawn out of us. Many of us had the feeling that what we had to offer was irrelevant, that our gifts were worthless. John Paul was the only game in town and the most we could hope for was to be in the cheer squad. A situation had developed in which we were all acolytes, mere spectators in our own church and community. As a result, many good people now feel marginalised and have withdrawn to the edges of the church. This sense is often reinforced by the tendency of admirers of John Paul to accuse their fellow Catholics of disloyalty and question their faith and commitment because they resisted the papal super star. It was as though the Wojtyla way exhausted Catholicism, that there were no other options. Many of us felt that no matter who the next pope was, at least the burden of the cult of the messianic papal personality had been lifted from us. We could look to the future and hope for a more encouraging, low-key, Christ-like leadership.

Whether these expectations will be fulfilled remains to be seen, for the course of the papal election, and its outcome, surprised many observers.

Following well-established rules and customs, the church was run by the college of cardinals during the two-week interregnum between the death and burial of John Paul and the beginning of the conclave. The whole period is technically called *Sede vacante*, which loosely means 'the (papal) chair being empty'. During this period the cardinals operated according to very strict rules that reach right back into papal history and that were most recently revised by Popes Paul VI in October 1975 and John Paul II in February 1996. These rules cannot be changed by the cardinals during the interregnum.

The most important person in the interregnum period is the Cardinal Camerlengo, or Chamberlain of the Holy Roman Church, the 78-year-old Spanish Cardinal Eduardo Martinez Somalo. The Camerlengo was assisted by the Apostolic Camera, a small office, originating in the eleventh century, that aided him in the administration of the temporal goods of the Holy See during the *Sede vacante*. A rotating committee of three cardinals was chosen by the cardinal electors to assist the Camerlengo in preparing for the conclave, and making the day-to-day decisions that could not be deferred. However, the cardinals are strictly bound not to make any important decisions, above all any rulings that would be binding on the next pope. Their daily meetings were presided over by the Dean, Ratzinger.

After the pope's death, all cardinals who were heads of Vatican departments ceased to hold office except the Camerlengo and the Major Penitentiary, the American Cardinal Francis Stafford, former archbishop of Denver. The Penitentiary deals with confessional matters, and the idea is that forgiveness should always be available, pope or no pope. Cardinal Camillo Ruini, the vicar of the pope for the diocese of Rome, also remained in office so that the government of the local church could continue.

During the *Sede vacante* the cardinals met daily in general congregations (meetings), again chaired by Ratzinger as Dean, and it was during these congregations that he clearly impressed his brother cardinals. They also spent a lot of time networking informally and getting to know each other. There is no doubt that they discussed the kind of man they wanted and felt that the church needed as the next pope. Catholics believe that the whole profiling process is somehow guided by the Holy Spirit, but it will be worked out in very practical ways and will be determined by theological and ecclesiastical politics. Cardinals aged over 80 could participate in these discussions, but they were excluded as soon as their colleagues entered the conclave. There was deep resentment among some octogenarian cardinals back in 1970 when Paul VI prevented them from participating in papal elections. According to rumours, this sense of exclusion emerged again during the pre-election period and a number of the over-80s said bluntly that their exclusion was unjustifiable. There were other complaints that some cardinals felt they had been left out of pre-conclave discussions. The African Cardinal Wilfred Fox Napier of Durban told a journalist that he was isolated at a religious house in a remote Rome suburb and that he did not know where these informal discussions were occurring. No doubt this also applied to other cardinals who were not part of the inner circles.

Of course, many of the cardinals had already formed loose constellations with theological, ecclesiastical, political or regional interests in common. They did this very discreetly and obliquely before John Paul died. When asked about their discussions, especially by the media, they denied that anything remotely like this was happening. Those working in the Vatican will have been the most active in this type of discussion because of their proximity to each other and their common interests. Most cardinals will argue that the aim of the secrecy is to avoid party politics in the church, but the real reason is because Vatican affairs, still very much influenced by the Latin mentality, are always played out obliquely and behind closed doors.

This secretive approach has been criticised by some commentators. For instance, the American sociologist-priest Andrew Greeley has pointed out

that the original and traditional approach to the election of the Bishop of
Rome was for a wide cross-section of church membership to participate
democratically in the election and Greeley explicitly referred to the dictum
Qui praesidet super omnes, ab omnibus eligatur ('He who presides over all
must be chosen by all'). He said that the cardinals today are 'a collection of
elderly males who speak only for themselves … A drastic reform of papal
elections is absolutely necessary.' Here Greeley speaks for many in the
church who think that it would be better if the College of Cardinals were
joined in the election process by senior bishops from across the world, as
well as by representatives of priests and laity. As the College of Cardinals
is further internationalised, perhaps some of the elitist attitudes will dis-
appear and the church will become more open and drop its tendency to do
things in this secretive, arcane, Latin way.

In the period before the funeral, some cardinals were reasonably outspoken about the type of pope they wanted. Among the English-speakers,
Cardinal Cormac Murphy-O'Connor of Westminster sat down with a
number of print journalists at the English College in Rome, and US Cardinals Justin Rigali (Philadelphia), Roger Mahony (Los Angeles), William
Keeler (Baltimore), Theodore McCarrick (Washington, DC) and Edmund
Szoka (retired) all talked to CNN. Cardinal George Pell (Sydney) talked
to both Australian and foreign media. However, once the *novendiales*
(the nine-day mourning period) began Ratzinger, as Dean, tried to impose
silence on his colleagues. He was successful in the sense that no one spoke
out publicly, although a few Italian cardinals seemed to be leaking stories
to Marco Politi of the newspaper *La Repubblica*. Certainly an argument
can be made out to support the secrecy and media blackout. The *National
Catholic Reporter*'s John Allen commented that many cardinals from the
non-European and Anglo-American world were not used to dealing with
an aggressive, and at times hostile, media and that cardinals could end up
spending their whole time talking to journalists. He argued that they
needed time to reflect, pray, network and talk among themselves before
they entered the conclave. However, an opposite argument can also be
made. In the contemporary world, especially among people with democratic traditions, there is always suspicion of elections held behind closed
doors. Interested and committed Catholics wanted to know what their
leaders thought. The cardinals do not own the church. Nor have they
always had a monopoly over the voting. It is only since the mid-1100s that
the popes have almost always been elected by the cardinals.

It is often forgotten that the fundamental role of the pope is to be bishop of the diocese of Rome. In fact, during the first 700 years of church history it was usually the clergy and lay-people of the city, as well as the bishops from the towns immediately surrounding Rome, who played the major role in the election of the pope. The ancient popes would have agreed with Andrew Greeley and considered the present method of electing the pope by the College of Cardinals highly irregular and gravely wrong. There was a genuine communal and democratic sense operating in the first millennium church that many Catholics today are now trying to recover.

However, by the late eighth century the franchise had gradually become limited to the senior clergy of Rome, with approval from the people of the city. These were the priests who ministered at the 'titular churches'; that is, the oldest churches in the city. The title 'cardinal' (from the Latin *cardo* meaning 'hinge', or 'door', or even the beam used to support the door) was first applied to these parish priests from as early as the seventh century. They came to be known as 'cardinal priests'. The title was also slowly extended to the senior deacons of Rome. These were ordained men who were not priests, but who were in charge of church administration and the distribution of social welfare to the poor. In the eighth century the title of cardinal was also extended to the bishops of the central Italian dioceses immediately around Rome. With the pope and local clergy, these bishops formed the Roman Synod, often advising him on doctrinal issues and assisting him in the administration of the Roman church. They eventually evolved into a group of 'cardinal bishops'.

As the senior pastors and administrators, cardinal priests, deacons and bishops gradually assumed control of the Roman church during a papal vacancy. They also came to have an increasing say in the election of the new pope. In order to break the influence of secular rulers in papal elections, Pope Stephen III (768–72) decreed in 769 that only cardinal deacons and priests of the Roman church could be eligible for election as pope, and that the laity should have no vote. Lay participation had sometimes led to riots, disturbances and vicious factional infighting in Rome, and it was for this reason that churchmen tried to exclude the laity of Rome. However, the laity still retained the right to approve the election. Despite this, in the ninth and tenth centuries the papacy came more and more under the influence of external lay forces, especially the Mafia-like clans who controlled the *rioni* or districts of the city and its immediate surroundings from their fortified mansions. Many of the popes of this period were actually members of these families, and were often utterly unworthy of ecclesiastical office, let alone the papacy.

But from about 1030 onwards a reform movement that originated in Germany permeated Rome which gradually gathered strength. The greatest figure in the campaign to break lay control of ecclesiastical office was Pope Gregory VII (1073–85). The reformers realised that the papal election process was the key to making sure that a worthy person was elected. They eventually broke the control of the Roman clans over papal elections. At the same time, the papacy turned away from the narrow preoccupations of the political and ecclesiastical government of Rome and central Italy, and began to reassert its claims to universal jurisdiction over the whole church. Simultaneously, in the decades between 1050 and 1100, the cardinalate increasingly became an institution of the broader church. There were more and more cardinals of non-Roman and even non-Italian origin.

After experiencing a disputed election himself, Pope Nicholas II (1058–61) and the Lateran Synod of 1059 issued a Papal Election Decree, *In nomine Domini*, in April 1059 which bestowed on cardinal bishops alone the right to elect the pope. The other cardinals and the rest of the Roman clergy and people were then asked to express acquiescence. Pope Nicholas was trying to maintain the tradition of wider involvement because the papal election was not considered valid unless there was subsequent consent granted by the other cardinals, the Roman clergy and people. But the limitations of this process were quickly evident, and the right to participate in the election gradually spread to all cardinals, whether they were of episcopal, priestly or deacon rank This was enshrined in the election decree *Licet de evitanda* of the Third Lateran Council of March, 1179, which required that for a papal election to be valid a two-thirds majority of cardinals present must vote for a candidate. However, the notion was maintained for quite a long time that the lesser clergy and the laity of Rome still played a part in the process by their public acquiescence after the election. This fiction has subsequently disappeared.

From the twelfth century onwards, the college of cardinals has elected the pope in an enclosed meeting called a 'conclave', from the Latin '*cum clave*', meaning 'with a key'. This referred to the fact that the cardinals were locked up, sometimes with graduated fasting, until they elected the pope. Almost all medieval conclaves were held in the Lateran palace next to the cathedral church of Rome, St John Lateran. The Vatican was only used when the Lateran was not available, such as in 1378, the first conclave in Rome after the popes returned to the city after a 60-year residence in

Avignon. That election led directly to the Great Western Schism, when for thirty-five years there were two then three rival claimants to the papacy. The Council of Constance (1414–18) was called by the Emperor Sigismund to heal the Schism. All three pretenders to the papacy were dismissed, and Pope Martin V (1417–31) was elected by a mixed group of cardinals, bishops and lay people representing the Council.

Most modern conclaves have been held in the Sistine Chapel (which was built between 1475 and 1481 for Sixtus IV), surrounded by Michelangelo's amazing and now gloriously restored paintings of the creation (painted between 1508 and 1512) and last judgement (painted between 1534 and 1541). From the early fourteenth century the cardinals were strictly isolated from outsiders in uncomfortable circumstances until the new pope was elected. Even in twentieth-century conclaves the cardinals and their assistants did not always have separate rooms. They resided in the cramped and very inconvenient makeshift area surrounding the Sistine Chapel. The purpose of locking them away was to try to hasten papal elections. The reason for this was that in the late thirteenth and early fourteenth centuries there were long breaks between popes because of sharp divisions among the small number of cardinals in the conclave, who could not agree on who should be pope.

During the conclave that followed John Paul II's death, the cardinal electors resided in the purpose-built and much more comfortable 'Domus Sanctae Martae', a motel-style building of 130 suites and single rooms with dining facilities, erected in 1996 within the Vatican, next to the rather ugly modern Hall of Audiences on the left side of St Peter's Basilica. In keeping with the rule that a conclave could not begin less than fifteen days, and no later than twenty days after the death of the previous pope, the cardinals determined just before the funeral that the conclave would begin on Monday, 18 April 2005.

To be elected pope, a candidate must win a two-thirds majority plus one. This is a long-established rule. It was introduced during the papacy of Alexander III (1159–81) whose papacy was bedevilled by a series of anti-popes. So he made sure that the Third Lateran Council decreed that to be elected pope a candidate must gain a majority of two-thirds of the votes of the cardinal electors. In 1945, Pope Pius XII (1940–58) tightened this rule further to require a two-thirds majority, plus one. The purpose of requiring the two-thirds majority was to force the cardinals to compromise and reach an agreed consensus about the candidate in order to preclude the danger of a disputed election. It also avoided the problem of an elected pope's authority being weakened by having to deal with a large minority of disgruntled cardinals who had opposed his election. The two-thirds majority requirement prevented damaging splits between a small majority and a large minority.

However, in the Apostolic Constitution, *Universi Dominici Gregis* of 2 February 1996, John Paul II issued a new set of rules governing the election process. It is hard to discern why he suddenly issued this Apostolic Constitution; he gives no coherent explanation for it in the text of *Universi Dominici Gregis*, and no subsequent explanation has ever been forthcoming. Among a number of changes, he made a seemingly minor, but nevertheless extremely significant modification to the two-thirds majority requirement. He decreed that after the first day when, due to spiritual and liturgical preparation only one or two scrutinies (ballots) would be held, scrutinies are to proceed at the rate of four per day, two in the morning and two in the afternoon. If after three days no one has been elected, a day of prayer and discussion is to be held. If after a further twenty-one ballots (with a day's break after each set of three days) no one has received the two-thirds vote required, the Camerlengo can invite the cardinals to vote for another election procedure. At that point, the cardinals can decide to drop the requirement of a two-thirds majority and decide to elect by an absolute majority; that is, elect the cardinal who gets more than half the votes. This also means that they can vote to eliminate all candidates except those two who received the largest number of votes in the previous ballot.

The US Vatican specialist Father Thomas J. Reese highlights the possibility of problematic results from this change in procedure:

> If an absolute majority of the electors favour a candidate in the first ballot of the first day of the conclave, all they would have to do is to hold firm for about twelve days through about thirty votes until they can change the rules and elect their candidate. There is no incentive for them to compromise or move to another candidate. In fact, the incentive is reversed. The majority is encouraged to hold tight, while the minority is encouraged to give in since everyone knows the majority will prevail.

The problem with this change, as Reese points out, is that in a difficult and contested election there is no incentive to compromise. What has actually happened in most modern conclaves is that two or three candidates have emerged relatively quickly with large blocks of cardinals supporting them. But none could get the requisite number of votes. The two-thirds requirement forced a compromise, or persuaded the 'great electors' (the leading cardinals from various factions) to look for a compromise candidate, someone who would eventually be acceptable to the large majority from both blocks.

What John Paul's change does is to encourage a small majority to hold out against a large minority. It could prove to be disastrous in a strongly contested election. In the view of a number of commentators it actually indirectly influenced the result of the April 2005 conclave. Not only may the cardinals have felt pressured to come up with a quick election result in order to look unified, but once the strength of Ratzinger's vote was revealed in the first couple of ballots, supporters of other candidates realised, even unconsciously, that he was unbeatable. If there was a sizeable opposing minority, all his voters had to do was to hang together until they could force a change in the voting method to a simple majority. This change in the rules is disastrous and must be reversed at the earliest opportunity, preferably in the papacy of Benedict XVI.

Since the beginning of the twentieth century, the composition of the college of cardinals has become more and more internationalised. Italians no longer hold the majority. In the first conclave of the twentieth century, which elected Pius X, more than half the cardinal electors (38 of the 62) were Italian. In the April 2005 conclave there were 115 cardinals from 52 countries. Only 20 electors were from Italy. While the continuing growth of the ethnic diversity of the College of Cardinals gives the whole church a much better representation in the election process, it was expected that it would also make the actual election process more problematic, fraught and difficult to predict. There was less chance that cardinals will know each other well, and while many of the present-day cardinals, having studied in Rome, are likely to be able to speak reasonably good Italian, this is by no means assured. The use of Latin was no solution because there have always been only a very small number of cardinals who speak this language with any fluency. It was expected that cultural differences, expectations and priorities would also mean that communication problems between some groups would be enhanced.

So it seemed that the conclave that began on Monday, 18 April 2005 was going to be complex and possibly extended over several days. There was a feeling at least among commentators and journalists that the cardinals were fairly divided. This may have reflected the frustration of those trying to understand and comment on a situation in which there was hardly any information available. There was, in fact, a complete lack of briefing for the world media who were trying to cover the conclave. The only group that offered anything in the way of a detailed briefing was the International Movement We Are Church (IMWAC), which held three press conferences in the days before the conclave. IMWAC represents progressive European Catholic opinion, and it brought US Benedictine Sister Joan Chittister, Italian feminist theologian Adriana Valerio, psychoanalyst Luigi de Paoli, Sri Lankan theologian Father Tissa Balasuriya and me to Rome for the briefings. These conferences were very well attended by a cross-section of the world media. No other progressive or conservative Catholic group offered anything similar, even though it was clear that the media were hungry for anything they could get.

But, in the end, all the theories and pundits were proved wrong. The long slow demise of John Paul II meant that commentators like myself minutely examined the college of cardinals looking for potential popes on the basis of a profile. We felt that the cardinals would debate the kind of pope they felt that the church needed and that they would then look around for someone who more or less fitted the profile. So commentators saw it as their task to try to second-guess the cardinals.

Here is the profile that I developed to brief journalists:

The cardinals won't want a Wojtyla clone. But they won't be looking for the opposite either. Ideally they will look for someone around 68 to 72 who speaks perfect Italian, and who also has a good grasp of English and Spanish, the two most broadly spoken languages in the church. He will need to be at least reasonably progressive on political and economic issues with a strong sympathy for the conditions of life for the poor of the third world. But to be *papabile* (electable) he will need to be cautious and preferably conservative on theological issues and committed to defending the core beliefs of Catholicism, while remaining open to the other churches and religions. He will need to have some comprehension of Islam and not be inflammatory in attitudes towards it. There is considerable likelihood that there will be a reaction against the Roman curia among the electors. This means that curial cardinals are unlikely to be elected. There is a lot of resentment towards the Vatican Curia outside Rome, even among quite conservative churchmen, about the way the bishops have been marginalised and their authority limited by the heavy-handedness of the Roman bureaucracy during the Wojtyla papacy. So the cardinals will be looking for someone willing to support decentralisation and a retreat from the kind of centralised micro-management that has characterised recent years. I also think that to be *papabile* the candidate would need to be a spiritual person who is able to interpret Catholic belief and practice in terms that make sense to contemporary life and society. It is in this sense that a cardinal with wide pastoral experience with real people, who has worked in parishes, or in education, or in some form of hands-on ministry will appeal to his colleagues, especially if he is a man of genuine goodness. Someone without outspoken opinions, especially outspoken progressive views and, to a lesser extent, without abrasive reactionary views, will be preferred by the cardinal electors.

How totally wrong I was!

So, what really happened? If you believe what a number of cardinals had to say after the conclave, they didn't worry about a profile at all, but claiming they trusted in the Holy Spirit, they simply looked around for the right man and found him in Joseph Ratzinger. There is probably some truth in this claim, although the reality is much more complex.

In fact several factors were operative in the election of Benedict XVI and they go back to the mid to late 1990s as it became obvious that John Paul's health was failing. There is no secret that there was an active group who were working for the election of Ratzinger. This group wanted the continuation of the major policies of the Wojtyla papacy, but shorn of John Paul's dalliance with mega-events like the interreligious days of prayer at Assisi, his turning of the worship of the church into populist displays, his tendency to proclaim an endless succession of saints and blesseds, and what they felt were embarrassing *mea culpas* and apologies to all and sundry. Nevertheless, many commentators, including myself, simply did not think that those who supported the CDF cardinal's candidacy would be able to pull it off as easily as they did. I certainly thought that the other cardinals would have thought this out more thoroughly and organised other possible runners, and that their analyses would have revealed the flaws in the arguments being put forward by the Ratzinger supporters.

But I had underestimated the simplicity and a lack of imagination of the majority of cardinals. And perhaps I had attributed more faith to them than they actually had. They seem to have surrendered to fear and abrogated their responsibility to find a more creative solution to the needs of the church and the world. As the Brazilian Dominican theologian and activist Frei Betto commented after the election of Benedict XVI: 'Many cardinals appear to be imbued with fear rather than faith'.

In the week before the cardinals went into the conclave, Rome was swept by rumours that there was a strong move in favour of Ratzinger. According to the same rumour, or to another that was conflated with it, there was a counter-move by European cardinals, among them Cardinal Danneels of Brussels, to shore up support for Dionigi Tettamanzi of Milan. This certainly seemed an unlikely combination but, according to the rumour, Ratzinger already had close to fifty votes by the weekend before the conclave began. Clear divisions began to emerge among the Italian cardinals and they began to leak to the media, especially to Marco Politi of *La Repubblica*. The problem was that no one had any idea how much truth there was in this, although Politi certainly turned out to be right when, just after the John Paul funeral, he predicted a Ratzinger papacy.

To begin to understand the speed with which the CDF prefect was elected you have to backtrack to see how the coalition that put Ratzinger forward was built. In chapter 4, I explained how he is profoundly influenced by the theology of Saint Augustine and by the Swiss thinker Hans Urs von Balthasar. Essentially, his theological view is deeply imbued with a kind of pessimism about the world and human affairs. His spirituality is deeply Christocentric and he sees Catholicism as the real light of the world which is lost in sin and despair. He feels that European culture especially has abandoned its Christian roots and has thus 'developed a culture that excludes God from the public consciousness, either by denying him altogether or by judging that his existence cannot be demonstrated, is uncertain and, therefore, somewhat irrelevant to public life.' This sentence comes from a speech that Ratzinger gave at Subiaco, Italy, just nineteen days before he was elected pope. Subiaco is the place where Saint Benedict began the movement that became Western monasticism. The then CDF prefect was particularly concerned with the explicit rejection of a recognition of the place of Christianity and God in European culture, specifically in the proposed EU constitution. He felt that the dominant post-modern emphasis on relativism and crass secularism had become so ingrained in Western culture that the church must confront it.

He is not alone in this view of the contemporary world. There is a group of Catholics, including many cardinals, which believes that this analysis is correct, and that a confrontation cannot be avoided with what they conceive of as aggressive secularism. If that means being totally out of tune with the times, then so be it. Their preoccupations tend to be with western Europe and the Anglo-American world. They seem to have little sympathy with or experience of poverty, inequality, over-population, environmental exploitation and destruction, let alone the non-Christian world of Asia. They are conscious of Islam, although they tend to see it as a threat in Europe. In fact, several of them, including the former CDF prefect himself, have opposed the admission of Turkey to the EU on the grounds that this predominantly Islamic nation has little in common with the culture of Europe. This group is particularly critical of Catholics who advocate dialogue rather than confrontation with contemporary culture. It is especially critical of those who think the world might have something to teach the church and that God might be active outside Catholicism and especially outside the ambit of Christianity. Essentially, what is happening is that the consequences of the theological emphases of Karl Rahner and Hans Urs von Balthasar are being played out in practice in the life of the church.

The Balthasar approach represented by Ratzinger was especially favoured in the Wojtyla papacy and had grown to become a powerful force in many places in the hierarchy. The strength of this group was that it had a clear program for the internal renewal of the church. It wanted to maintain what it saw as the best elements of the Wojtyla papacy such as doctrinal clarity, holding the line on sexual ethics and gender issues, the emphasis on equity and social justice (although in this area they are probably a good bit more muted than John Paul II himself), a clear statement on the uniqueness of Christianity and a renewal of missionary activity, and the re-evangelisation of countries and cultures seen as lost to secularism and consumerism such as western Europe, the UK and Australia.

But while the CDF prefect was the leading exponent of this approach, he always remained the theologian. It has been left up to others to make this vision of a more militant, muscular, uncompromising Catholicism a reality. Over the last years of the Wojtyla papacy, as John Paul's health increasingly failed, a party, or perhaps more precisely a constellation, of influential clerics have been forming around the notion of making Ratzinger pope. It is not as though they are all in perfect agreement, but there is a general consensus among them about how the church should relate to contemporary culture. They felt that Ratzinger would be the only reliable one to continue this aspect of John Paul II's policy. To some extent this constellation has been chronicled by Sandro Magister, a journalist and commentator in the Italian news magazine *L'Espresso*. Magister characterises this group as 'neo-conservative', but for the English-speaker this term could be misleading, because of its popular associations with American politics. Some associated with the Ratzinger push in the US would be 'neo-cons' in the commonly used sense. They are sympathetic to most aspects of George W. Bush's policies, including his neo-rationalist approach to the economy. They would be Republican voters. They were fierce opponents in the last US election of John Kerry and those Democrats who lean towards more small 'l' liberal policies on gender, social and defence issues.

While many of the pro-Ratzinger Italians are close to the Italian government of Silvio Berlusconi, none of them are 'neo-cons' in the American sense. Nor are they unreconstructed reactionaries. While in my view their analysis of the contemporary church, world and culture is simplistic and in many ways wrong, their position is consistent and clearly articulated. They are really the anti-relativistic and anti-post-modern party of 'capital "T" Truth'. They believe that there is an objective, unassailable, eternal truth that can be known and that its fullness is to be found in the Catholic Church. They maintain that most western European countries are dominated by militant secularism and post-modernism that is explicitly anti-religious, creating a cultural crisis of the first magnitude which the church must confront.

Who are they? In Italy they centre around Cardinal Camillo Ruini, the papal vicar for the diocese of Rome and the president of the Italian Bishops' Conference. Ruini, who was not elected by the Italian episcopate but imposed on them by John Paul II, is a key if divisive figure in Italian Catholicism. Like Ratzinger, he has articulated views that reflect a jaundiced view of progressivism, whether Catholic or secular. He maintains that Catholicism is locked in a grand struggle for the very soul of Europe, which the church originally nurtured, but that it has now rejected its historical roots. At a Mass in St Peter's basilica during the *novendiales* he told the congregation that the church should not be 'folded in upon itself, not timid, not lacking in trust ... [but should be] burning with the love of Christ for the salvation of all'. Others who support Ruini are Cardinal Angelo Scola, Patriarch of Venice, Archbishop Carlo Caffarra of Bologna, as well as his predecessor in Bologna, the bluntly-spoken Cardinal Giacomo Biffi. The new religious movements in Italy are also supportive of a more aggressive, evangelical Catholicism, especially Communion and Liberation founded by the Milanese priest Luigi Giussani. As president of the Bishops' Conference, Ruini also controls *Avvenire*, the daily newspaper owned by the Conference, which gives him a platform to air his views. However, in Italy there is a strong group, including many bishops, who are very much opposed to the Ruini approach. While there is an articulate group of progressive Catholics, most of the Italian bishops, clergy and people take a much more tolerant, pastoral approach to moral, political and social issues than Ruini.

In Europe there are several other cardinals who would have had much sympathy with the Ratzinger diagnosis of the ills that affect European society. Among them would be his former student from the 1970s, the Dominican Christoph Schönborn, the archbishop of Vienna, and Jean-Marie Lustiger, the retired archbishop of Paris. Schönborn became especially important as a numbers man and organiser as the conclave approached.

While this movement is largely European in origin and inspiration and is essentially deeply Euro-centric, there are also adherents elsewhere in the English- and Spanish-speaking worlds. In the United States the leading clerical exponents of the pro-Ratzinger view would be the archbishop of Chicago, Cardinal Francis E. George, Cardinal Avery Dulles, son of former US Secretary of State John Foster Dulles. Cardinal Dulles is a prominent US Jesuit theologian who is over 80. The other key figure is Father Richard John Neuhaus, a convert from Lutheranism to Catholicism, whom I quoted above.

Neuhaus is a classical neo-con. Staring out as a radical leftist Lutheran pastor in the Brooklyn ghetto of Bedford-Stuyvesant in the 1960s, he moved from a revolutionary opposition to the Vietnam War to a strongly pro-capitalist stance in the mid-1970s and argued for the compatibility of Christianity and what subsequently came to be called 'democratic capitalism'. He is the editor of the magazine *First Things* and the founder and president of the Institute on Religion and Public Life. In 1990 he converted to Catholicism and a year later was ordained a priest for the Archdiocese of New York. He has considerable influence within the Bush White House, and is widely respected by the Protestant Evangelicals who provided the groundswell of support that propelled Bush back into the Presidency in 2004. Neuhaus's support for the election of Ratzinger as pope is quite overt and his closeness to Chicago's Cardinal George is also well known. Sandro Magister says that other cardinal members of this pro-Ratzinger group include Marc Ouellet, the recently appointed archbishop of Quebec, Jorge Mario Bergoglio, cardinal of Buenos Aires, and Francesco Javier Errazuriz Ossa, archbishop of Santiago. Ouellet taught for many years in seminaries in Latin America and at the Lateran University in Rome and worked briefly in the Roman curia, as also did Ossa. The inclusion of Bergoglio in this group is surprising.

Another cardinal in this coalition is the much-travelled George Pell, archbishop of Sydney. He is well known among anti-progressive Catholics in the United States where he frequently features as a lecturer. Since the early 1990s when he was Auxiliary Bishop of Melbourne, Pell has been active in building a network of contacts with like-minded American Catholics and Neuhaus is a key part of that group. Pell has also built many contacts in the Vatican, many of them drawn from a ten-year stint from 1990 as a member of the Congregation for the Doctrine of the Faith. He is a frank admirer and firm supporter of Ratzinger, and told a number of people openly that he would vote for the CDF prefect in the conclave. Neuhaus frankly acknowledges Pell's role in the group. Writing from Rome on 11 April 2005 in *First Things* he muses that 'The only plausible English-speaking *papabile* is the formidable George Pell of Sydney, Australia. He is a friend and I confess I would rejoice in his election, but that seems an unlikely prospect.'

As the health of Pope Wojtyla continued to decline over the last eighteen months of his papacy and particularly from early 2005, the curial cardinals who wanted Ratzinger to be elected began to play a much more active role in gathering the required votes. I have already noted Ruini's work in promoting Ratzinger. In addition, a series of meetings were held at the Opus Dei headquarters in Rome at 73 Viale Bruno Buossi, moderated by the powerful Opus Dei Cardinal Julián Herranz from the Pontifical Council for the Interpretation of Legislative Texts. Linked closely to the Opus were the curial Cardinals Dario Castrillón Hoyos and Alfonso Lopez Trujillo, both from Colombia. Intimately linked to this group was the other Opus Dei cardinal, Juan Luis Cipriani Thorne, the archbishop of Lima, Peru. Support from the Opus and its allies is not because Ratzinger is particularly close to the secretive organisation, but he would be perceived as sufficiently conservative to please them. No doubt there were others in the curia connected with this group who were ready to give their votes to the CDF prefect. One of the advantages this group had was that virtually no one took it very seriously simply because commentators did not think Ratzinger would ever get up as pope. It was felt he was too old, and as a long-serving prefect of the CDF he had made too many enemies. As a result they were able to move quietly in gathering the numbers. There was also an assumption that an opposition must be forming, but it merely proved to be a figment of reformist Catholics' imagination.

So when Pope John Paul II finally died there was already a solid block of support for the CDF prefect as pope. The key issue was that this group had a program for the next papacy: They knew what they wanted and they were far better organised than anyone else. The *Sede vacante* period also clearly consolidated Ratzinger's candidacy. As Cardinal Dean he was by far the most prominent cardinal, preaching very effectively and pastorally at Pope Wojtyla's funeral, chairing the thirteen daily general congregations as the cardinals gathered to administer the church during the *Sede vacante* and think about the kind of pope they wanted.

The other reality is that more moderate or progressive cardinals (although 'progressive' is a bit of a misnomer in referring to any cardinal) were completely disorganised. Many of the Africans and Asians seemed to be at sea, and the Latin Americans, especially the Brazilians, simply did not have the resources to organise a campaign. In fact one of the mysteries of the April conclave is where were the moderates? While they are clearly in the minority among the cardinals, there seemed to be absolutely no preparation. In a way this is inexcusable. It is not as though the European moderates such as Cardinals Danneels, Murphy-O'Connor and Kasper were lacking resources like the Latin Americans. There just seemed to be no political nous, no intelligent apprehension of what was happening around them. They seemed to be totally disorganised, and once the voting began, seemed to be steamrolled by the Ratzinger juggernaut.

So as the conclave began Ratzinger was *the* candidate. At the Mass *pro eligendo*, for the Election of the Pope, celebrated on the day the cardinals entered the Sistine Chapel, he preached what was essentially a kind of policy speech at the Mass. This sermon is especially worth examining. It is made up of a series of meditative comments on the biblical texts set for the Mass. His somewhat confrontational tone surprised many. He spoke of the necessity to journey towards what Saint Paul called 'the maturity of Christ' although, ever the scholar, Ratzinger could not resist saying: 'More precisely, according to the Greek text, we should speak of "the measure of the fullness of Christ" to which we are called so as to be true adults in the faith.' So how do we become true adults in the faith? By avoiding being 'tossed by waves and swept along by every wind of teaching arising from human trickery (Saint Paul to the Ephesians, 4:14)'. The CDF prefect continued:

> This description is very relevant today! How many winds of doctrine have we known in recent decades, how many ideological currents, how many ways of thinking? The small boat of thought of many Christians has often been tossed about by these waves, thrown from one extreme

to the other. From Marxism to liberalism and even to libertinism; from collectivism to radical individualism; from atheism to a vague religious mysticism; from agnosticism to syncretism ... Every day new sects are created and what Saint Paul says about human trickery comes true. Having a clear faith, based on the creed of the church, is often labelled today as fundamentalism. Whereas relativism, which is letting oneself be tossed and "swept along by every wind of teaching" looks like the only attitude that is acceptable to today's standards. We are moving towards a dictatorship of relativism which does not recognize anything as certain and which has as its highest goal one's own ego and one's own desires.

'Relativism' in this context really means post-modernism, and while one might sympathize with his view of this already-fading movement, it was surprising to find such a discourse in a sermon for the election of the pope. It conjured up for those who knew their church history the condemnations of Pius IX (1846–78) and the 1864 Syllabus of Errors. These comments overshadowed his much more beautiful words about Jesus as 'the measure of true humanism' and of the Christian's call to friendship and intimacy with Christ. But all-in-all, it seemed a confronting, almost off-putting performance. He seemed to be saying: 'This is who I am. I'm not compromising. Take it or leave it! I'd be just as happy to retire to my home in Bavaria.' Perhaps that is exactly what it was. Knowing that the votes were there, it was an attempt to escape the papacy by presenting himself for the last time as the *'Panzer Kardinal'*, the watchdog of orthodoxy. In other words, it was a genuine attempt to put the cardinals off electing him. Other more cynical observers saw it as an attempt to shore up votes and to gain new ones. But the simple fact was it was an honest statement of what Joseph Ratzinger really believed.

On Monday afternoon 18 April 2005, 115 cardinals entered the conclave. Two who were eligible to vote, Filipino Cardinal Jaime Sin, former archbishop of Manila, and Cardinal Adolfo Suarez Rivera, former archbishop of Monterrey, Mexico, were too ill to join their colleagues. Assisting the cardinals in the conclave were the Master of Pontifical Ceremonies, Archbishop Piero Marini, who acted as the legal notary, the Secretary of the College of Cardinals, Archbishop Francesco Monterisi, two doctors, a couple of nurses, and domestic workers in the 'Domus Sanctae Martae'. After Marini called *'Extra omnes'* ('Everyone out!'), a final spiritual exhortation was given by the 86-year-old Czech Jesuit Cardinal Tomás Spidlík, an expert on Eastern Christian spirituality and Christian art, an appropriate qualification for preaching in the Sistine Chapel. Then he and Marini left and the cardinals were alone for the first scrutiny.

This must have taken some time because those of us waiting in the piazza of St Peter's saw no smoke from the little chimney atop the Sistine Chapel until 7.30 p.m., almost an hour and a half late. Perhaps Spidlík had spoken at considerable length or, more likely, the cardinals were nervous —after all, no one had done this since September 1978—and took their time working through the rather elongated and complex voting process? When the smoke finally came it looked white at first and people started cheering. But it soon turned to grey and then black. No one had been elected. Waiting in the piazza you become aware of the theatricality of it all. In a world of instant communication, here we were reading smoke signals, the colour of which depended upon the skill of the Pontifical Master of Ceremonies in mixing the chemicals! It was also a quite manipulative process, making everyone dependent on primitive signals from a closed group of male electors who are not particularly representative of Catholicism at large, and whose average age is 71.

So what happened in this first scrutiny? Given the oath of pontifical secrecy taken by the cardinals, with an excommunication attached to anyone breaking it, the best we can hope to do is intelligently piece together a probable scenario from the tit-bits of information provided by cardinals after the conclave. The different cardinals' accounts resemble the widely differing accounts of an accident given by eye-witnesses. So all we can do is some detective work, and anyone who tells you they know exactly what happened is fooling themselves—and you. Also, as Sandro Magister has pointed out in his 'What Really Happened at the Conclave' (www.chiesa, 2/5/05), the actual dynamics among the cardinals within the Sistine Chapel are very important. Surrounded by one of the greatest artistic masterpieces of human history 'a very peculiar atmosphere is created among the cardinals', a unique 'monoculture'. According to Magister, basing himself on Benedict XVI's own account, the trend to Ratzinger was inexorable and there was no other strong alternative candidate. He refers to what Benedict himself said: 'As the voting process gradually showed me that the guillotine, so to speak, was to fall on me, my head began to spin. I was convinced I had done my life's work and that I could hope to end my days in tranquillity' (quoted in *L'Osservatore Romano*, 27/4/05). But then a fellow cardinal reminded him of the text he had used in the homily for the funeral of John Paul II: 'Follow me'. The cardinal continued, 'If the Lord now says to you "Follow me" remember what you preached. Do not refuse.' While this does indicate that there was an unstoppable move towards Ratzinger from the start, it does not support Magister's argument that there were no other viable candidates. In fact, Pell of Sydney, using the Australian idiom, described the voting as 'a real horse race'. In other words there were a number of runners.

Allowing for the difficulties and contradictions, let us try to piece together what *might* have happened. The delay in the first scrutiny could be explained by the fact that there was a considerable spread of votes. The first ballot of a conclave is usually a kind of 'straw vote', testing the support of the major candidates. It is also a vote in which some cardinals show respect to other cardinals they want to 'honour' before they turn to their real candidate in the second scrutiny. What seems to have happened is that there was a wide spread of votes with Ratzinger gaining about forty or more. Probably the other cardinal with a substantial vote was the retired 78-year-old archbishop of Milan and Jesuit scripture scholar, Carlo Maria Martini. The Martini vote was really a 'stalking horse', a test to see how much support there was for the moderate reformers, because Martini is already a sick man. There were also a small number of votes in the first scrutiny for Ruini, Sodano, the Secretary of State, the German Walter Kasper, and Jorge Mario Bergoglio of Buenos Aires. Tettamanzi of Milan is reported to have had two votes and Scola of Venice one. The last two were clearly out of the race.

On Tuesday morning two scrutinies were held with the numbers firming up around Ratzinger. By this stage the moderates would have realised that it would be very difficult to stop Ratzinger and possibly many of Martini's votes moved to Bergoglio. It had become clear that there was hardly any support for the Italians. Some think that by the third scrutiny Ratzinger had up to sixty votes. There is a sense in which Bergoglio really belonged to the same camp as Ratzinger. Before the death of Pope Wojtyla, Ratzinger had said that he thought that Bergoglio would make a good pope. What is interesting is that ultimately there does not seem to have been much support for moderate candidates like Walter Kasper from the Pontifical Council for Christian Unity, or Godfried Danneels of Brussels. Perhaps they were too young, or more likely this indicates that the moderates were only a tiny minority and that the present college of cardinals is decisively on the conservative to reactionary side. Among the Latin

Americans only Bergoglio got votes; other cardinals like Claudio Hummes of Sao Paulo seemed to be right out of the race from the beginning.

In the end there was really no moderate opposition. In a way this is the great mystery of the April conclave: where were the moderates? The frightening answer might be that there are hardly any moderates in the College of Cardinals, and the few who are there were simply overwhelmed. If this is the case, then it is true, as the secular media maintained all along, that John Paul II had 'stacked' the deck with conservatives like himself. Personally, I don't want to think that, but it may indicate my own failure to grasp what has happened to the Catholic church and how out of touch its hierarchy is from its people.

By lunchtime on Tuesday it was clear that the momentum for Ratzinger was unstoppable, so any holdout cardinals were ready to capitulate. The cardinals were conscious that the church and world were waiting and that a short conclave would indicate that they were united and decisive. So it seems that in the first scrutiny on Tuesday afternoon—the fourth vote—the Bergoglio block plus many others went over the Ratzinger. Perhaps the Argentinean's supporters realised that they had reached the optimum number of votes they were going to get, or that Bergoglio made it clear he would not accept election. This easily gave the CDF prefect the 77 votes he needed, plus a lot more. The archbishop of Westminster, Cardinal Cormac Murphy-O'Connor, told the media that there was 'suspense' in the Sistine Chapel as the votes were called out and more and more of them went to Ratzinger. 'When the majority was reached after 77 or 78 votes, there was a sort of gasp all around, and then everyone clapped.' He said Ratzinger 'had his head down' as they awaited his acceptance. He still had the cold that he had throughout the *Sede vacante* period. After accepting, he sprang his first surprise. He said he wished to be known as Benedict XVI.

He explained this later at a general audience on 27 April.

I chose to call myself Benedict XVI ideally as a link to the venerated Pontiff, Benedict XV, who guided the church throughout the turbulent times of the First World War. He was a true and courageous prophet of peace who struggled strenuously and bravely, first to avoid the drama of war and then to limit its terrible consequences. In his footsteps I place my ministry, in the service of reconciliation and harmony between peoples, profoundly convinced that the great good of peace is above all a gift of God, a fragile and precious gift to be invoked, safeguarded and constructed, day after day with everyone's contribution.

While Pope Ratzinger does not mention it, Benedict XV (1914–21) was also the pope who stopped the so-called 'Modernist' crisis in its tracks. Under his predecessor Pius X (1903–14), a whole group of theologians, biblical scholars, historians and Catholic intellectuals, who were trying to reconcile Catholicism with the contemporary world, were condemned and persecuted. Benedict XV put an end to this 'heresy hunt'.

The new pope also emphasised that the name Benedict was that of the founder of Western monasticism and the co-patron saint of Europe. He continued: 'For that reason St Benedict is much venerated in Germany, and especially in Bavaria, my own land of origin. He constitutes a fundamental point of reference for the unity of Europe and a powerful call to the irrefutable Christian roots of European culture and civilisation.' In other words, he was issuing a clear and deserved rebuke to the small-minded European Union bureaucrats and secularist hacks who had made sure that all references to the role of Christianity in Europe's cultural heritage had been excluded from the EU constitution. Clearly, European culture and Christianity's role within it is very much on the mind of Benedict XVI.

What was the source of this strong and almost immediate consensus for Ratzinger in the conclave? We have already seen the group that had been working for several years to push the cause of the CDF prefect. So there was an impetus for him even before the conclave began. Also, his performance as Dean of the College of Cardinals in the *Sede vacante* period was outstanding. This is a more influential position than that of the Camerlengo because the Dean is in the forefront of liturgical celebration and gets to deal most intimately with his brother cardinals. There was also a deep sense of security about him. The cardinals knew what he stands for because he had told them plainly in the homily at the Mass for the election of the Roman pontiff.

Nevertheless, this does not mean that he will be a rabid reactionary. The more moderate and theologically aware cardinals, like Walter Kasper and Cormac Murphy-O'Connor, have made it clear that they expect Benedict XVI to pay particular attention to the question of collegiality and to involve the bishops in a much-needed reform of the Roman curia. This was another reason why Ratzinger was attractive to his brother cardinals. He had not climbed the greasy ladder of political opportunism required to make your way in the curia. He had come in laterally, had worked in the curia for twenty-four years and knew it thoroughly. But he always remained the theologian rather than the bureaucrat. Many observers think he will take the broom to the Vatican and thoroughly clean out the dead wood. It is certainly needed. What the cardinals seemed to want is the continuation of the general direction of the John Paul papacy with much greater attention to administrative detail. There is no doubt that his age is an important issue. By electing someone who is 78 the cardinals have certainly shown they want a short papacy. But there is a danger lurking here: his health has not been robust. What would happen if the church found itself having to deal with another grievously ill pope for several years? The question of retirement or removal has to be faced, or else the church could eventually face a tremendous constitutional crisis.

There is no doubt that Ratzinger's personal gifts were part of his attraction. He is a substantial theologian, one of the best of the post-Vatican II generation. He is also a person of obvious spiritual and cultural gifts, with a gracious, gentlemanly, even shy personality. But he also comes to the papacy with enormous baggage from his time at the helm of the CDF, as I discuss in detail in the next chapter. Given this baggage, the gracious and generous response of many progressive Catholics to the election of Benedict XVI was quite striking. Perhaps the most interesting came from Cardinal Martini. He told *La Repubblica*: 'It is certain that Benedict XVI has some surprises in store for us in light of the stereotypes by which he has been defined a little too hastily ... [He is] a man of great humanity, courtesy, and gentleness, ready to listen, even to ideas different from his own ... I am sure the new pope will not be rigid, but will listen and reflect.' This is particularly significant given that Martini admitted that he had frequently disagreed with Ratzinger when he was CDF prefect and Martini was a member of the Congregation. Hans Küng, who also had many disagreements, many of them public, with Ratzinger, issued a generous and conciliatory statement. This generosity of spirit contrasts strongly with the immature ranting and triumphalism of some of the so-called conservative clerics and laity that I saw in the Piazza of St Peter's on the day of the election, and have subsequently seen in print.

After the conclave Pope Benedict and the cardinals remained in the 'Domus Sanctae Martae' for the night. They had a modest champagne celebration and a meal together, and the new pope actually remained in the 'Domus' for another ten days and did not move into the papal apartment until Saturday 30 April. In an unremarkable move he reappointed all the curia heads 'until further provision had been made'. Sodano the senior cardinal bishop was appointed Dean of the College of Cardinals. This is a standard procedure for a new pope; they do not rush in and sack people immediately. The reappointment of these old curial hands is not indicative of what he will do later. It was simply an interim measure.

The good thing is he comes to the papacy as a known quantity, perhaps the best known cardinal of all. So what will he do as his papacy develops? What will be his priorities? What does his past tell us about him? What is his record?

Part Three

POPE BENEDICT XVI

7

THE ORIGINS OF BENEDICT XVI

We know more about Pope Benedict XVI than any other possible candidate for the papacy, with the possible exception of Cardinal Carlo Maria Martini, who as former archbishop of Milan is especially well known in Italy. Certainly, as Joseph Ratzinger, no other churchman in recent times has raised such passions. The darling of conservatives as a champion of orthodoxy and suppressor of heresy, he was the *bête noire* of progressives and was cast in the role of grand inquisitor. Both views are caricatures, over- and under-estimating him at the same time. Since his election, most progressives have been generally generous and courteous in their responses while quietly harbouring unspoken suspicions. The feeling is, 'We should give him a chance'. This is reflected in the response of Margaret Hebblethwaite, wife of the late Peter Hebblethwaite, author of many books on the papacy, particularly an excellent biography of Pope Paul VI. Her ministry is now in Paraguay, and she was in Rome for *The Tablet* to cover the conclave. At first she was disappointed by the election of Ratzinger and was struggling to be positive, but by the time she wrote the article 'The reconciler reaches out' (*The Tablet*, 30 April 2005) she was much more upbeat.

What we saw in the past week in Rome was not just the predictable enthusiasm of the huge crowds who will cheer anyone who is pope, but also an unforeseeable effort by Pope Benedict to change his tone and win over his former critics. Dismay and depression at his election were not disguised in Rome in private, although all public pronouncements studiously refused to acknowledge those reactions. But since Sunday people have been saying 'Cardinal Ratzinger is no more. *Viva* Pope Benedict XVI!' It is like Simon being transformed into Peter.

The secular media were not so kind. Indulging in those ingrained British prejudices, being anti-Catholic and anti-German, the Murdoch-owned tabloid *Sun* newspaper ran a cheap and tasteless headline 'From Hitler Youth to ... Papa Ratzi'. The conservative *Daily Telegraph* in an equally crude headline called Benedict 'God's Rottweiler'. This led the *Sun's* equivalent in Germany, *Bild*, which normally runs with a semi-nude woman on the front page, to wax righteous about 'English insults to the German pope' and to comment, 'If you read the British tabloids yesterday, you would have thought Hitler had become pope. Only the devil could come up with such a thing. Oh, you English, with your complexes ... The pope in his goodness will include you idiots in his prayers. Yes, you the editors of the *Sun* and the *Daily Mirror*. Even idiots go to heaven' (*Deutsche Welle*). But, in fact, in some ways the German papers were harshest of all on Benedict. The *Frankfurter Allgemeine Zeitung* said 'Ratzinger is the Counter-Reformation personified' and the *Berliner Zeitung* described him as 'autocratic, authoritarian' and 'as shrewd as a serpent'. *Die Tagenzeitung*, commenting on his desire to be 'a simple worker in the Lord's vineyard' said 'Simple he is not, humble hardly'!

In contrast, in a very perceptive piece, the *International Herald Tribune's* Roger Cohen spoke of the effect of Ratzinger's election on the culture and psyche of Germany. The Nazi past still weighs heavily on Germans. Cohen quotes writer Peter Schneider: 'The burden the Third Reich left the generations that followed has been heavier than we imagined. Of course, we are not guilty. But we feel responsible.' Feeling responsible means that it is hard for Germans to develop any sense of national pride. Cohen says, 'The raising of Ratzinger to the pinnacle of the church amounts to a consecration of Germany's post-war achievement. As *Die Welt* put it: "This papal election is also a gesture of forgiveness for the most shamed European nation. The world's conscience has accepted German atonement."' Referring to Ratzinger's role in the 'remarkable reconciliation of the church with the Jews', Cohen says that 'In a sense Pope John Paul II overcame Europe's physical division. It could be that Pope Benedict XVI overcomes the Continent's historical wound, for which Germany bears a terrible responsibility.' However, he warns that 'not all the signs are encouraging'. Revealing his own secularist bias, Cohen warns that Pope Benedict has called for the exclusion of Turkey from the European Union based on the 'disturbing suggestion of a quasi-mystical notion of what constitutes the true or pure essence of Europe' (*International Herald Tribune*, 23–24 April 2005). Certainly, I would have thought that historically and culturally Europe is essentially 'Christian' and that to deny that is to deny reality.

When we turn to the Catholic response to the election of Benedict XVI, many are much more sceptical than Margaret Hebblethwaite and those of us who at first cautiously welcomed the new pope. Certainly, there is a real sense in which Ratzinger has no record of interest in Latin America, Asia or Africa, except to condemn liberation theology, the opening up of Catholicism to the other great world religions, and the widespread use of condoms to prevent the spread of AIDS. There is certainly something profoundly Euro-centric about the former CDF prefect. So it is understandable that one of those most critical of the election of Benedict XVI is the Brazilian Dominican and activist Frei (Friar or Brother) Betto, a maverick liberation theologian who has deliberately refused to be ordained priest. Born in 1944, he spent four years in prison in the 1960s under the Brazilian military junta, and is the author of thirty-four books on spirituality, social justice and activism on behalf of the poor, a number of them bestsellers in Brazil and Latin America. Over the years he has been close to Cardinals Paulo Evaristo Arns and Claudio Hummes of Sao Paulo, both strong supporters of liberation theology and justice for the poor. However, since the condemnation of liberation theology by Ratzinger's CDF, Cardinal Hummes has placed some distance between them. However, Betto is still a friend and spiritual guide of Brazilian Workers' Party president Luiz Ignacio Lula da Silva, and has served as an adviser on the Zero Hunger program, 'which aims not just to take care of physical nutrition, but also mental and spiritual nutrition. It aims not only to satisfy hunger for bread but also for beauty.' In the past twelve months there have been some tensions between Betto and da Silva over the president's increasing closeness to neo-liberal economic policies and the failure of land reform and environmental programs to protect the Amazon basin. But they are still close personally.

Betto is scathing about Pope Benedict.

The election of Cardinal Joseph Ratzinger as pope is a worrying sign that the direction of the Catholic church is more confused and lost than we imagined. The opposite of fear is not courage, it is faith. Many cardinals appear to be more imbued with fear than with faith. To elect as pope a man responsible for the church's orthodoxy … constitutes a gesture of retractation and defence before a world which is perturbed, which expects from Rome more than anathema, censure, mistrust and segregation … During the period in which he headed the CDF, he punished 140 Catholic theologians … His obsession is Nietzsche, whose ghost he identifies in post-modern culture … I am not aware of whether the new pope has any social sensitivity. The image of the poor and the tragedy of poverty are not recurrent in his pronouncements and writings … May God allow the new pope to come down from the pedestal of theological academicism and become a pastor, embracing the most evangelical and forgotten papal title—'Servant of the servants of God'.

Whether this represents merely the opinion of Betto or has wider sympathy in Brazilian government and presidential circles is impossible to tell, but for reasons we shall see later it is understandable that people with a background in liberation theology would be upset with the election of Ratzinger.

The new pope's past statements on women also do not encourage those committed to a change in their role in the church. As Sister Joan Chittister said: 'The history of this pope's understanding of women is a limited one'. Joelle Battestini of the Australian Ordination of Catholic Women group said succinctly: 'I fear the worst'.

Many Catholics felt a deep sense of relief that Cardinal Ratzinger did not choose the style 'John Paul III'. It would have been too much to bear. Choosing the name 'Benedict' is significant. It points in a different direction altogether from the Wojtyla papacy. This does not mean there will no references to the late pope and his policies, or that there will be a total historical disjunction. But it does mean that Benedict XVI is setting out in his own direction. There is a real possibility that the new pope is breaking with his past as CDF prefect and doctrinal enforcer for John Paul II. Betto also recognises this.

What offers a thread of hope is the fact that Ratzinger adopted the name Benedict XVI. Usually this indicates the interest of the new pontiff in following the work of his predecessor of the same name. Benedict XV … was an open man. He stopped the persecution of the "modernists", gave value to ecumenism, promoted dialogue between Catholics and

Anglicans, showed an interest in the Eastern churches and, above all, fought colonialism and struggled with impartiality for the ending of the First World War.

So who is this man? Can he and will he change? And where will he lead the church? Certainly at first sight his record, as Betto has pointed out, is at best very mixed. He brings much baggage to the papacy. So what does his record tell us?

Joseph Alois Ratzinger was born in Marktl am Inn in the diocese of Passau in rural Bavaria in the far south-eastern corner of Germany, very close to the Austrian border and Salzburg, on Holy Saturday, 16 April 1927, the youngest of three children. His sister Maria, who served as his secretary until she died in 1991, was the eldest, and his brother Georg, who also became a priest, was second. Georg eventually became the director of the Regensburger Domspatzen, a thousand-year-old boys' choir in Regensburg cathedral. The Ratzinger family subsequently lived in several small towns because Georg Ratzinger senior was a member first of the Bavarian State Police (*Landespolizei*) and then the uniformed national police (*Ordnungspolizei*). The many moves the family had to make were caused by the father's police career, but also due to transfers and demotions resulting from his strong Catholicism and overt anti-Nazism. Georg Ratzinger junior says that 'Our father was a bitter enemy of Nazism because he believed it was in conflict with our faith'. He eventually retired with his wife Maria to Traunstein in 1938, where the family lived in somewhat straitened circumstances. It was here that Joseph spent his adolescence.

As was clearly shown by the career of Pope Wojtyla, birthplace is important. Benedict XVI is profoundly Bavarian. Bavaria was originally part of the Roman province of Raetia with its capital at Augusta Vindelicorum (Augsburg), and it was part of the Roman empire from as early as the age of Augustus (31 BC to AD 14). In the reorganisation of the empire by the emperor Diocletian after 284 it became part of the province of Raetia II, part of the larger division, the diocese of Italia. Even though the barbarian tribes crossed the Rhine on the last day of 407 and much of the Western Roman Empire collapsed, Roman rule survived in Raetia until 488 when the area was invaded by both the Franks and the Baiuvarii from northern Germany, after whom the area was renamed. Here they intermingled and intermarried with the local Celtic and Roman populations. Seventy years later the Bavarian tribes were united under a local dukedom and they remained independent with their power at times reaching right across the Alps and down into northern Italy. For several centuries the dukes of Bavaria recognised the suzerainty of the Merovingian Franks to the west and north until the Frankish ruler (later emperor) Charlemagne deposed Duke Tasillo III in 787–88 and annexed Bavaria into his kingdom.

The conversion of Bavaria was a complex process. Christian enclaves survived from Roman times and the Bavarian dukes were probably Christian from the early sixth century. In the seventh and eighth centuries continental, Irish and English missionaries were all active in Bavaria, and the great Englishman, St Boniface (680–754) reorganised the dioceses of Bavaria in 739–40. After the break-up of the Carolingian empire in the ninth century and the invasion of the Magyars in the tenth, the situation in Bavaria became chaotic, but the dukes managed to maintain their position. Finally, in 1180, Bavaria was handed over by the German Emperor Frederick I Barbarossa to Otto of Wittelsbach, and his descendants ruled Bavaria until 1918. The area always remained staunchly Catholic, even during the Reformation. It became a kingdom in 1806 and from 1866 was part of the Prussian-sponsored German empire.

At the end of the First World War, with the abdication of the Kaiser and Germany descending into chaos, the utopian Jewish socialist and dreamer, Kurt Eisner, led a revolt that deposed the last Wittelsbach king, Ludwig III, on 7 November 1918 and declared himself minister-president of Bavaria. His socialist republic was relatively moderate. It lasted only until 21 February 1919 when Eisner was assassinated by Count Anton Arco-Valley, a young, vicious anti-Semite. Bavaria collapsed in disorder and eventually the communists and anarchists seized power. On 6 April 1919, inspired by what had happened in Hungary, a 'Bavarian Soviet Republic' was proclaimed in Munich. It was run by incompetent independent socialists—at one stage they actually declared war on Switzerland! It was soon replaced by a much more hard-line communist regime which began to seize the property of the wealthy and distribute it among the poor and the workers. While seen as uncouth and radical, this regime was not particularly violent, with only eight people killed as spies. Many of the leaders were Jews, a fact commented on in reports to Rome by the then papal nuncio to Bavaria, Archbishop Eugenio Pacelli, later to become papal Secretary of State and Pope Pius XII. After attempting to organise an army along the lines of the Red Army, the Bavarian Soviet Republic was violently overthrown by the right-wing freebooter squads of *Freikorps* (Free Corps) and about 800 people were executed in revenge. The *Freikorps* were paramilitary units that sprang up all over Germany made up of demobilised officers, ex-soldiers and fanatical nationalists who blamed the socialists and the Jews for the terrible situation in Germany in 1919.

This period of revolution is important in order to understand what subsequently happened in Bavaria. The state remained a stronghold of the right throughout the inter-war period, although this did not mean that everyone was pro-Nazi, even though the Nazi party began in Munich and its first attempt at revolution against the Weimar Republic, the Beer Hall *Putsch*, was staged there in November 1923. After the Second World War it was part of the American zone of occupation, was rebuilt and is now a prosperous industrial region and a stronghold of the Christian Socialist Union (CSU), as the Christian Democratic Party is called in Bavaria. The CSU have maintained a stranglehold on the state since 1946, and every minister-president since 1957 has been a CSU member. In Oberbayern (Upper Bavaria—the 'Upper' here referring to the Alps) an Austro-Bavarian dialect is spoken and the whole area has much in common with nearby Salzburg. Traunstein, where Ratzinger spent much of his adolescence, is only thirty kilometres from Mozart's birthplace. Nowadays the population of Upper Bavaria is almost four million, which includes 1.3 million people in Munich.

The whole area between Munich and eastwards towards the Austrian border is completely Catholic. So in his childhood and youth, just like Karol Wojtyla in Poland, Joseph Ratzinger had no experience of living with other faiths and religious pluralism. Even today travelling through southern Germany, and especially among older people in rural and small-town Bavaria, you have a strong feeling of claustrophobic provincialism and of a conservative, mono-lingual population who live in their own world. This is an inward looking, secure community with roots reaching back many centuries. It is characterised by a deeply ingrained folk religion that is often found in rural areas and small towns. Also, we tend to forget how much regionalism still characterises Germany as a result of the fact that the country was only very recently united; the geographical, religious and social lineaments of the Holy Roman Empire, abolished by Napoleon in 1806 can to some extent still be discerned. Bavaria is particularly determined to maintain its identity with the Federal Republic. We forget that the country was only truly united under Bismark in 1871, and then only superficially until the Weimar Republic after the First World War, and the Hitler era united the whole country. While very rooted in their own regions, Catholic Germans also have a strong sense of their common European tradition. They tend to be defined by their local provinces, but nevertheless see themselves as Europeans. This harks back to the medieval period long before the birth of nation states.

At Easter 1939, when he was 11, Joseph followed his older brother Georg into the high school seminary in Traunstein. Up until the 1970s it was not uncommon even for a young adolescent to enter the high school seminary, a kind of boarding school for those thinking of becoming priests. He entered 'with joy and great expectations because my brother had told me many exciting things about the place and because I developed good friend-ships with the seminarians in my class. However, I am one of those people who are not made for living in a boarding school. While at home I had lived and studied with great freedom ... and had built a childhood world of my own. Now I had to sit in a study hall with about sixty other boys and this was such a torture to me'(Joseph Ratzinger, *Milestones: Memoirs 1927–1977*, 1998, p. 25). He also hated the two hours every afternoon devoted to sport. Forced by wartime conditions, the seminary had to move a couple of times. Young Joseph gradually became accustomed to living with others: 'I came to terms, then, with being in the seminary and experienced a wonderful time in my life. I had to learn ... to come out of my solitary ways and start building a community with others' (*Milestones*, p. 27).

The seminary was closed down in late 1942 and Ratzinger, like every other member of his school class was forced to join the Hitler Youth. In 1943, at the age of 16, he began military service in an anti-aircraft unit. In September 1944 he joined the *Landsturm* (work detail) and he spent some time on the Hungarian frontier preparing tank-traps for the advancing Russians. Eventually he was drafted into the infantry and was assigned to a barracks in Traunstein. He says in *Milestones* that after Hitler's suicide 'At the end of April or the beginning of May—I do not remember precisely—I decided to go home. I knew that the city was surrounded by soldiers who had orders to shoot deserters on the spot.' This is very vague. Given that the Führer's suicide was only announced on 2 May 1945, it is likely to have been early May when Ratzinger deserted. But it was hardly a brave action. The entire country was collapsing. He was briefly held as a POW by the Americans, and by autumn 1945 he was back in the seminary.

Ratzinger, like other young Germans of his time, especially Catholics, was an unwilling participant in the Hitler Youth and the war. His family, like others in small-town and rural Catholic Bavaria, were strongly anti-Nazi, specifically because the regime attacked the church and tried to replace Catholicism with an ideology of race. Any attempt to link him or his immediate family to the Nazi regime is utterly without foundation, despite the fact that most Bavarians were right wing and conservative in political attitude. But it was their very conservatism and their deeply rooted Catholicism that preserved and insulated them from the worst of the Nazi propaganda regime. While certainly very law-abiding and tolerant of an interfering and paternalistic government, they were not prepared to surrender their faith to the absurdities of Nazi racial theory or to attempts to replace Catholicism with National Socialist ideology. Thus the headlines like 'From Hitler Youth to ... Papa Ratzi' of tabloid newspapers like the *Sun* are without foundation and grossly unfair.

In autumn of 1945 the Ratzinger brothers entered the major seminary at Freising, thirty-five kilometres north-north-east of Munich, close to where Franz Josef Strauss Airport is located today. A diocese was established in Freising in 739 and was united to Munich in 1818 to form the archdiocese of Munich-Freising. At the seminary Joseph began his study of philosophy. He describes what life was like for 'the 120 or so seminarians who now came together in Freising to set out on the road to the priesthood'. He says they were full of gratitude that they could begin their studies and they had 'a hunger for knowledge that had grown in the years of famine ... when we had been delivered up to the Moloch of power, so far from the realm of the spirit'. Despite war damage and the fact that part of the building was requisitioned as a hospital, there was still a good reference library at the seminary. He says,

Our interests were varied. We wanted not only to do theology in the narrower sense but to listen to the voices of man today. We devoured the novels of Gertrude von Le Fort, Elizabeth Langgässer, and Ernst Wiechert. Dostoevsky was one of the authors everyone read, and likewise the great Frenchmen [Paul] Claudel, [George] Bernanos, [Francois] Mauriac. We also followed closely the recent developments in the natural sciences ... In the domain of theology and philosophy the voices that moved us most directly were those of Romano Guardini, Josef Pieper, Theodor Häcker, and Peter Wust. (*Milestones*, pp. 41–3)

Others who influenced him were the theologians Michael Schmaus and especially Henri de Lubac. He showed great interest in German and French literature and in a theology tinged with an existentialist leaning. He developed an enthusiasm for the liturgical movement which was eventually to have a strong influence on changes in Catholic worship, and no doubt this came through his studies of the great liturgical pioneer Guardini.

He was clearly not attracted to the conventional neo-scholastic theology that was taught at Freising and in many seminaries of the time. Neo-scholasticism refers to the attempted revival in nineteenth and twentieth century of medieval philosophy generally and that of Saint Thomas Aquinas particularly. But it quickly atrophied into a 'system' that turned inward and away from an encounter with modern thought and that certainly lacked any sense of the historical context of Aquinas and the other great medieval thinkers. All of the theologians and Catholic writers mentioned by Ratzinger had turned away from the rigidities of this seminary philosophy and turned outward towards modern thought. As he says himself, he did not want to do theology 'in the narrower sense'; that is, in the neo-scholastic way. However, it is worth noting how profoundly, if understandably, Euro-centric his Catholicism was. Ratzinger says that as a student he had 'difficulties penetrating the thought of Thomas Aquinas, whose crystal-clear logic seemed to be too closed in on itself, too impersonal and ready-made'. Perhaps the cause of this was the kind of Thomism, or approach to Aquinas' thought, that was taught at Freising. Ratzinger says his lecturer 'presented us with a rigid, neo-scholastic Thomism that was simply too far afield from my own questions'(*Milestones*, p. 44). Clearly he was a student whose interests faced out into the world rather than someone preoccupied with the minutiae of ecclesiastically circumscribed philosophy and theology.

It was at Freising that he was first attracted to Saint Augustine (354–430), the bishop of Hippo Regius in North Africa, who in many ways is the key to his whole theological attitude. At the core of the great bishop's thought is the primacy of love and the centrality of commitment in the search for God. As his *Confessions* show, Augustine's faith is profoundly personal and is rooted in an examination of God's interaction with him. Nevertheless, it is significant that much of his theology is developed in controversial circumstances and is deeply haunted by a sense of humankind's fall from grace, the brevity and incompleteness of all worldly affairs, and our inheritance of a kind of moral disease which can be only cured by God's gratuitous goodness. Running through Augustine is a deep feeling of the Christian's alienation from the world and a sense that we 'have no abiding city' here and inhabit merely 'a vale of tears'. This is why Ratzinger is so suspicious of religious and theological movements that originate in the world and are accused of using alien (i.e. Marxist) analysis of social and even church structures, like liberation theology. He is particularly critical of notions that argue that the modern church can be reformed by its own sinful members. The young Ratzinger was also influenced by the Jesuit Erich Przywara (1889–1972), one of the most important Catholic intellectuals of the twentieth century who is, nevertheless, hardly known in the English-speaking world. He was one of the pioneers in introducing the theology of the great English Cardinal John Henry Newman to German readers. Editor of the Munich-based Jesuit journal *Stimmen der Zeit*, Przywara presented a very open vision of Catholicism in contact with the philosophical and cultural currents of his time. He was also a great student of Augustine.

After two years in the seminary, in 1947 Ratzinger entered the Herzogliches Gregorianum, the theological faculty associated with the Ludwig-Maximilians Universität of Munich. At the university he was influenced more by his own personal reading than by the lecturers. This spread out from Augustine to a deep assimilation of the fathers of the church, the early theologians whose thought is basic to the later development of theology. Thus he places himself within the context of a broad movement of twentieth-century Catholicism which was deeply concerned with recovering both a strong scriptural sense and a knowledge and assimilation of the early theology and liturgy. This tendency is generally known as the *ressourcement* (recovery) movement. Not surprisingly, his thesis topic was 'People and House of God in Augustine's Doctrine of the Church'.

Here it needs to be stressed that Ratzinger's exploration of these sources was essentially theological in contrast to a more empirical reading which would have characterised a trained historian. This is an important distinction. Nowhere does Ratzinger show any contextual or historical sense. Like his latter-day friend Balthasar, he is essentially a theologian. Historians tend to be much more aware of relativity, of change and context. Thus historians understand that for the believer, faith is always lived out within the context of history. Thus our theological understandings are determined and limited by the constraints of culture and human experience. We can never exhaust in one theological approach or doctrinal statement the transcendent and mysterious realities that underlie and give context to belief. To have faith is to explore the mystery and this is a dynamic and ongoing process. While committed to the truth, Catholics discover it as a process not as an accomplishment. Truth is dynamic, not static.

Ratzinger passed his final university examinations in mid-1951 and he returned to Freising seminary to prepare for ordination. But he had not finished his thesis. 'The seriousness of this preparation [for the priesthood] demanded the whole person, without any reservation, and yet I had to combine it with the writing of my [thesis] ... My brother, who was with me on my road to the priesthood, did everything possible to relieve me of all practical tasks relating to our preparation for priestly ordination and our first Mass. My sister ... used her free time to produce in exemplary fashion a clean copy of the manuscript, and so I was able to hand in my work by the required deadline' (*Milestones*, p. 99). He then devoted himself full-time to preparation for priesthood. On 29 June 1951 Joseph and Georg Ratzinger were ordained together in Freising cathedral by Cardinal Michael von Faulhaber, the archbishop of Munich. Significantly in view of his later election to the papacy, 29 June is the Feast of Saints Peter and Paul. For a brief time after ordination he worked in a Munich parish.

Following parish work he returned to teach theology at Freising seminary. In July 1953 he defended his thesis and graduated doctor of theology *summa cum laude*. While continuing his theological teaching he also worked on his *Habilitationsschrift*, the postdoctoral lecturing qualification required in Germany to obtain a university post. The focus of his study this time was Saint Bonaventure (1217–74), the most significant of Saint Francis of Assisi's successors as head of the Franciscans, and later the Cardinal Bishop of Albano. Very much an Augustinian, Bonaventure emphasised the centrality of mystical illumination and knowledge bestowed gratuitously by God. Through Bonaventure, Ratzinger became aware of the teachings of Joachim of Fiore (1132–1202), an Italian Cistercian abbot who deeply influenced many of the Franciscan spirituals, a radical group with whom Bonaventure had to deal. This movement believed that a new spiritual age had begun with Saint Francis in which there was no real need for clerical intervention. They looked forward optimistically to a 'new age' in which the kingdom of God on earth would be ushered in and an *ecclesia spiritualis* (a spiritual church) would be established. It was this kind of 'false messianism', as Ratzinger would see it, that he later discovered in liberation theology. He defended his thesis 'The Theology of History in Saint Bonaventure' in February 1957. In 1958 he became a lecturer in theology at the University of Munich and was professor of fundamental theology at Freising seminary.

One of his fellow students at the time was Uta Ranke-Heinemann. A member of an influential German family—her father Gustav was President of the Federal Republic of Germany from 1969 until 1974—and a distinguished feminist theologian, Ranke-Heinemann, now aged 77, has a complex view of Ratzinger.

> We were doctoral students together at the University of Munich in 1953 and 1954, which was the first time a woman was allowed to get a doctorate in Catholic theology ... We had to defend our theses in Latin. In preparation we translated our theses together from German into Latin. He was very intelligent. He was the star student ... we all admired his intelligence. But there was something more about him I admired. He was a rather shy student, not obsessed with his ego. I liked his humble intelligence. I still do like many passages in his books ... Many people have been astonished that I've always sort of defended Ratzinger, even though I've said many of his opinions are totally wrong.

Ranke-Heinemann draws an interesting contrast between the pope and his predecessor. 'The enormous difference between John Paul II and Ratzinger is intelligence. Ratzinger is much, much more intelligent. Quite frankly, John Paul was tedious without end. He was obsessed with Mary ... Ratzinger has much more of what the French call *esprit de finesse*. And John Paul II had none!' She says that once a small Italian newspaper misquoted her as saying that Ratzinger 'had a total absence of *humanità*— humanity. But what I actually said was he "always had the aura of a cardinal, and the highest intelligence, with the total absence of the erotic".'

Here I want to pause to reflect on the larger cultural and social context in which Ratzinger grew to manhood. Nazism dominated this whole period from 1933 to 1945. Ratzinger has said unequivocally that the Catholic church was the principal source of resistance to the Nazi ideology and social practice. He tends to present a picture of a church united in opposition to the worst aspects of the attempts to impose a theory of racial supremacy, eugenic elimination of the 'unfit', and the replacement of Christianity with a kind of Nazi folk religion, as well as moves to control education and all social activity. Germans of his generation and background have tended to excuse the church's failures in the Nazi era by focusing on undoubted examples of at times heroic Catholic resistance. Certainly within his family, and in the smaller cities and towns of Bavaria and other strongly Catholic areas in Germany, there was genuine opposition to open Nazi attacks on the church, its role in education and social services, and especially to the removal of symbols such as the crucifix from schools and public buildings. At the same time these Catholic areas were strongly resistant to Nazi ideology and attempts to replace church worship with pseudo-Germanic folk liturgies.

Significantly, the city of Munich and the Ludwig-Maximilians Universität saw two of the only overt demonstrations against the Nazis during the war. An ad hoc group of young Catholics gathered around Walter Klingenbeck, an apprentice mechanic. Outraged by the Nazis' behaviour, they distributed a flyer headed 'Down with Hitler' in early 1943. Captured by the SS, Klingenbeck was beheaded in August that year. A group better known to posterity is the *Weisserose* (White Rose) movement. Inspired by the professor of philosophy, Kurt Huber, a small group of students secretly opposed the Nazi regime. It included the Catholic brother and sister, Hans and Sophie Scholl, who had been influenced in their opposition to the Nazis by Cardinal Clemens August von Galen, bishop of Münster and his public protests against the killing of mentally ill persons. The White Rose group also included Christoph Probst who became a Catholic in jail, just before his execution. The group had drafted a leaflet in early 1943 that was scattered around the university and the city. All were captured by Gestapo and beheaded.

Oddly, Ratzinger never mentions any of these heroic dissidents. Nevertheless this kind of obstinate defiance is often mentioned by German Catholics of his generation as symptomatic of the church's opposition. The most he says is that the church alone was 'the alternative to the destructive ideology of the brown rulers [Nazis]; in the inferno that swallowed up the powerful, she had stood firm with a force coming to her from eternity. It had been demonstrated: The gates of hell will not overpower her' *(Milestones*, p. 42). There is some truth to this assertion, but it is not the whole picture which is much more mixed.

Firstly, reaction from Ratzinger's own profession of theology was far from unanimous in its opposition to Nazism. Robert A. Krieg of the University of Notre Dame recently published a major study of the reaction of theologians to National Socialism, *Catholic Theologians in Nazi Germany*. He confronts the question: Why didn't the church resist the Nazis more forcefully and why did it compromise and sometimes capitulate so easily? To answer this question Krieg looks at five influential theologians, three of whom more or less compromised with the Nazi regime, and two of whom stood against it. A number of factors were operative and each of these men differed from the other and none can be taken as representative of Catholic attitudes generally. In other words, there is no easy answer to the question.

Some, such as Kurt Eschweiler, a dogmatic theologian who was actually buried in his Nazi uniform, were essentially authoritarian and the Nazi preoccupation with order in society appealed to them. Others, like the historian of the reformation Joseph Lortz, were seduced by the grand vision of western civilisation that Hitler outlined. They felt this could be infused by Christian spirituality. For a brief time the philosopher Martin Heidegger, himself originally a Catholic, shared this idealised notion of Nazism. This kind of intellectual 'cloud cuckoo-land' was seemingly totally divorced from Nazi violence in the streets and the almost cosmic barbarity of the 'final solution'. Like Heidegger, Lortz soon realised his mistake. Perhaps the best known in the English-speaking world of all German Catholic theologians in the first half of the twentieth century was Karl Adam. In many ways he understood the kind of hunger for spirituality and order that characterised much of western society in the 1930s. He agreed with Oswald Spengler, whose book *The Decline of the West* (1926) argued that European culture was degenerate with modern individualism rampant. Adam felt that there was a need to recover a sense of society and authority, and that a new synthesis between faith and culture was required. He saw the Nazis as providing this. Again there is this sense of unreality running through his thought that ignores the inherent violence, authoritarianism and racism embedded in National Socialist ideology. Adam, even as late as 1943, was still writing anti-Semitic material.

Not all theologians hid their heads in the sand. Two particularly stand out. The Italian-born Romano Guardini, one of Ratzinger's intellectual mentors, lost his professorship because he early recognised the barbarism at the essential core of Nazism. The strongest opponent of the Nazis among Catholic theologians was Englebert Krebs at Freiburg University. He openly opposed the Nazis and spoke in defence of the Jews. He too lost his university post. During the war, both of these theologians, like Heidegger, simply retired and didn't speak.

In some ways the response of the bishops parallels that of the theologians. While there were bishops who made heroically strong stands, such as 'the lion of Münster', von Galen, and Bishop Konrad von Preysing of Berlin, there were others who capitulated or equivocated. Before Hitler came to power the bishops condemned National Socialism, but this was softened after the Nazis formed government in January 1933, and especially after the Enabling Act of 23 March 1933 which gave Hitler dictatorial power. Despite the reservations of many, the Vatican persuaded the Catholic Centre Party (*Zentrumspartei*) to support the Enabling Act. Cardinals Adolf

Bertram of Breslau and von Faulhaber of Munich issued pastoral guide-lines that the earlier condemnations of Nazism should be ignored and that Catholics 'must be loyal to the lawful authorities and fulfil their civic duties conscientiously, rejecting any illegal or subversive activities'.

The simple fact is the church did not forcefully resist the Nazi dictator-ship. Perhaps part of this was a kind of sense of inferiority and a desire to conform given that Catholics were always seen as second-class citizens since Bismarck's *Kulturkampf* in the 1870s. Given the large-scale theological and intellectual failure of Catholicism to make a stand, ordinary Catholics simply did not have the moral guidance, social passion and educated argu-ments to oppose National Socialism. Only a tiny group of Christians and Catholics were prepared to join and support the courageous students of the White Rose movement, and the military and political leaders who formed the core of the 'July Plot' of 1944 against the Nazi tyranny. There was no truly prophetic voice from German Catholicism. It was simply left up to isolated and brave individuals to make a stand. All the church really did was to maintain its own institutions and a somewhat circumscribed form of pastoral life. There was a total lack of prophetic passion and indignation at the terrible things that the Nazis carried out. The bishops only seemed obsessed with maintaining the structures of the church—schools, churches, organisations.

Part of the problem was that the bishops were actually crippled by the behaviour and attitude of the Vatican which was determined to control the German episcopate and, through it, the church in Germany. It is easy, of course, to be critical at this distance, but the simple fact is the Nazis gained respectability in Germany because of the Concordat between the Hitler government and the Vatican, negotiated by the then papal Secretary of State, Cardinal Eugenio Pacelli. Pacelli was absolutely besotted with the idea of a concordat (an agreement between civil and ecclesiastical author-ities) with Germany.

For instance, in 1931 the Catholic Centre Party had stood as a bastion against the Nazis, especially under the leadership of Chancellor Heinrich Brüning. In the middle of the Depression the party was in government with the support of the Socialists, and Brüning was leading a country caught up in rampant inflation, massive unemployment and the increas-ingly threatening growth of the Nazi movement. Visiting Rome in August 1931 he had a meeting with Pacelli. Brüning, whose *Memoirs* are the source of this story, says that Pacelli demanded that he seek Nazi support for his minority government so that he could out vote the Socialists and smaller parties and fulfil the Secretary of State's favourite scheme, a concordat between Germany and the Vatican. Brüning bluntly refused to do this. He considered it unrealistic. He had much more pressing priorities and was utterly unwilling to compromise with Nazism. On leaving Pacelli the chancellor commented acidly that he hoped 'the Vatican would fare better at the hands of Hitler than with himself, a devout Catholic'. This was prophetic given the church's losses during the Nazi period.

As a Catholic, Brüning probably understood Pacelli's political and diplomatic manoeuvrings better than most. In a revealing passage, later excised from the *Memoirs*, he explained: 'All successes [Pacelli believed] could only be attained by papal diplomacy. The system of concordats led him and the Vatican to despise democracy and the parliamentary system ... Rigid governments, rigid centralisation, and rigid treaties were supposed to introduce an era of stable order, an era of peace and quiet.' Elsewhere Brüning commented 'I am convinced the Nazis are neither religious nor tolerant'. This was the core of the problem. Essentially many Catholics and most of the bishops were caught up in the authoritarian, hierarchical *führerprinzip* system that had dominated Catholicism since the First Vatican Council of 1870 when papal infallibility and primacy had been defined. Pacelli's closest ally in the *Zentrumspartei* was Monsignor Ludwig Kaas. He said bluntly: 'In the state there is the leadership principle; at the Vatican the same holds'.

The great fear of Catholics was not of the right but of the left, of Bolshevism rather than Fascism. What is also significant is that the Jews were often linked to the left. Catholics in the 1930s were conventionally anti-Jewish rather than anti-Semitic. Religious anti-Judaism is not the same as racial anti-Semitism, but it does create the ambience in which racism can flourish. After all, Catholics were still praying for the 'perfidious Jews' who had executed Jesus as late as 1962 in the Good Friday liturgy. In the 1930s the Jews were incorrectly identified by right-wing Catholics as proponents of secular liberal values that were thought to undermine the identification of Catholicism with European culture. Secular liberalism was seen as the product of a 'Masonic–Jewish alliance' and the myth of Jewish world financial dominance was often mentioned. Jews were also cast in the role of leaders of socialism and communism, even though the vast majority of European Jews were actually poor, conservative and orthodox. But these caricatures deeply infiltrated conservative Catholic consciousness. Linked with the Bolsheviks, the Jews were seen as setting out to destroy Christian civilisation. The Nazis were easily able to exploit these presumptions.

So to say that the church stood four-square against the Nazis, 'prevailing against the gates of hell', as Ratzinger suggests, is to rewrite history completely. The actual Catholic response leaves much to be desired.

After his *Habiliationsschrift* Ratzinger was only briefly back in the Freising seminary. From 1959 to 1969 he taught theology at state universities. He was ordinary professor of fundamental theology at the University of Bonn from 1959 to 1963, and was then professor of dogmatic theology at the University of Münster. In 1966 he moved to Tübingen University, again as professor of dogmatic theology. Meanwhile the Second Vatican Council had been called by Pope John XXIII in 1959. The pope wanted a renewal of the church and an opening-up of Catholicism to the world. After a long preparation, Vatican II began in October 1962 and lasted through four sessions until December 1965.

Ratzinger played an important role both in the preparations for the Council and at all four sessions. In 1961 he published, with the great Austrian Jesuit theologian, Karl Rahner, the influential book *The Episcopate and the Primacy*, in which they argued persuasively that the papal office is not something separate from and over and against the bishops. They maintained that the pope must always act as a member of the church and of the college of bishops. As the traditional formula puts it, the pope is *primus inter pares*, first among equals. The practical result of this is that the bishops need to play a much more active role in working with the pope in the government of the world church. This received its conciliar expression in the doctrine of the collegiality of bishops—the notion that bishops all work as colleagues with the Bishop of Rome in the government of the universal church. It is important to recall this because as cardinal of the CDF Ratzinger retreated from this doctrine, although since being elected pope he has spoken favourably about episcopal collegiality.

This kind of theology was unacceptable, even incomprehensible, to the Roman curia and its theologians who managed to keep complete control of the preparations for the Council. While they took suggestions from bishops these were carefully vetted and everything that did not fit the Roman viewpoint was eliminated. They set up pre-conciliar commissions that they loaded with their own people who prepared documents that faithfully represented the Roman line. The aim of the curia was a closed, in-house Council approving, but not debating, previously prepared documents. The presupposition was that the Roman curia's views were the only possible ones. Eventually they were forced by Pope John and pressure from many bishops to appoint theologians, like Rahner and Ratzinger, from outside

Rome and with different views, but these were not there long enough nor in sufficient numbers to able to exercise influence to modify the stodgy and inward-looking documents the curia had prepared for the Council.

But there were other powerful forces at work in the wider church. In the period after the First World War, theology had undergone an extraordinary process of renewal. Some of the leading lights in this *nouvelle théologie* as it was called in France, were actually Ratzinger's intellectual mentors: thinkers like Guardini, Rahner, De Lubac, Yves Congar, Pryzwara and many others. A whole new way of conceiving of Catholicism and its relationship with the world had emerged. Also there were many broad-minded, theologically literate bishops and archbishops, especially in France and Germany, who were simply not prepared to let the curia get away with its plan of action. They wanted a Council that would be open to the world, democratic, collegial, rooted in the Bible, the liturgy and the fathers of the church, ecumenically sensitive, with lay participation and with observers from the Orthodox, Protestant and Anglican churches. Renewal, what John XXIII called *aggiornamento*, was in the air.

The person who captured the prevailing mood best was a young 32-year-old Swiss-born theologian who in 1960 had become a professor in the Catholic faculty at the prestigious Tübingen University, the equivalent of Cambridge University in Germany. His name was Hans Küng. Two of his books, *The Council and Reunion* (German edition 1960, English translation in 1961) and *Structures of the Church* (1962), which were translated into many languages, captured the imaginations of many thoughtful Catholics and really set the mood for the coming Council. He argued that the church could achieve Christian unity if Catholicism was committed to making the Bible an essential part of its spirituality, renewing its worship and emphasising the common priesthood of all believers. In other words, reform of the church and Christian unity went together. He became an instant celebrity, touring the world talking about the Council and firing people up with enthusiasm. In the definitive *History of Vatican II*, J. Oscar Beozzo shows how difficult it was for anyone to penetrate the secrecy which surrounded the preparation of the Council documents, and he says that 'The explosive spread of Küng's idea of a necessary and sufficient connection between reform and unity' captured people's imaginations and really set out a whole popular agenda for the Council.

Joseph Ratzinger was far less prominent. He was simply an academic theologian at Bonn University. It was here that he came to know the Cardinal Archbishop of Cologne, Josef Frings, who was a member of the

Central Preparatory Commission for the Council. He eventually invited Ratzinger to come to Rome with him as his *peritus*, his theological expert. Frings was no mean theologian and scripture scholar himself. He had also had long pastoral experience as a priest, seminary rector and bishop. It was in Rome early in the first session of the Council in 1962 that Ratzinger first met Küng. They were the same age and in some ways from similar backgrounds, although Küng was Swiss, and that is a significant difference.

Küng says in his memoirs *My Struggle for Freedom* (English trans. 2003) that they first met at the Caffè San Pietro on the Via della Conciliazione just down from the piazza of Saint Peter's. Küng wrote later: 'He seems to me very friendly, though perhaps not completely open, whereas to him I possibly seem all too spontaneous and direct. For me he is more a *"timido"* with an invisible spiritual anointing, whereas to him I perhaps seem audacious, with more worldly charms. But all in all he is a very congenial contemporary, with whom one can argue on the same level about all the questions which have arisen.' Nevertheless, Küng felt that even then Ratzinger was rather cautious. Perhaps it is closer to the truth to say that he was simply shy, especially in the company of a theologian who had a widespread international reputation. Küng comments, somewhat acidly, that nevertheless Ratzinger was characterised by a 'clericalistic narrowness' as a result of which he 'concentrates the collegiality of the church directly on the collegiality of the bishops ... [whereas] the structure of the early church is formed both by the college of the apostles *and* the community'.

Küng also makes a mordant comment in his *Memoirs* about Balthasar who was not invited to the Council. He says that the Council was pastoral and outward looking and not concerned with the issues that preoccupied Balthasar—the Greek and Latin fathers and mysticism. 'Some of the things that happen in the Council seem to him, an utterly apolitical aesthete, to be a false accommodation to the dominant spirit of the time ... He becomes a reactionary.' What is significant is that something similar happened to Ratzinger after the Council, and he ultimately joined forces with Balthasar.

However, a different side of Ratzinger is revealed in the speeches and actions of Cardinal Frings. Perhaps it was the great cardinal himself who was the courageous one, perhaps he was egged-on by his *peritus*; it might even have been the combination of both. Certainly Ratzinger was associated with the most important theologians, such as Rahner, Congar, Schillebeeckx and Küng, in trying to circumvent curial control of the pre-conciliar agenda. On the day before the Council opened, he gave a talk in Rome to the German-speaking bishops on the proposed schema on revelation,

God's self-disclosure to us through Christ, the Bible and the church. This was to become the most important theological issue confronting the Council because it intimately affected Catholicism's self-understanding and its relationship with the Protestant and Anglican churches. Ratzinger, among others, played an important role in the development of the fine document *Dei Verbum* on revelation.

Dei Verbum was the result of hard, even fierce, debates through all four sessions. The pre-conciliar schema had been substantially drawn up by a committee presided over by the Cardinal of the Holy Office, the powerful and almost blind Alfredo Ottaviani, assisted by the Dutch Jesuit, Sebastian Tromp, who had been one of Küng's professors at the Gregorian University in Rome. The schema was a restatement of a notion which had gained acceptance in the years after the sixteenth-century Council of Trent (its final session was in December 1563). This was that there were two separate sources of revelation: the Bible was one, church tradition the other. From tradition the church could learn things that were not contained in scripture. This approach was simply unacceptable to Protestants, for whom the Bible was absolutely central and complete. Much of the Tromp document was taken up with an attack on the views on revelation of a fellow Jesuit theologian, the German Josef Geiselmann of Tübingen University. He had argued that Trent had never made a sharp distinction between Bible and tradition as the 'two-source theory' claimed, and that the theory originated in the seventeenth century. Geiselmann said that tradition was actually the church's ongoing, dynamic interpretation of the Bible within the context of the demands of contemporary life. Thus tradition was really the church's evolving self-understanding, guided by the Holy Spirit. In other words, tradition was not separate from scripture. It was really the church's continuing, active interpretation of its relationship to historical and contemporary reality using scripture as its guide. Such a view was much more biblical and more acceptable to Protestants.

When the schema on revelation prepared by the Ottaviani–Tromp committee was introduced to the Council early in the first session (10 October to 8 December 1962) Cardinal Frings was scathing on its contents and no doubt Ratzinger played a major part in preparing his speech. He told the bishops:

> The primary purpose of a Council is to provide for the pastoral needs of the day, to teach the truth, to stimulate its preaching in such wise that it will be received. At the First Vatican Council [in 1870] complaints

were raised against the professional [and obscure] tone of the schemata
... Here the approach is even further exaggerated ... Why speak of two
sources of revelation? This is not traditional. Neither the fathers, nor
the scholastic theologians, nor Saint Thomas Aquinas himself, nor the
previous councils knew anything about this way of explaining our
teaching. It is not traditional and only in recent centuries, as a result of
a false historicism, have certain theologians tried to explain the matter
thus ... What is said here ... is at once offensive to our separated
brothers in Christ and harmful to the proper liberty required in any
scientific procedure.

But this was nothing compared to Frings' stinging attack during the
second session on 8 November 1963 on the Holy Office, the direct pre-
cursor of the Congregation for the Doctrine of the Faith and the direct heir
of the Roman Inquisition. Again this is significant, because the very institution that Ratzinger was later to lead was attacked by the Cardinal who
had brought him to Rome as a *peritus*. Frings said the Holy Office still
acted inquisitorially by condemning people without a hearing, without
clear charges and without giving them an opportunity to defend themselves. He spoke of 'methods and behaviour ... [which] are the cause of
scandal to the world'. This was greeted with long applause. He went on to
suggest that lay people could easily qualify for many tasks in the curia.
Even though it was forbidden, there was more applause. Later that day the
pope asked Frings for proposals to reform the Holy Office. Sadly, however,
there have only been cosmetic changes at the Holy Office and although its
name is now the CDF, the reality is the same. Nowadays people 'delated'
(reported) to the CDF are never informed who has accused them—usually
they do not even know they have been delated until much later, there is no
presumption of innocence, the CDF does not usually deal with them
directly but through intermediaries, they do not know who is assessing
their work, they do not know who is judging the assessment with prose-
cutors acting as judges, and they do not even know who is defending them.
They are usually never given a chance to defend themselves verbally.
Everything is in writing and usually direct letters from the accused are
ignored. It is a Kafkaesque process that is characterised, above all, by extraordinary discourtesy and rudeness. And Ratzinger presided over all this
from November 1981 to April 2005 and did nothing about it.

But this is getting ahead of ourselves. Back at the Council, Ratzinger
played an important role behind the scenes. There is certainly evidence
that as the Council progressed he had considerable influence on Frings. It

is thought that Frings' attack on the Holy Office led Pope Paul VI (1963–78) to ask Ratzinger among others for ideas on the reform of the Roman curia. He played an important role on the subcommittee dealing with the role and function of bishops and the doctrine of collegiality through which pope and bishops together are responsible for the universal church. Ratzinger had some reservations about focusing too exclusively on this issue. For him Catholicism was better imagined as one church made up of a communion of local churches, thus making the Eucharist the centre of the bond of unity. He was also continuously engaged in the ongoing group reformulating the text of *Dei Verbum* on revelation. In 1965 he published the small book, *Revelation and Tradition*. He was also involved in the committee formulating the uninspiring 'Decree on Missionary Activity'. This, too, ran into trouble during the break between the third and fourth sessions of the Council, but was eventually passed.

Throughout the Council, Ratzinger was viewed as part of the reformist majority, although both he and Frings showed little enthusiasm for the final document of the Council, 'The Pastoral Constitution on the Church in the Modern World' (*Gaudium et Spes*), approved on the second last day, 7 December 1965. What Ratzinger objected to was the strongly Thomistic tone and optimistic feel of the Constitution and the failure to recognise the endemic presence of sin in the world.

So what happened to the progressive theologian of Vatican II who was eventually to become inquisitor and then pope?

In 1966, Hans Küng was dean of the Catholic theology faculty at Tübingen. He says he was anxious to build up a kind of stellar group of theologians that included Rahner and Ratzinger. Rahner never came, but Ratzinger did. He seemed the ideal choice. Küng says: 'Although he is only 37, he enjoys great respect, as his career so far shows. He has his own direction of research and at the same time he is very open to contemporary questions—a basis for good collaboration. I had also found him personally congenial at the time of the Council' (*Memoirs*, p. 453). Just three years later, in summer 1969, Ratzinger resigned and left for Regensberg. Why? Küng says, 'Time and again people puzzle over how so gifted, friendly, open a theologian as Joseph Ratzinger can undergo such a change: from progressive Tübingen theologian to Roman Grand Inquisitor' (*Memoirs*, p. 457).

Küng has his own theories, but before we look at those let us try to understand it from Ratzinger's own perspective. In one sense he would argue that others have changed and that he has remained steadfast. In one way that is true. There is a consistency between the pre- and post-Council Ratzinger. He always remained an Augustinian. For him the world, especially a culture divorced from faith, has little or nothing to offer the church. That is why he never supported the Council document on 'The Church in the Modern World'. It all sounded too optimistic, too convinced that the world could teach the church. Although he only makes passing reference to him, what Ratzinger really objected to was the remote but pervasive influence of the thought of the Jesuit palaeontologist and cosmologist Pierre Teilhard de Chardin (1881–1955) in the document. The French Jesuit's optimistic vision of the world and of the whole process of material evolution moving towards greater spiritual complexity and a kind of cosmic consummation in Christ was regarded as unrealistically optimistic and lacking any real sense of the fallen human condition by the future CDF prefect. For him the world needed a redemption that could only come from Jesus' crucifixion. Divorced from this, the world had nothing to offer, and could often explode in what were essentially demonic outbreaks.

This was why Ratzinger reacted so badly to the student radicalism and riots of 1967–68. These occurred right across the United States, Europe, especially in Paris, and also in Britain and Australia. The riots culminated for the sheltered academic theologians of Tübingen in April–May 1968 when their radicalised students adopted Marxist terminology to describe the New Testament as an exploitative text and the death of Jesus on the cross as a 'sado-masochistic glorification of pain'. Ratzinger says he was horrified, and no doubt he was. He says that he increasingly came to see this lack of respect for authority and the constant demands for more rights, for example gay rights, as symptomatic of an abandonment of Catholic teaching and moral standards. Küng adopted a much calmer viewpoint. He saw student radicalism for what it was—delayed adolescence—and treated it as such. Revolting students were certainly a dreadful nuisance, but nothing more. Of course, most of these same student 'radicals' were to go on to become neo-conservatives, captains of industry and comfortable 'baby boomers' whose selfishness is well known. These are the people who now insist on charging their own children to go to university after getting a free tertiary education themselves. But by any objective standards, Ratzinger's response to student radicalism in 1968 seems very much like a massive over-reaction. Despite the student revolt, at Tübingen he was still able to write what is generally considered his masterpiece, his *Introduction to Christianity* (1968, English trans. 1969), an exposition of the Apostles' Creed.

The year 1968 also saw the publication on 24 July of the encyclical *Humanae vitae* by Pope Paul VI. This was the Vatican's response to the contraceptive pill. The pope's teaching against the pill caused a storm of protest right across the Catholic world, especially in developed countries where the use of contraception was already widespread. So Catholics could not avoid the issue. Theologically, the *Humanae vitae* affair confronted the church with the question of the status of non-infallible (Paul VI made it clear that this was not an infallible decision) but authoritative papal teaching that was ignored and even directly rejected by the very people to whom it was directed. As a result, the church today is still confronted not by the question of contraception (most people of fertile age have made up their own minds on this issue), but the status of non-infallible papal teaching power, the 'ordinary magisterium' as it is called.

Ratzinger left Tübingen in 1969 and returned to Bavaria, to the newly established University of Regensberg. Regensberg is one of the most beautiful cities in Germany. Much of its medieval character has been preserved and the Dom (cathedral) of Saint Peter is an example of pure German gothic architecture. His brother Georg was for many years the director of the cathedral choir. It was not bombed during the war, and Ratzinger has subsequently made the city his home. At the university he began working with Johann Auer on a nine-volume collection on Christian doctrine, *Kleine Katholische Dogmatik*. In 1977 he published the volume which deals with eschatology; that is, death, heaven, hell and the second coming of Christ.

At Regensberg, he moved further and further away from his erstwhile colleagues at Tübingen. Küng says that even while he was on the faculty 'my colleague who for all his friendliness always seems somewhat distanced and cool, had kept something like an unenlightened "devotional corner" in his Bavarian heart and shown himself to be all too stamped by Augustine's pessimistic view of the world and Bonaventura's Platonising neglect of the visible and empirical (in contrast to Thomas Aquinas)' (*Memoirs*, p. 457).

In the early 1970s, Ratzinger co-operated with Hans Urs von Balthasar in a short book *Two Say Why: Why I am Still a Christian*. Around the same time the two had founded the theological journal *Communio* as a kind of response to the more progressive *Concilium*. In the *Two Say Why* book, Ratzinger is exceptionally pessimistic about the state of the church. For sure, it was a difficult, silly, even tragic time when many excesses occurred, such as rejection of long-established devotions, so-called home Masses that were really kitchen table Eucharists, outright discounting of church teaching, and catechetical chaos. But in historical context these extremes were understandable. The lid had been kept on in the church for far too long and once it was removed an explosion occurred. While there was a massive amount of talking and adult education, the Council's vision was really not enshrined in church structures. There was also an absolutely determined and often destructive group of people who utterly refused to accept the Council. These people blocked renewal at every turn. Ratzinger has sympathy for these people. He says: 'To them it seems as though the church is betraying its essential nature, selling out to the way of the world and losing its soul. They are disillusioned, like any lover whose great love has been betrayed' (*Two Say Why*, p. 66). Yet, in practice, these people often acted with extraordinary viciousness towards those who tried to implement the conciliar changes. Nowadays the besieged group is different. The people who feel deeply betrayed now, especially by people like Ratzinger, are those who have worked for years in ministry often without any recognition (let alone ecclesiastical honours like the title 'cardinal') to bring about the Council's reforms with integrity

In *Two Say Why* Ratzinger paints an almost apocalyptic vision. 'How was it possible for this Babylonian captivity to arise at a moment when we had been hoping for a new Pentecost? How was it possible that just when the Council seemed to have reaped the ripe harvest of the last decades, instead of enjoying the riches of fulfilment, we found only emptiness? How could disintegration emerge from a great surge toward unity?' (p. 68). This is an extraordinarily pessimistic reading of what happened in the church of the late 1960s and 1970s. I lived right through this period and worked in parishes, seminaries and adult education, and I certainly would not interpret those years so negatively. And I am not alone in my more positive evaluation of the period. This negative assessment seems so relentless. 'The church is becoming extinguished in men's souls, and Christian communities are crumbling. In the midst of a world striving for unity the church is falling apart in nationalistic partisanship, in culmination of the alien and glorification of self' (p. 67). He admits that positive things have happened since the Council: an accessible liturgy, an awareness of social problems, a better understanding between the churches, but 'in spite of all the signs of hope, the church that has emerged from this process is not a modern but a thoroughly shaky and deeply divided church' (p. 73). However, he says he stays a Catholic because it is in the church alone that he can meet Jesus Christ, and it is only the church's faith that can redeem humankind. Neither Marx, nor Freud, nor Jung are able to bring redemption, 'to build a world free from pain, sickness and sorrow ... to fight against pain and injustice in the world is a thoroughly Christian impulse.

But to imagine that one can inaugurate a sorrow-free world through social reform and the abolition of government and the rule of law, and demand that this be accomplished here and now, represent an erroneous doctrine, a serious error concerning the nature of man' (p. 85).

In all his writings from about 1970 onwards, there is a tendency towards exaggeration and caricature of views with which he disagrees. An example of this are his 1985 interviews with Vittorio Messori in *The Ratzinger Report: An Exclusive Interview on the State of the Church*. There is much in the book that I certainly agree with, especially when he talks about 'a shattered catechesis' (p. 72). This is an interesting and important example. The context in which he considers the crisis in religious education is what he calls 'an individualistic theology'. 'In this subjective view of theology, dogma is often viewed as an intolerable straight-jacket, an assault on the freedom of the individual scholar' (pp. 71–2). But he gives no examples of 'subjectivist theologians' and I don't know a single reputable Catholic who asserts such an extreme form of individualism. He claims that 'theology can no longer transmit a common model of the faith', asserting this as an established fact, when it is not. He says the result is that 'catechesis is exposed to dismemberment and constantly changing experiments. Some catechisms and many catechists no longer teach the Catholic faith in its harmonic wholeness ... rather they try to make some elements of the Christian patrimony humanly "interesting" (according to the cultural orientations of the moment)' (p. 72). The simple response to this is: What is wrong with engaging the students through grabbing their interest and establishing the relevance of belief and faith in their lives? Also, there was never a time in which Catholicism was taught 'in its harmonic wholeness'. Every age has its own emphases, every historical period focuses on what seems important to it.

The CDF prefect seemingly knows very little about religious education on the ground. Many Catholic schools are making heroic efforts to try to give their students a genuine initiation into Catholicism and an encounter with Christ, but they understand that this involves both the cultivation of what has been called the 'Catholic imagination', as well as an informed intellect. By 'imagination' I mean the development of a way of viewing the world which is essentially symbolic, sacramental, poetic and profoundly community oriented. It is an attitude to life which transcends the purely empirical. Andrew Greeley has shown that Catholic schools in the United States continue to nurture this kind of 'Catholic' attitude, as many do in Australia. The Catholic imagination is nurtured in students through the way the school operates as a community, through the ministerial and caring attitudes of the staff, through the ethos that is created. While instruction is important, it is really the articulation of a deeper process whereby a living faith is conveyed. The process is so much more sophisticated and complex than Ratzinger suggests. Also, while there was real confusion in religious education in two decades immediately after the Council, this has now changed. A more comprehensive religious education is certainly being offered.

I have already talked about Ratzinger's relationship with Balthasar in chapter 4. They are the founders, together with Henri de Lubac, Walter Kasper and Karl Lehmann, of the scholarly review *Communio* (begun in 1972) designed as an antidote to the progressive Dutch-financed *Concilium* (begun in 1965). All the founders of *Communio* were subsequently appointed cardinals; none of the founders of *Concilium* have ever got beyond simple priest! This tells you everything about the bias of the Wojtyla papacy. Significantly, Kasper and Lehmann, after their appointments as diocesan bishops in Germany, have moved back from a conservative to a moderate-to-progressive stance.

Both Ratzinger and Balthasar are essentially intellectuals who view the world from a cultured, scholarly and abstract non-experiential perspective. Both are influenced by the fathers of the church and they look back to them as a resource to be recovered today. Both tend to espouse a kind of dichotomy between an evil world and a world that is redeemed by the love of God. Both identify openness to the world, the kind of approach espoused by the Council in 'The Church in the Modern World' as dangerous because it 'baptises' secular and religious movements from outside the church and thus runs the risk of losing a specific Christian identity. Both tend to see creation and salvation as inextricably intertwined. Creation is secondary to salvation and it is only in Christ that we can discern the connection between the two. Essentially, both are Augustinians who perceive a great divide between the world and God, between our apprehension of the divine and God's self-revelation in Christ. Both felt that there was a complete collapse of the vitality of the church in the period after the Council when large numbers of priests, brothers and sisters abandoned ministry and religious life. They argue that Mass attendance has dropped precipitously and many Catholics today are merely nominal. But it remains to be seen if these results were the direct consequences of Vatican II, or were inevitable given that the Council was really part of a much larger social change process. And both are great lovers of Mozart, which is something very much in their favour.

Finally, and most importantly, Ratzinger and Balthasar are not historians, although they, like many theologians, dabble in history. Both evinced considerable interest in the *ressourcement* movement and wanted to get behind the arid scholasticism of the post-reformation period and recover biblical, patristic and medieval sources so that these could be used as resources for contemporary Catholicism. What they wanted to reclaim was what they saw as the church's genuine tradition, so often hidden by the accretions of the last few centuries. But the problem was they were theologians using history. History is one of those unfortunate sciences that everyone thinks they can 'do' without any professional training. But what happens is that history is distorted when it is mined for information and texts divorced from their context; in other words, the past treated as though it were the present. Of course, the great narratives, like the Bible, Shakespeare and all serious literature transcend their context and shine across the ages. The post-modernist attempt to reduce these texts entirely to their time, period and the individual subjectivity of their author is nonsense. But so is the failure to deny the past its own context. Ratzinger's attacks on relativism may well have some validity, but it does not mean that his going to the opposite extreme is correct, pretending that there were a whole range of 'Truths' whose expressions were somehow free of historical context. What is needed is some healthy historical sense, some feeling for context and process. Nothing exists outside of historical context: all dogmas, teachings and texts belong somewhere in the process and evolution of human experience and knowledge. What thinkers like Balthasar and Ratzinger have done is to turn history into an abstraction. They never engage with and attempt to understand, as does the historian, the 'stuff' of history, the people and processes, the unpredictability and serendipity. Their tendency is to 'absolutise', to turn history into ideology.

This can be seen in the way Ratzinger brings up legitimate criticisms of the post-Vatican II church, such as liturgical excesses and experiments gone wrong, or failed religious education programs. But just as you expect him to advance a balanced, middle-of-the-road position, he suddenly goes to the opposite extreme. The church is going completely to the dogs, the true vision of the Council has been lost as though he alone knows what the 'true vision' is: 'Today it is clear that, in spite of all the signs of hope, the church that has emerged from this process [of post-Vatican II renewal] is not a modern but thoroughly shaky and deeply divided church' (*Two Say Why*, p. 73). There is no sense that this was a period that Catholicism had to pass through after the Council, no feeling for historical context, no sense that change always implies the danger of making mistakes, and that mistakes can be corrected without going to the opposite extreme.

In the end it is hard to see how Ratzinger's thought is particularly original. What he really does is explore well-established themes at some depth, reflecting his conviction that his perception of objective truth is central to theology. Much of his theology reflects the earlier work of Johann Adam Möhler, the pioneering nineteenth-century Tübingen Catholic theologian. This is not to say that Ratzinger is not a good theologian or a man of great intelligence. It is just to say that historians reflecting on our age will not see him as an original thinker in the sense that Romano Guardini and Karl Rahner were. This is reflected in the fact that in the 1970s he was increasingly identified with the more conservative wing of the church. He was appointed to the International Theological Commission (ITC), which had been founded during the Council as a kind of advisory body to the CDF. This meant he had been noticed by Rome. However, the Congregation largely ignored the ITC and it quickly evolved into a kind of 'talk-fest' for theologians. Rahner described it as 'a theologians' club where intelligent theologians intelligently (impotently) dialogued with one another. I felt I didn't need to go to Rome for that.' At the same time as Ratzinger was retreating from many of his stances during the Council years, he manifested an increasingly pessimistic view of the post-Vatican II church. All this made him attractive to Rome.

So when the aged and progressive Cardinal Julius Döpfner of Munich died on 24 July 1976, Ratzinger was nominated as his successor. He says he heard rumours that he would be offered the see, but that he discounted them. So he claims he was surprised when offered the archbishopric by the papal nuncio, Archbishop Guido del Mestri. After consulting his confessor, he accepted. He succeeded to the see of Munich-Freising on 15 February 1977 and was ordained archbishop on 28 May. He was created cardinal priest of Saint Mary of Consolation in Tiburtina by Pope Paul VI in a consistory on 27 June that same year. He chose as his episcopal motto a text from Saint John's Third Letter (verse 8) 'Fellow worker in the truth'. He says that this text 'seemed to be the connection between my previous task as a teacher and my new mission. Despite all the differences in modality, what is involved was and remains the same: to follow the truth, to be at its service.' Then follows one of those typical Ratzinger caricatures and exaggerations: 'And because in today's world the theme of truth has all but disappeared, because truth appears too great for man, and yet everything falls apart if there is no truth' (*Milestones*, p. 153).

He had mixed success in his four years as Munich's archbishop. He was not particularly popular with the clergy, although part of this may be explained by the fact that he seemed to spend most of his time dealing with matters outside the archdiocese.

Firstly, there was the business of two papal elections in quick succession. On 6 August 1978 Pope Paul VI died quietly in his sleep. The conclave for the election of his successor began on 25 August and the new pope was elected the next day on the third ballot, a remarkably quick and, to most people, surprising choice. It was generally expected that there would be three major candidates. Cardinal Giuseppe Siri of Genoa, an outspoken critic of John XXIII and the Council, was supported by die-hard conservatives and some in the Roman curia. Some of the Italians and some Vatican II supporters favoured Cardinal Giovanni Benelli, formerly Paul VI's right-hand man and now archbishop of Florence. The other candidate was largely self-appointed: Cardinal Sergio Pignedoli who, so one story goes, so fancied himself that he went on a severe diet so he could fit into the white cassock the pope wears when elected. Many commentators, like Andrew Greeley, expected a long conclave and were literally astonished when Albino Luciani of Venice was elected in the third ballot. There is evidence that a number of cardinals had already informally planned what they were going to do before entering the conclave. Also, it is clear that the other two of the candidates (Siri and Pignadoli) were of such poor quality that they were actually unelectable. And Benelli had made many enemies as Paul VI's authoritarian hatchet man in the Secretariat of State. There is also evidence that Wojtyla from Cracow got some votes in this conclave. Clearly the cardinals were looking for someone from outside the Roman curia.

We do not know how Ratzinger voted in the conclave. Certainly, on the face of it, the rather simple, pastoral, smiling, direct and non-intellectual approach of someone like Cardinal Luciani would probably not have appealed to him. Throughout much of September he was in Ecuador attending a Marian Congress as a representative of the new pope. Back in Rome, all the evidence is that the papacy simply overwhelmed John Paul I physically and psychologically. The Vatican did nothing to care for his health, which was clearly fragile, nor did it support the steep learning curve he faced. As a result, he seems to have become emotionally disoriented. He had no real support from his secretary from Venice who was as inexperienced as he. He brought back Paul VI's secretary, the Irishman John Magee, who brought some order to the papal household. But no one was supervising the Vatican and, more importantly, no one was watching his medicine to prevent blood clotting, which needed to be taken carefully. The result was disaster.

The thirty-three-day papacy of Pope John Paul I was one of the shortest in history. He was found dead in his bedroom early in the morning of 29 September. He had died the night before. All types of absurd conspiracy theories abounded when John Paul I died, especially as a result of the Vatican's inefficiency and obsession with secrecy. His death was certainly not the consequence of some nonsensical conspiracy, as argued by David Yallop in a very silly book *In God's Name*. A man of genuine humility and personal warmth, John Paul I's sudden death was the result of natural causes. John Cornwell's book *A Thief in the Night* convincingly showed that the pope had suffered a pulmonary embolism; that is, an unusually large blood clot.

So Ratzinger was back in Rome in early October for the papal funeral and another conclave. Again the battle seemed to be between Siri and Benelli, although both their reputations were tarnished by their playing dirty politics before the conclave began. After four ballots it was clear that there was no consensus for an Italian, so the cardinals began to look elsewhere. Wojtyla quickly emerged. To the progressives like Cardinal Franz König of Vienna he seemed to be pastorally minded and intelligent, and therefore open to new ideas. The German-speaking cardinals supported König. This no doubt included Ratzinger, for he and Wojtyla were old friends, and Peter Hebblethwaite thinks he was active with König in soliciting votes for the Pole. The conservatives, like Siri and the curial Cardinal Silvio Oddi, were much shrewder. They knew that theologically Wojtyla was really conservative and he was deeply opposed to communism. Siri's votes went over to him, and Cardinal John Krol of Philadelphia brought the Americans onside. Wojtyla was elected after eight ballots. He chose the name John Paul II and the second-longest papacy in history began. Ratzinger says that the thing that won his sympathy was Wojtyla's 'uncomplicated human frankness and openness, as well as the cordiality that he radiated. There was his humour. You also sensed a piety that had nothing false, nothing external about it. You sensed that here was a man of God … a completely original person who had a long intellectual and personal history behind him … He had blazed his own intellectual trail.'

8

PREFECT OF THE CDF

After the conclave, Ratzinger returned to Munich. It quickly became obvious that he was very much in sympathy with the new Polish pope who had no patience with theologians who were perceived as dissidents. In 1979, a former colleague of Ratzinger's at Tübingen, Johann Baptist Metz, 'the father of political theology', that is, the idea that Christianity and spirituality inevitably involves the believer in social and activist struggles, was offered a chair in the Catholic theology faculty at the Ludwig-Maximilians Universität of Munich. Although the university is an auto-nomous, government-funded institution, appointments to theology chairs require episcopal approval according to the Concordat negotiated between the state of Bavaria and the Vatican in 1924. The archbishop can blacklist candidates with the education minister. This is what Ratzinger did to Metz, even though the priest had been an advisor to the German bishops and a consultant to the Vatican Secretariat for Non-Believers. Ratzinger knew that Pope Wojtyla had no patience with theologians who developed justifications for clergy interfering in politics, and he himself was deeply opposed to anything that smacked of 'liberation theology'. Ratzinger's action was widely criticised in Germany at the time, especially by Rahner.

Then there was the long drawn-out case of Hans Küng. This finally came to a head at Christmas time, 18 December 1979—the CDF regularly seems to send 'final notices' to theologians just before Christmas. The CDF declared that Küng could no longer hold a *missio canonica*, a mission to teach as a Catholic theologian. It led to an extraordinary response in

Germany. Küng, who remained in good standing as a priest and Catholic, was prevented by the bishop of Rottenburg-Stuttgart, Georg Möser, from retaining his chair at Tübingen. The university appointment was subject to a concordat between the Vatican and the state of Baden-Württemberg. The ecumenical institute which Küng headed was removed from the Catholic faculty and placed directly under the university president. Thus it was not subject to an episcopal veto.

Ratzinger's response to Küng's treatment was appallingly patronising: 'The Christian believer is a simple person: bishops should protect the faith of these little people against the power of intellectuals'! He also alleged that in Germany 'criticism of the papacy had reached a dramatic level' to which one newspaper, the *Frankfürter Rundschau*, replied: 'The removal of a theologian who has done more to bring back doubters to the church than all the German bishops with their formal declarations, leaves one speechless and bitter' (13/12/79). Küng told me later:

> The 'Declaration' led to protests both in Germany and across the world, especially the English-speaking countries. I suspect that the CDF and the German bishops totally underestimated the reaction that they eventually faced. The irony is that the whole thing gave me freedom. I only met Cardinal Ratzinger once subsequent to this Roman intervention and his appointment as prefect of the CDF. He said to me 'You look good.' 'Yes,' I said, 'I feel good, but this was obviously not the intention of your Congregation.' 'I do not know the intentions of my predecessor!' he replied.'

Ratzinger was soon back in Rome again for the Synod on the Family which ran from late September to 25 October 1980. Discussion during the first week was free-ranging, and controversial issues such as contraception, divorce, remarriage and the role of the family were freely canvassed. But then Ratzinger was brought in by the synod administration to structure the discussions along narrower lines. The bishops were split up into small language groups and thus lost the energy that comes from a big group led by influential speakers. Still, their recommendations were radical, but these were soon lost in forty-three 'propositions' which some bishops complained did not represent their discussions at all. In the end the Synod achieved little and the later encyclical *Familiaris consortio* reflected little or nothing of the bishops' real concerns. But Ratzinger had again made his mark in Rome.

John Paul made two efforts to get the Munich archbishop to come to Rome. The first was when he offered him the job of prefect of the Congregation for Catholic Education. Ratzinger said 'No' because he felt he had not been in Munich long enough. But before he was offered his next Vatican job, he found himself in an embarrassing situation. John Paul's globe-trotting travels had begun soon after his election. There had already been rather embarrassing but gentle public confrontations with two religious sisters: first, with Mercy Sister Theresa Kane in Washington, and then Handmaid of the Sacred Heart, Sister Danièle Souillard, in Paris. Both told the pope to his face that they were concerned about the role of women and of religious sisters in the church. The third woman to confront the pope was a lay woman, Barbara Engl, who spoke in Munich on behalf of Catholic youth organisations during the November 1980 papal visit to Germany. It was a freezing day, but young people had turned out for a Mass at which the pope spoke about Satan, which seemed totally inappropriate. This led Engl to depart from her approved speech of farewell to speak from quickly prepared notes. She told John Paul:

> Young people have the feeling ... that their concern for friendship, sexuality and partnership meets only with negative answers [from the hierarchy] ... Many young people cannot understand why the church should insist so strongly on celibacy for its priests, when there is an evident lack of priests ... Nor can young people understand why a greater sharing of women in the ministry should be ruled out. (*Süddeutsche Zeitung*, 20/11/80)

Ratzinger was deeply embarrassed, and the pope, who buried his head in his hands during the speech, was quickly hustled away on the pretext that he had another appointment.

However, it did not spoil Ratzinger's chances for a high Roman position. Again the pope asked him to come to Rome, this time as head of the CDF. Ratzinger says he could not resist a second request. So, on 25 November 1981, he was appointed prefect of the CDF. According to papal biographer George Weigel, Pope Wojtyla assured Ratzinger that he need not abandon his own theological work, but that he could continue to research and publish privately. He has certainly done this.

With the election of John Paul II, the CDF seems to have been encouraged to new levels of action against those theologians perceived to be 'dissident'. We have already seen the action against Hans Küng. Proceedings against the Dutch Dominican Edward Schillebeeckx were forced to a conclusion just before Ratzinger arrived in Rome. In 1979, Schillebeeckx was called to the CDF to explain his books on Christology and ministry. After protracted negotiations the case was concluded in June 1981 with the CDF issuing a 'Note' containing what it considered to be a list of clarifications, precisions and rectifications provided by Schillebeeckx. He himself has subsequently said that Rome was not really interested in his Christology. It was his views on ministry in the book *Ministry: Leadership in the Community of Jesus Christ* and the role of the priesthood that interested the CDF. He maintains that the Congregation's central interest is actually in practical things, especially when they concern ethics or the structure of the church, the hierarchy and the priesthood. Obviously, North America was also increasingly in the CDF's sights because Charles Curran's troubles with the CDF also began around this time, and dragged on for most of the 1980s.

However, it was liberation theology that was Ratzinger's first concern. This story goes back to the 1968 Conference of the Latin American Bishops (CELAM), held in Medellin, Colombia. Medellin was attended by Paul VI, and the majority of bishops present placed the blame for the social and economic injustices of the continent squarely on those with 'the greater share of wealth, culture and power ... [those who] jealously retained their privileges, thus provoking explosive revolutions of despair'. Medellin thus placed the church hierarchy in direct confrontation with the wealthy power brokers, the economic interests of US corporations, and the military strongmen of the national security states.

Even before Medellin, *communidads de base*—grassroots communities of Christians—were flourishing. These were groups of poor people who reflected on their experiences of oppression in the context of the Bible. In fact, liberation theology is the product of the experiences of these base communities. The founder of the movement, the Peruvian priest Gustavo Gutierrez, says that this type of theology can only emerge after those who develop it have made a serious commitment to the poor and are willing to experience life from the bottom. Inevitably, this involved the church in politics and in confrontation with military governments and the rich. It also meant opposition to economic policies of globalisation and the 'Thatcherite' economic rationalism that was then being applied ruthlessly in Latin America, especially in Chile.

Priests and members of religious orders who stood with the poor were sometimes murdered. Those churchmen with vested interests, or those who belonged to highly conservative organisations like Opus Dei, which were often close to Latin American military governments, or those who opted to be the chaplains to the rich and to the emerging middle class, were deeply affronted as their integrity was either implicitly or explicitly questioned by liberation theology.

However, it was not all about politics and clerical sensibilities. It is important to comprehend the actual process of liberation theology, because then it is understandable why it was so profoundly opposed by Ratzinger. Liberation theology is not so much a specific theological interpretation of revelation as a way of actually *doing* theology. The living experience of the poor is its absolute starting point. This is in contrast to the traditional way of doing theology, which begins with dogma or church teaching. Liberation theology turns the process upside-down and proceeds from the lived experience of those at the bottom of the social scale, and then moves through belief, reflection and prayer to worship and ministry. Theology follows and is based on ministry. Thus liberation theology is the systematic reflection on the belief that emerges from the lived experience of the poor.

In contrast, the European way of doing theology—which is basic to the Ratzinger approach—begins with the dogma proposed by the church and the tradition that flows from the Bible, liturgy and the fathers, and belief and reflection flows *a priori* from theology and church teaching. Thus liberation theology is subversive of hierarchical and intellectualistic approaches to faith and the church, and reflects the different cultures that characterise third-world countries. I do not think we should underestimate the importance of the contrast between continental European ways of doing theology and those that, despite setbacks, are still growing in the developing world. For the ideas developed in Latin America in the 1970s quickly spread, and inspired Catholics in other parts of the third world, particularly Asia.

By no means all the bishops at Medellin embraced liberation theology. The most powerful enemy of this approach was the staunchly conservative Archbishop (now Cardinal) Alfonso Lopez Trujillo. In 1974 he took over the secretariat of CELAM. The *éminence grise* of Lopez Trujillo was the Belgian Jesuit Roger Vekemans. Based in Bogota, it was Vekemans who coordinated the opposition to liberation theology by making connections between the Colombian and German hierarchies and right-wing elements

in Rome. Lopez Trujillo organised the CELAM conference at Pueblo
in Mexico in 1979. This was attended by the newly elected John Paul II.
At Pueblo, while the pope stressed the church's commitment to 'human
advancement, development, justice, and the rights of the individual', he
also emphasised that the church does not need to fall back on 'ideological
systems in order to love, defend and collaborate in the liberation of man'.
For 'ideological systems' read 'Marxism'. While never mentioning liberation theology, he said that some reduced the Kingdom of God to secular
notions and created a false dichotomy between the people and the poor on
the one hand, and the official church with its 'sacred magisterium' on the
other. The theme that liberation theologians used—'Marxist [sociological]
analysis'—was now to recur constantly, and it was used as a way of cari-
caturing what liberationists were doing, and tagging them with a secular
revolutionary brush. It is significant that Lopez Trujillo was made archbishop of Medellin itself in 1979 and a cardinal in 1983. In 1991 he was
moved to Rome to head up Pontifical Council on the Family. His influence
on John Paul II was considerable.

The CDF also began investigations of individual liberation theologians:
Guitierrez was accused of advocating a 'people's church' in conflict with
the hierarchy, and of reducing the 'vertical' dimensions of the gospel to
'mere' personal relationships. Nothing much came of this investigation
because the CDF tactic was to try to get the Peruvian bishops to condemn
him. The bishops could not agree among themselves; in fact, at that stage,
many of them supported Guitierrez. As a result, the whole composition of
the Peruvian hierarchy was gradually changed by the Vatican with progressive bishops being replaced by reactionaries, including eventually the
first Opus Dei cardinal, Juan Luis Cipriani Thorne.

In many ways Ratzinger's first target as CDF prefect was the Brazilian
Franciscan friar Leonardo Boff. Ratzinger had actually been his *Doktorvater*,
his thesis supervisor. What happened was that after Boff's book *Church,
Charism and Power* was published in 1981, detailing many abuses of ecclesiastical power from history, he was attacked as a heretic by his other
Doktorvater, Bonaventura Kloppenburg, also a Franciscan and now a
fierce enemy of liberation theology and a bishop in Brazil. Boff wrote to
Ratzinger, which was a mistake because in May 1984 he was charged by the
CDF with 'a pitiless, radical assault' on the institutional church's use and
abuse of power and of lacking 'serenity' and 'moderation' and challenging
the hierarchical authority of the church. Perhaps the erstwhile Bonaventura
scholar feared that Boff was reviving the ideas of the Franciscan spirituals

who were all too deeply influenced by the millennial notions of Joachim of Fiore and his faith in a new kind of 'liberationist eschatology'. Targeting Boff also served as a shot across the bows of the then progressive Brazilian bishops' conference. Not only was it the largest episcopal conference in Latin America, but many of the bishops were supporters of liberation theology. In early 1984 Ratzinger informed the Latin American bishops that liberation theology was 'in the final analysis unacceptable'.

When Boff was summoned to Rome he was accompanied by his fellow Brazilian Franciscans, Cardinals Aloisio Lorscheider and Paulo Arns, which pitted Ratzinger against two other members of the college of cardinals. In August 1984 the CDF issued an *Instruction* on 'certain aspects' of liberation theology. It admits the obvious: that Latin America has experienced 'shocking inequality … crushing poverty … and the seizure of the vast majority of wealth by an oligarchy of powers bereft of social consciousness'. But it falls back on accusing liberation theology of using 'concepts borrowed from various currents of Marxist thought … [and of] containing errors which directly threaten the truths of faith regarding the eternal destiny of individual persons'. The CDF's attack on 'communism' and 'Marxism' caused some embarrassment for Cardinal Agostino Casaroli, the Secretary of State, who at that time was trying to improve relationships with the Soviet bloc, and he took the extraordinary step of distancing himself from the document. Boff was 'silenced' for a year after this *Instruction* was issued. But even after that he was still subjected to a whole series of petty restrictions imposed on him by the CDF through the Franciscan order. Ratzinger was already descending to the niggling nastiness that came to characterise so much of his administration of the CDF.

What is significant in this controversy over liberation theology is that it highlights the deeper struggle that was (and is) going on for the very soul of the church. Fundamentally, this struggle is all about history. For Boff, the church, like Jesus, is rooted in the historical process and is only truly incarnated in and through particular cultural realities. It is in the poverty and exploitation of the third world, especially Brazil, where Boff finds the church to be most truly itself. For him theology is also caught up in the historical process and it is only through reflection on living experience, on the 'stuff' of history, that the church can discover God's will for itself. For Ratzinger, the church transcends history. It is not the Jesus of history who provides Ratzinger's primary theological focus. It is the risen and ascended Christ who stands in splendour outside the world process both as saviour and as judge who provides his focus. The CDF prefect worried that the attempts of Boff and his colleagues to read back through the resurrection to the radical prophet of Galilee endangered Christ's eschatological significance, his relevance for all times and places.

So, as Ratzinger sees it, this was (and is) not just a squabble over who has political control in the church. It is about the very meaning of Catholicism. But this does not mean politics are not important. Liberation theology's opponents constantly accuse people like Boff of politicising the church by constantly identifying God with the poor. If God has a preferential option for the poor, then the rich and powerful have placed themselves outside God's ambience. Thus the structures that they erect to protect their interests are evil and must be overthrown. Once you say that your attitude is certainly political, if not revolutionary.

Ratzinger was relentless with Boff. Having attempted to 'silence' him in 1985–86, and having attacked other liberation theologians, Ratzinger was back on the case in 1991–92. He eventually banned Boff from teaching and writing. Boff responded by resigning from the priesthood, commenting that 'Ecclesiastical power is cruel and merciless. It forgets nothing. It forgives nothing. It demands everything.' A sad but true comment!

After the departure of Boff, liberation theology seemed like a spent force. But it is interesting to see how opponents of the movement have gained ecclesiastical preferment and its supporters have been marginalised. Cardinal Alfonso Lopez Trujillo, the Colombian we have already met, is a particularly aggressive foe of the movement. This is the man who argued on BBC TV that condoms are 'porous' and do not prevent the spread of AIDS. Dario Castrillón Hoyos, another Colombian profoundly opposed to liberation theology who nevertheless had a reputation for kindness to the poor in his own diocese, is now the prefect of the Congregation for the Clergy. Cardinal Jorge Medina Estevez, a Chilean and a friend of the murderous dictator Pinochet is now retired but he was prefect of the Congregation for Divine Worship and Sacraments. It is he who was responsible for the 'gutting' of the International Committee for English in the Liturgy (ICEL).

Unfortunately, liberation theology has been to a considerable extent marginalised by this struggle. Slowly the episcopates of Latin America have been transformed by the appointment of conservative bishops, and the base communities driven to the edge of the church. Peru, for instance, now has a number of Opus Dei bishops, including Cipriani Thorne of Lima, a close confidant of the now-disgraced Fujimori regime. The religious tragedy of Catholic Latin America continues with the conversion of Catholics, especially those who have attained middle-class status, to the American Protestant fundamentalist sects. However, the significance of liberation theology cannot be underestimated and its influence continues; it has articulated a whole other way of doing theology.

Parallel with the attack on liberation theology was the attempt to rein in moral theology. Ratzinger chose as his target Charles Curran. Choosing a leading figure in a theological movement seemed to be the CDF prefect's methodology—that you frighten the disciples by picking off the leader.

While they may not specifically know his name, Charles Edward Curran has had a pervasive and profound influence on the way most contemporary Catholics, particularly those from the English-speaking world, form their consciences and act on moral, and especially interpersonal issues. Curran is a warm, generous friendly person with a raucous laugh and a great ability to enliven a theological point with a funny story. His own bishop, Matthew Clark of Rochester, says of him: 'He lives simply and has a remarkable ability to combine a life of serious scholarship with generous availability to a variety of persons'. Unlike many academics, he enjoys teaching.

Perhaps precisely because of his influence, popularity and American nationality, the CDF began a major investigation of Curran in 1979. The United States was the homeland of so-called 'situational ethics', which the French superciliously refer to as 'Anglo-Saxon morality', and American Catholic moralists are often unjustly tarred with this brush. So Rome could make an example of Curran. After a protracted process, on 25 July 1986 Ratzinger wrote to the chancellor of the Catholic University of America in Washington, DC, where Curran was employed as a tenured professor, to inform him that Curran was neither 'suitable nor eligible to exercise the function of a professor of Catholic theology'; the chancellor was instructed to take the 'appropriate action'. The chancellor at the time was the archbishop of Washington, Cardinal James Hickey. On 2 June 1988, the board of trustees of the Catholic University declared that Curran could not teach Catholic theology at that institution. This led to a civil case which finally came to an end on 28 February 1989 in which the judge found in favour of the university. After brief stints as a visiting professor at Cornell and the University of Southern California, Curran became Elizabeth Scurlock University Professor of Human Values at Southern Methodist University in Dallas, Texas, in 1991 where he remains.

Richard McCormick says that 'the Curran affair ranks as among the most significant developments in moral theology in the past 50 years'

(*Theological Studies*, 50 (1989), p. 17). At the heart of the Curran case is the theological question of the right to dissent from authoritative, but non-infallible papal teaching. Throughout the 1980s and 1990s the CDF attempted increasingly to constrict the role of theologians to that of apologists for the papal magisterium, and to blur the distinction between infallible and non-infallible teaching. Curran has strongly defended the right of Catholics to dissent from non-infallible teaching.

At another level, the Curran case has widespread ramifications for other moralists. Curran criticised the physicalism in some papal teaching in moral matters; for example, contraception, sterilisation, homosexuality and the principle of double effect. The problem with physicalism comes from identifying the moral act with the physical structure of the act. Contraception, for example, according to the official teaching is wrong because it interferes with the physical act of marital relations. However, outside the area of sexuality, Catholic teaching does not identify the human moral act with the physical structure of the act. Killing is a physical act, but not all killing is wrong. It is murder that is morally wrong. Thus one must distinguish between physical and therefore non-moral evil and intentional acts that are truly morally evil. In this light many theologians such as Franz Böckle, Josef Fuchs and Richard McCormick developed a theory of proportionalism—one can directly do physical or non-moral evil (for example, interfere with the physical structure of the marital act) if there is a proportionate reason. In the 1960s and early 1970s, Curran frequently wrote about these controversial issues in sexual ethics. Hence it is not surprising that he was targeted by the CDF.

In the 1990s the CDF turned its attention to Asian theology as the case of Father Tissa Balasuriya demonstrates. For most of his life, Balasuriya has struggled to integrate his Catholic faith with his Sri Lankan culture. He has questioned the old missionary approach—salvation through conversion and conformity to a form of Catholicism that is essentially European and Roman; in other words, Catholicism expressed as a form of ecclesial colonialism. This dispute really goes back to the days of Vatican II when Balasuriya and a number of others, including Oblate Father Michael Rodrigo who studied with him in Rome, tried to get the church to be more open to the world and to adopt the fundamental change of attitude which was implicit in the whole approach of the Council. Rodrigo was murdered in 1988 while celebrating Mass in a remote area because of his opposition to those who exploited the rural poor. But Balasuriya has not been alone;

some other Sri Lankan Catholics have been working along similar lines. For those who think along these lines it is the poverty and the religiousness of the masses of Asian people that form the starting point of both theology and ministry. The Jesuit Aloysius Pieris has worked with base communities that include members of all religious faiths who are experiencing oppression and poverty. It is in this experience that theology finds its origins. He says: 'Spirituality is not the practical conclusion of theology, but the radical involvement with the poor and the oppressed, and is what creates theology.' Another group that works along the same lines is the Satoyada community in Kandy led by another Jesuit, Father Paul Casperz.

However, many of the bishops found it hard to adjust to the conciliar reforms. The church establishment has remained essentially conservative, and is close to right-wing elements in the country, including the military. It is this conflict about missionary method and cultural integration which is at the core of the attack that Bishop Malcolm Ranjith (now papal nuncio to Indonesia) and others launched on Balasuriya in 1992. This was quickly taken over by the CDF, which in the second half of the 1990s had become increasingly concerned with 'Asian theology'. The CDF views Balasuriya as a 'relativist', one who equates all religions and philosophies, and who reduces 'Christian spirituality' to 'social action'.

But Balasuriya has been discussing the issue of cultural integration for a long time. In *Jesus Christ and Human Liberation* (1976) he describes the image of Jesus traditionally presented by western missionaries to Asian converts. Jesus was represented as someone sent by God to save humankind from the effects of original and personal sin. He became man in obedience to God in order to make reparation for our sins through his death. His act of obedience in embracing the human condition and dying on the cross redeemed all humanity. Salvation for the individual was mediated by the church. There was no other form of salvation. Thus the great religious traditions, such as Buddhism, were insufficient for salvation. But the very process of conversion meant that new converts were, to a considerable extent, cut off from their culture and forced to adopt a religion that was Roman and western. In the traditional missionary approach, the emphasis on the personal unworthiness of the convert and obedience was important. This was precisely what the colonial power demanded in the civil sphere from the 'natives'. There was no conscious collusion, of course, but both church and state were working out of the same set of presuppositions. However, as Balasuriya points out, the gospels could have been used to present a very different image of Jesus: one who cared for the poor and oppressed and worked for human liberation. But the Jesus who was presented to Asian converts was passive and obedient. In contrast, Balasuriya presents a Jesus who is active and liberating, a fully 'conscious human being capable of suffering, being angry and even tempted'.

A similar image of Mary was presented by the missionaries. In place of the strong woman concerned with social justice and liberation described in the first chapter of Saint Luke's gospel (Luke 1:51–53), Mary was presented in the traditional approach as passive, domesticated and obedient. Sri Lankan Catholicism, like much of the popular Catholicism of Asia, is deeply devotional and Mary and the saints play an important 'mediating' role. The social radicalism of the Mary who praises God for showing 'the strength of his arm' and 'scattering the proud-hearted', for bringing 'down the powerful from their thrones' and lifting up the lowly, for filling 'the hungry with good things' and sending 'the rich away empty', is replaced by the passive Blessed Virgin, the 'purest of creatures', the Mary who is both 'sweet mother [and] sweet maid'. In *Mary and Human Liberation* (1990), Balasuriya describes her as 'a loving mother and sister of all; a woman among women, a human being among us; one who faced the difficulties of being united to Jesus for a better humanity'.

There is a sense that Balasuriya's challenge is as much politico-social as it is theological. As such it is seen as deeply subversive by many in the church establishment, especially in a country that is as deeply divided as is Sri Lanka. The CDF process against him led eventually, in 1998, to the radical and draconian penalty of excommunication. He is the only theologian to have been so drastically treated since Vatican II. The only other well-known example of excommunication of a theologian in the twentieth century is that of the Italian priest Ernesto Buonaiuti, who was accused of 'modernism'. Yet Balasuriya's consistency and strength of character, as well as worldwide public pressure, forced the CDF to compromise and abandon the excommunication a year later. In the process it has made Tissa Balasuriya one of the best known priests and theologians in the world.

But Balasuriya has not been alone. In 1998 another Asian Catholic was investigated: the Indian Jesuit Anthony De Mello (1931–87). De Mello, whose writing takes the form of brief stories in the Buddhist and Taoist tradition, is still very popular and widely read. Ten years after his death the CDF has accused him of a 'progressive distancing from the essential contents of the Christian faith'. In the place of Christ he is accused of substituting 'an intuition of God without form or image, to the point of speaking of God as a pure void'. Strangely, the CDF does not seem to have noticed that this is very close to the language used by the great Catholic mystics when they speak of God—for instance, the 5th-century mystical writer called the Pseudo-Dionysius, and the sixteenth-century Spanish Carmelite Saint John of the Cross, who is a doctor of the church. But the crux of the CDF criticisms is that De Mello equates Jesus with the other great religious leaders, such as the Buddha, and of seeing institutional Christianity, as well as other systems of religion, as 'major obstacles to the discovery of truth'.

At about the same time, the CDF began an investigation of the influential Belgian Jesuit Jacques Dupuis, who taught at the Gregorian University in Rome and who died not long after the investigation. Dupuis' work was premised on the fact that in this age of the wider ecumenism Catholicism now accepts the fact that non-Christians can be saved outside the church, and is moving on from the question of asking *whether* salvation is possible for members of other religious traditions, to *how* these traditions mediate salvation to their members. Dupuis also talked about the need for Christianity to listen to and learn from the other great religions. The Congregation specifically targeted his book *Toward a Christian Theology of Religious Pluralism*. The CDF's actual concerns were not clear, but Cardinal Franz König, the former archbishop of Vienna, quickly came to Dupuis' defence in an article in *The Tablet* (16 January 1999). König suggested that the CDF's problem may arise from the fact that

the members of the Congregation, most of whom are Westerners, are, of course, very much afraid that interreligious dialogue will reduce all religions to equal rank. But that is the wrong approach for dialogue with the Eastern religions. It is reminiscent of colonialism, and smacks of arrogance ... The Indian way of thinking is very different, and we must learn to understand other sorts of spiritual life.

Ratzinger replied to König's article with a letter to *The Tablet* denying 'colonialism and arrogance' in the CDF, and asserting that it is moving with 'maximum discretion' in the Dupuis affair. But certainly not with maximum speed. It took almost three years for the CDF to reach a decision. On 26 February 2001 it published a notice saying that the book contained certain 'ambiguities' but did not accuse Dupuis of doctrinal error. A shy, retiring man who was devastated by the CDF investigation and suffered an emotional collapse, Jacques Dupuis died on 28 December 2004 of an illness that was certainly exacerbated by the Congregation's examination.

While the relationship between the CDF and speculative theology over the years has been a fraught one, the Congregation under Ratzinger has attempted to be part of the development of theology. In 1999, for instance, the CDF participated in a major conference on the history of the Inquisition at which a subtle and unreal distinction was made between 'the church' on the one hand and 'the children of the church' on the other. 'The church', the Congregation argued, had no need to repent or be sorry because it had never been in error or made mistakes, but 'the children of the church' could repent of their sins, such as persecuting people for their religious beliefs, or for being Jews or Muslims. The Italian Jewish historian Carlo Ginsburg, an expert on the history of the Inquisition, rightly said that this was an evasion of responsibility. It was unreal to ask the dead to forgive. Rather he wanted an admission of shame from the church for what it had done. I described the distinction between the 'church' and its 'children' as 'unreal' because the church *is* its sons and daughters. It is not some ethereal reality, untouched by history and culture. While it certainly has its 'triumphant' aspect in the sense that it is identified with the risen Christ, it is also rooted in historical processes and cannot be divorced from them. The things that you eventually find wearying in all of this are the constant evasions, the perpetual self-justification, the inability to assume responsibility and simply say 'sorry', not just for the personal sins of the church's 'children', but for the systemic and real failure of the institutional church itself. The church is nothing other than the historical community of Catholics in union with the risen Christ.

The CDF gained some kudos for participating in this symposium. But the Congregation's recent track record is not good in relationship to systematic theology. In fact, as the CDF document *Instruction on the Ecclesial Vocation of the Theologian* (24 May 1990) makes clear, Rome's view of the role of theology is restrictive; it could even be interpreted as destructive. The *Instruction* admits that theology always occurs within a cultural context and it certainly recommends the value of 'freedom of research'. But this freedom is immediately limited not only when the papal magisterium or teaching authority speaks in a definitive way, but even when it does not act definitively. The Congregation says that everything the magisterium says 'has a validity beyond its argumentation', which seems to suggest that logic and argument have no real role in papal teaching, which is patent nonsense. The *Instruction* denies that there is such a thing as a theological magisterium and it makes the papacy alone the sole judge of theological truth. In practice, the theologian is reduced to being an apologist for the magisterium. The problem with these assertions is that they are at best a restriction of the genuine Catholic theological tradition, and at worst a complete of distortion of it.

This approach to theology was further highlighted and imposed in the Apostolic Letter *Ad Tuendam Fidem* (30 June 1998), which was published with a detailed commentary by Ratzinger himself, to which I will refer later. The purpose of the Letter was to define in the narrowest possible sense the limits of dissent, and to force Catholics to accept all levels of church teaching, almost as though they were equal. Thus the question of the ordination of women or the validity of a saint's canonisation was in effect placed on the same level as the divinity of Christ and the presence of Christ in the Eucharist. Otherwise, Catholics were told that they risked being 'out of communion' with the church. A 'profession of faith' has been imposed which has to be taken by all priestly and episcopal office-holders in the church, and by everyone teaching theology professionally, as a way of making sure that all persons in any type of influential position, both ordained and lay, conform to the narrow orthodoxy articulated in this Letter. The first clause of the oath covers everything defined in the Word of God and in divine revelation. The second focuses on doctrines on faith and morals definitively put forward by the church. The third covers the teaching of pope and bishops even when they are not intended to be definitive.

It is the second category that has caused the most comment. In explanation the CDF Secretary, Archbishop Tarcisio Bertone, has said that this category includes 'all those teachings in the dogmatic or moral area which are necessary for faithfully keeping and expounding the deposit of faith, even if they have not been proposed by the magisterium as formally revealed'; that is, they are not formally defined as infallible. Bertone is saying that *de facto* they are actually infallible. This is a whole new category of doctrine which the CDF seems to have almost single-handedly invented, or if not invented at least expanded far beyond what was previously accepted. This is further distorted by the fact that while technically all the congregations of the Roman curia are equal, the CDF still maintains a unique status. Because its role is to safeguard faith and morals, it not only exercises a power of jurisdiction; it actually shares in the teaching role of the pope. 'The documents issued by this congregation [the CDF] expressly approved by the pope participate in the ordinary magisterium of the successor of Peter' (*Instruction on the Ecclesial Vocation of the Theologian*, 18). Because of its central role, all the other bodies of the curia are obliged to refer all matters touching on faith and morals to the CDF, and to abide by its judgement.

As is well known, I have had personal experience of the CDF's ways of operating. In *From Inquisition to Freedom* I have outlined in detail how the Congregation treats those it examines. Now that I am four years out from my own encounter with the CDF I want to conclude this chapter by reflecting on what happened.

It was clear that in the late 1990s there were concerns among a few Catholics in the UK and Australia about people such as Sister Lavinia Byrne and myself who were prominent in the secular media and who were considered by conservatives as having an 'undesirable' influence, and whose presentation of the church was seen by reactionaries as too 'soft' and accommodating. Certainly, both 'cases' began in the home country. Lavinia Byrne was probably 'delated' (reported) by a reactionary Catholic women's group, and while he has never acknowledged it, all the circumstantial evidence points to Cardinal George Pell of Sydney as my accuser. The vast majority of people targeted are priests or members of religious orders. It is clear that the CDF is not interested in lay people, or perhaps it realises that they are not so vulnerable to its machinations. I use the word 'machination' purposely. This is the only way that the behaviour of the Congregation can be interpreted. It has no notion of human rights, is manipulative in its processes, and doesn't even abide by its own 'Regulations'.

The CDF now says it operates according to a set of 'Regulations' issued on 29 June 1997. These 'Regulations' reflect nothing of the positive approach called for by the Council and Paul VI in the Apostolic Letter *Intergrae Servandae* (7 December 1965) on the reform of the CDF. Commenting on these 'Regulations' the respected Jesuit canonist at Washington's Georgetown University, Ladislas Örsy, asks 'Are Church Investigation Procedures Really Just?' (see *Doctrine and Life* 48 (1998), pp. 453–65). He examines the 'Regulations' in the light of the church's concern with human rights and of the widespread concern for fair legal processes. Örsy finds them defective in a number of ways. Firstly, there is no precise definition of the offence. Secondly, they do not distinguish between judge, prosecutor and investigator. The CDF carries out all roles, and often the same person acts in the various roles. Thirdly, the accused is given virtually no chance to put his or her case. Fourthly, there is no presumption of innocence. Fifthly, there is no right of appeal. And finally, the secrecy provisions mean that justice is not seen to be done, especially when the penalty is automatic excommunication. 'To rush into imposing an extreme sentence (perhaps even without ever having listened to the author) can hardly be a sign and symbol of justice' (p. 464). What Örsy calls for is the creation of a climate of trust and he argues that if the CDF thinks that norms are needed to pre-

vent doctrinal deviations, 'norms are even more needed to secure legitimate freedom for creative thinking' (p. 466) in the church. In other words,
theologians and those who attempt to communicate the faith need some
form of protection from arbitrary investigation and judgement. His conclusion is that overall the 'Regulations ... are not signs or symbols of justice. They have their roots in past ages which did not have the same vision
of the dignity of the human person and the same respect for honest conscience that is demanded the world over today' (p. 465).

The first thing that struck me about the Congregation in the very first
correspondence I received from them was the superficiality of the consultor's assessment of my book *Papal Power*, which was under investigation.
The three pages sent to me from this anonymous priest could have been
the work of a first-year theological undergraduate (perhaps it was). Most
of the criticisms were actually inferences drawn by the consultor from the
book rather than clear statements of mine. Quotations were constantly
divorced from the context in which they occurred. According to the CDF
'Regulations' it is the task of the consultor to determine what is 'clearly and
certainly erroneous', and what will cause 'grave harm to the faithful'.
Precisely how they attain this remarkable level of judgement is not spelled
out; again it is just presumed. Surely such a procedure demands much
wider consultation, discussion with the accused, and the advice of his or
her peers, as well as an attempt to understand the perceived problems
within the cultural context from which they emerge? Most of the consultors work part-time for the CDF. He (there are no 'shes' listed among the
thirty-one consultors in the 2004 *Annuario Pontificio* (pp. 1082–3)) will normally be a Roman-based priest with some theological or legal training who
assesses the whole matter for 'doctrinal error' or lack of 'doctrinal clarity'.
Most of these reviewers, who have spent most of their careers in Rome, are
lecturers in the parochial world of the Roman ecclesiastical seminaries and
universities. They would not be consultors if they did not adhere strictly
to the narrow orthodoxy that prevails in Rome. A number of them have
other important positions in the Vatican. Most are lacking in any pastoral
experience and would be lost in an ordinary parish.

Tissa Balasuriya had a worse experience of the incompetence of CDF
consultors. He says:

> In my response [to the Congregation] I put side by side what the CDF
> consultor claimed I said, and what I actually said. My problem was with
> the CDF's methodology. I showed fifty-eight specific instances where
> the consultor's 'Observations' on the text of my book contained unproved

generalisations, misunderstandings, misrepresentations, distortions and falsifications. They were really unhappy about this, but there were so many mistakes that I had to protest. Actually, the 'Observations' were first sent to me in Italian, and I asked for an English translation. So they sent me the English translation of the Italian including in the footnotes quotations from the text of *Mary and Human Liberation*. It suddenly dawned on me: 'This is not what I wrote.' Their translation from Italian did not correspond to the actual English text of my book. So I was able to show that in the process of translating English into Italian and then back again, that they had actually injected heresy into what I had said! ... It is a very good example of the way the system operates, because nobody listens when you protest, nobody in authority is held accountable; the accused alone must explain themselves. In my response to the 'Observations' I asked Cardinal Ratzinger 'to inquire into these grave misrepresentations and render justice to me by taking due action against such misrepresentations, distortions and falsifications'. I received no response to this because everyone else involved in the process is presumed to be right. They also hide behind the mask of anonymity. This lack of accountability leads to basic miscarriages of justice which must be reformed for the sake of the church. Dealing with these arbitrary methods is one of the key issues facing those who want to reform the CDF' (*From Inquisition to Freedom*, pp. 95–6).

The second thing that struck me about Ratzinger's Congregation was the sheer discourtesy of its staff and procedures. It ignored me and operated as if I did not exist. My letters went completely unanswered and I was treated as a schoolboy and all dealings were with my religious superiors— who behaved admirably. Dealing with the CDF is a form of shadow boxing; you never actually 'meet' them. All discussion passes through the accused person's superior, conducted completely in writing. It is meant to be kept strictly secret. It is argued that this protects the accused person's reputation, but actually it renders them more vulnerable because they have to deal with a powerful bureaucracy on their own. That is why I 'went public' quickly, so that the CDF had to think seriously about its own reputation and public image before it used arbitrary measures. The CDF's 'Regulations' show no care for justice, and any sensitivity for those being investigated is totally lacking. They are simply a set of cold, objective norms that treat the accused as a non-person, issued by the very authority that will act as investigator, judge and jury. Reading them, you are struck with the un-Christ-like feel that they reflect. The CDF's discourtesy reflects the Congregation's lack of pastoral sensitivity.

This discourtesy is vividly illustrated in Ratzinger's 'Commentary' on the Apostolic Letter *Ad tuendam fidem* (30 June 1998). Among other issues, the Letter discussed a category of 'definitive' but non-infallibly defined doctrine. In his commentary Ratzinger said that this second-level teaching is, in fact, infallible. As examples of second-level definitive teaching he includes a hotchpotch of issues such as the condemnation of euthanasia, the validity of the canonisation of a particular saint, the legitimacy of a papal election, and even the decision of Leo XIII in the Bull *Apostolicae curae* (1896) declaring the invalidity of Anglican orders. The gratuitous reference to Anglican ordination is astonishingly maladroit and insulting; it reveals a complete lack of ecumenical courtesy and sensitivity. And this happened right at the very time that Cardinal Edward Cassidy, the then president of the Pontifical Council for Christian Unity, was visiting the archbishop of Canterbury. Cassidy said he knew nothing in advance about the 'Commentary' by Ratzinger.

A similar lack of sensitivity can be found in the CDF document *Dominus Jesus* (DJ) of 6 August 2000. Fundamentally, DJ is concerned with the unique role of Christ and is addressed to those involved in the wider ecumenism and in relations with the other great religious faiths. It was largely prepared by Archbishop Angelo Amato, Secretary of the Congregation, whom the Italians ironically say is 'neither an angel nor a lover'. It basically attacks the kind of theology that, it says, questions the uniqueness of Christ and the Catholic church. It says this theory is wrong:

> Therefore the theory of the limited, incomplete or imperfect character of the revelation of Jesus Christ, which would be complementary to that found in other religions is contrary to the church's faith. Such a position would claim to be based on the notion that the truth about God cannot be grasped and manifested in its globality [sic] and completeness by any historical religion, neither by Christianity nor by Jesus Christ' (DJ, 6, *Zenit* translation).

But then it goes on to say that the Orthodox churches are 'true particular churches', but that 'the ecclesial communities which have not preserved the valid episcopate and the genuine and integral substance of the Eucharistic mystery are not churches in the proper sense'(DJ, 17). Not only is this insulting to the non-Orthodox churches; it certainly denies the intention and probably contradicts the text of Vatican II on ecumenism. The whole context of the Council was profoundly ecumenical. It was essentially about reaching out to other Christians and to the wider world, and any other interpretation is a distortion. My own commitment to the Catholic church does not blind me to the profound Christian truths and traditions that the other churches have emphasised—for example, the Protestant emphasis on the Bible when the Catholic church neglected scripture for centuries before the present-day revival of biblical study within Catholicism. The Vatican's own *Ecumenical Directory*, approved by the CDF, recognises 'the rich diversity of spirituality, discipline, liturgical rites and elaborations of revealed truth that have grown up among the churches'. Note there the word *churches*. The *Ecumenical Directory* is right; any other view is insulting to other Christians.

But this doesn't seem to trouble Ratzinger and the CDF authors of DJ because many in ecclesiastical leadership at the highest level seem to be moving in an increasingly sectarian direction and watering down the catholicity of the church and even unconsciously neglecting elements of its teaching. This word 'catholicity' is important. It is derived from the Greek word *katholikos* that means 'general', 'broad' or 'universal'. The *Shorter Oxford Dictionary* defines catholicity as 'the quality of having sympathies with or being all-embracing; broad-mindedness; tolerance'. Catholicity also has a profound theological meaning. Cardinal Avery Dulles has a fine book entitled *The Catholicity of the Church* (1988). Catholicity, he says, is characterised by (1) inclusiveness, which means openness to various cultures and opposition to sectarianism and religious individualism; (2) by an ability to bridge generations and historical periods; (3) by an openness to truth and value wherever it exists; (4) a recognition that it is the Holy Spirit who creates the unity of the church through whose indwelling we participate in the life of God.

This is the kind of Catholicism that I, and many others, have embraced throughout our lives. Its foundations, which are deeply embedded in church history, were given modern expression in the vision of the church articulated at the Council. For Catholics like myself, our benchmark is a church that is defined as the living sacrament of God's presence and the place where God's sovereignty is acknowledged, expressed through a participative community of people dedicated to the service of the world and characterised by collegiality and ecumenism. It is precisely this image of Catholicism which I think is being distorted by many at the highest level in the contemporary church by documents like DJ. It gives voice to a wider movement that is slowly but pervasively turning the church in a sectarian direction.

Sectarianism is incompatible with genuine catholicity. It is the antithesis of the kind of openness to the world, tolerant acceptance of others and a sense of religious pluralism that most thinking Catholics have been formed in and have embraced over the last three or four decades. Thus many Catholics find themselves involved in a corrosive disjunction between what they believe and have experienced, and the views expressed at the highest levels of the church. The reason is because those who claim to articulate Catholic belief, especially in the CDF, seem to be abandoning their *catholic* spirit. As a result there is a turning away from the other Christian churches, and a rejection of the search for common ground with the other great religious traditions. Thus more and more thinking Catholics who have been educated and live in pluralist, democratic and tolerant societies, find themselves in conflict with church hierarchs who seem to be moving in an ever-more sectarian direction. Sometimes there is a hankering after a more genuinely Catholic approach—as you find in John Paul II's encyclical *Ut unum sint* (1995), where he went so far as to ask the other churches for advice on papal primacy. But ecclesiastical reality indicates that this hankering is, in fact, merely ecumenical wishful thinking, while the hierarchical reality is exclusivist.

There is also an emerging unspoken assumption among some very senior church leaders, including Ratzinger, that the contemporary western world is so far gone in individualism, permissiveness and consumerism that it is totally impervious to church teaching. Claiming to assume the broader historical perspective, these churchmen have virtually abandoned the secularised masses, to nurture elitist enclaves which will carry the true faith through to future, more 'receptive' generations. Ratzinger has gradually adopted this view, but seems oblivious to its dangers, particularly to the loss of the genuine catholicity of the church.

One of the first to articulate this sectarian tendency was my friend John D'Arcy May of Trinity College, Dublin, in his article 'Catholic Fundamentalism: Some Implications of *Dominus Jesus* for Dialogue and Peace-making'. (The article is one of a series of essays in the book, *Dominus Jesus: Anstoessige Wahrheit oder anstoessige Kirche* edited by Michael Rainer.) It was the opening sentences of May's commentary that struck me between the eyes.

There is no reason, in principle, why the Roman Catholic church, despite its enormous size and global presence, could not become a sect. Sectarianism is a matter of mentality, not size ... The deep shock *Dominus Jesus* caused in ecumenical circles consisted precisely in their exposure to the specifically Roman Catholic form of fundamentalism. Certainly Ratzinger has flirted with sectarian notions. For instance when talking about the church of the future he said 'it will be reduced in its dimensions, it will be necessary to start again. However, from this test a church would emerge that will have been strengthened by the process of simplification it experienced, by its renewed capacity to look within itself'. In *The Ratzinger Report* he spoke favourably of the new religious movements within Catholicism, specifically mentioning those that were most sectarian in tendency. (pp. 42–3)

However, Ratzinger has qualified this recently in an interview with the German journalist Peter Seewald. He now says:

The process of numerical reduction, which we are experiencing today, will also have to be addressed precisely by exploring new ways of open-ness to the outside, of new ways of participation by those who are out-side the community of believers. I have nothing against people who, though they never enter a church during the year, go to Christmas mid-night Mass or go on the occasion of some other celebration, because this is also a way of coming close to the light. There must be different forms of involvement and participation ... The church cannot be a closed self-sufficient group.

In other words the church is not as closed and as elitist a community as he had previously suggested. He is also more cautious about the danger of making predictions as to what the church of the future will be like. 'I think we will have to be very cautious ... because historical develop-ment has always produced many surprises' *(Zenit*, 1 October 2001). It certainly has!

Earlier I said that Ratzinger brings a lot of baggage with him to the papacy. He may well claim that the reason for this is that in his years at the CDF he was merely following the policies set by John Paul II. There is some truth to this but it is also true that he was given a lot of autonomy by the pope and that he pretty much set his own priorities.

So how does he explain and justify his role at the CDF? He told Messori in *The Ratzinger Report* that working at the Congregation has given him an understanding of what 'the universal church means'. He says that 'faith is the highest and most precious good—simply because truth is the fundamental life-element for man. Therefore the concern to see that the faith among us is not impaired must be viewed—at least by believers—as higher than concern for bodily health' (p. 22). Heresy still exists, he says, but 'in a multi-layered intellectual age like ours … [the "heretical" theologian] frequently opposes his own theological hypotheses to the magisterium by asserting that the teaching office does not express the faith of the church but only the "archaic Roman theology". It is contended that it is not the Congregation [for the Doctrine of the Faith] but they, the "heretics", who represent the "authentic" meaning of the transmitted faith' (p. 26). Putting the boot in, he says that some theologians these days are 'stamped by the typical mentality of the opulent bourgeoisie of the West. The reality of the concrete church, of the humble, simple people of God, is something altogether different from that which is imagined in the "laboratories" in which "Utopia" is distilled' (p. 20). This interview occurred in 1985 at the very time the CDF's sights were not set on 'bourgeois theologians' but on those who represented the poor of Latin America, the proponents of liberation theology. One has the distinct feeling that Ratzinger does get carried away and say things that are exaggerated and sometimes patently silly. The caricature of the bourgeois theologian is typical of the way he puts down those who differ from him. Some of these interviews betray a nasty streak, a tendency to attribute very negative motivations to those who disagree with him or who have come under his purview.

Finally, there is evidence that he saved the church from two disasters that may have resulted from Pope Wojtyla's obsessions with Marian doctrine and contraception.

Firstly, there were persistent rumours coming from Rome from the 1980s onwards that John Paul II wanted to define the teaching of the encyclical *Humanae vitae* (1968) condemning contraception as infallible. This is something Paul VI, who issued the encyclical, resolutely refused to do. Certainly Pope Wojtyla seemed very preoccupied with contraception and issues to do with sexuality. They crop up constantly in his writings and speeches, and support for the encyclical became one of the touchstones for him of genuine orthodoxy. While it is impossible to prove that Ratzinger talked him out of an infallible definition, if that was his intention the CDF prefect would have been the only person who probably could have achieved that.

Wojtyla's second preoccupation was Marian doctrine. He believed that the Blessed Virgin had saved his life when he was shot in the piazza of Saint Peter's by the Turkish assassin. He wanted to honour her by using infallibility to elevate her to the title of 'Coredemptrix'; that is, that she actively shared in the redemptive work of Jesus. This would be anathema to the Protestant churches. The idea and title has been around since about the seventeenth century. Vatican II refused to take it up and most modern popes have avoided using the term. But not John Paul II, whose use of it encouraged Mark L. Miravalle, professor of Marian theology at the charismatically inclined Franciscan University of Steubenville, Ohio. Miravalle has been trying to whip up interest in the title and support for its definition. Fortunately, even conservative churchmen realised the consequences of any attempted definition, especially without a wide-ranging consultation of the bishops and the church. In 1996 Ratzinger wisely advised the pope to back off and leave this ambiguous title alone. Fortunately John Paul II followed this advice. The theological advisor is now Pope Benedict XVI.

9

FIRST DAYS IN THE PAPAL *APPARTAMENTO*

James Michael Harvey is back in his old job as prefect of the Papal Household. The titular Archbishop of Memphis (in Egypt, not Tennessee—bishops in administrative posts are given an extinct diocese of which they are the nominal bishop) has accompanied Benedict XVI on a number of his outings since he moved into the papal apartment two weeks after his election. Monsignor Mieczyslaw Mokrzycki is back working with Harvey in the household, but Dziwisz has had a big promotion: he is now the archbishop of Cracow and will no doubt soon be a cardinal. The future of Archbishop Piero Marini is far less certain. Closely associated with the style of pontifical ceremony characteristic of John Paul II, which was very much geared to television, and which included all types of extraneous elements such as dancing and local customs, Marini may well be moved sideways as Benedict returns to a more traditional Roman manner of celebration. At the time of writing his position was probably under papal review.

Pope Benedict, however, has made one break with tradition. He has three personal assistants, but only two of them are priests. The other is a woman. Clearly, women are no longer to be relegated to domestic roles in the papal *appartamento*, like the Polish nuns of Wojtyla's time. For the first time in recent papal history the pontiff has a 'right-hand woman' as well as an official priest secretary, German Monsignor Georg Gänswein, 49, who worked with Ratzinger at the CDF, after his long-time secretary, Josef

Clemens, was ordained a bishop and appointed secretary of the Pontifical
Council for the Laity. Mokrzycki acts as assistant secretary.

The woman is Ingrid Stampa, 55, slim, black-haired with rimless
glasses and usually dressed in dark clothes. Although sometimes referred
to in the Italian media as 'housekeeper', she is actually a very distinguished
expert on medieval music and the viola da gamba (an instrument from the
late medieval and Renaissance periods, and the forerunner of the modern
cello) and a former professor at Hamburg's *Musikhochschule* and teacher of
one of today's best known viola da gamba players, Hille Perl. Being a good
musician himself—Benedict plays the piano—perhaps they will be able to
give a concert together! (It has been widely reported that Stampa is a lay
affiliate of the Schoenstatt Movement, a secular institute with many
branches founded in the early twentieth century. This is not correct. She
is being confused with Sister Birgit Wansing, a Schoenstatt Sister of Mary,
who acted as secretary of Ratzinger in the CDF for fourteen years.) After
Ratzinger's sister Maria, who acted as his secretary and housekeeper, died
in 1991, Stampa joined the cardinal's staff as a kind of personal assistant-
cum-housekeeper. She has become his trusted friend, ghostwriter and
translator. Fluent in three languages, Stampa has also translated some of
the books of John Paul II into German. Ratzinger has a reputation for consulting and trusting those closest to him and with whom he is comfortable,
especially if they have a track record of loyalty. Keeping Stampa on his staff
sends a message to the church: lay people and women have an important
role to play, even right at the very top of the ecclesiastical structure. She will
now influence the 'rear door' access to Benedict, a way in for those unable
to get a hearing from the pope through the hierarchical power structure.
Her position gives her a lot of power and real influence on papal policy.

Stampa was immediately able to clear up a confusion regarding
Benedict and his affection for cats. Rome is full of stray felines and Cardinal
Ratzinger often fed those that were around the Vatican. The Italian media
reported that Benedict took two cats with him into the Apostolic Palace
even though all animals and pets are forbidden in the Vatican. Stampa
was able to point out to the media that the 'two cats' are actually made of
porcelain!

So what can we expect from a Ratzinger papacy? As I write this one
month after his election it is still hard to tell the direction the new pope will
take. Even his old sparring partner Hans Küng has said it is important
to give him one hundred days. However, one thing the cardinals clearly

wanted was a short papacy; presumably, with a 78-year-old, they have it. It is clear they think the church needs breathing space to sort out its direction after twenty-six years of John Paul II. Most of them were astonished at the immense crowds, particularly the young people, who came for the lying-in-state of Wojtyla. They didn't want to lose what they felt was an initiative the church had gained in a very secular world through the personal popularity of John Paul II. They felt that one of the biggest crowds in history had to be saying something. But the problem is, what, specifically? Was it just a media event? Or did it bespeak a deep spiritual hunger that had not been met by a post-modern education in which everything goes and relativism reigns supreme? Were the young people who flocked to the lying-in-state prepared to hear and apply the 'hard' teachings that were dear to the heart of John Paul and Benedict? I don't think any of us has the answer to any of those questions, but the cardinals felt they had to build on it somehow.

But they had not thought this out, or had only done so superficially. There are very few natural leaders in the contemporary college of cardinals. With a few exceptions they are men of mediocre ability. It is significant that when they looked around for someone to elect as pope, they chose one of the couple of cardinals left who were appointed not by John Paul but by Paul VI.

So when they asked themselves the difficult question of why had all these people come to Rome, they come up with answers like that of Cardinal Francisco Javier Errázuriz Ossa of Santiago. He says Wojtyla somehow fulfilled 'the thirst for fatherhood, the thirst for God and also the thirst for values ... He was a father in the real sense of the word. There are all kinds of fathers, but John Paul was a man anchored in God, a man everyone could reach.' He maintains that Wojtyla was able to express in words what young people were seeking: 'He affirmed the search, then he went directly to these people and elevated their sights to what God was offering them'. He may well be right that John Paul articulated some ideals for the young, but it is Ossa's almost childish emphasis on 'fatherhood' that is significant. Perhaps all this is a projection and the cardinals themselves were looking for a kind of father figure on whom they could depend, a sense of security that nothing has changed so that they don't have to take responsibility. As a close collaborator of Pope Wojtyla, Ratzinger was seen as 'safe', someone who would not rock the barque of Peter, or steer it into stormy waters and demand that they provide some real leadership for the Catholic community. This talk about 'fatherhood' is found among many Catholic conservatives such as Michael Scanlon at the Franciscan University of Steubenville, Ohio, who says 'the young are hungry for real fatherhood'. The idea is hardly original.

The cardinals clearly want Benedict to carry on the legacy of the previous papacy. But does this mean the new pope is trapped by the emphases of the old? This is certainly a danger. Perhaps his decision to speed up the beatification process of Wojtyla indicates a kind of sanctification of the previous pope's policies. But it also might be a way out for Benedict. It might indicate that Wojtyla is being promoted (to the status of 'blessed') in order that the conservative *Santo subito* brigade can be made happy and get them off Benedict's back and stop them harping on the past. There is a well-known Vatican saying *promoveatur ut armovetur*—'let him be promoted that he may be removed'. If Wojtyla is promoted to the beatification process, which can take however long the Vatican wants it to take, he is off the immediate agenda, so to speak. They can always say that it is 'something under consideration'. And Benedict will be free to move in his own direction.

There are clearly some Wojtyla legacies that Benedict will not be carrying on into the new papacy. He will not be, and probably does not want to be, 'John Paul III', living in an incestuous, symbiotic relationship with the media. He will not turn the papacy into an endless media event and attempt to use modern communications as a propaganda tool. Nor will he travel the world as a kind of catechist-missionary. He will not be an idiosyncratic pope, doing his own thing. He will be much more traditional in a good sense, paying greater attention to the inner workings of the Roman curia and the church. He will deal with the 'nuts and bolts', the traditional tasks of the pope.

Most importantly, he has already shown that he understands that he is primarily the Bishop of Rome rather than 'bishop of the world', as John Paul attempted to cast himself. Benedict has a good knowledge of the tradition and he understands that his primary task is to be the 'vicar of Peter' rather than the 'vicar of Christ', a title that only gained currency in the period between Gregory VII and Innocent III. Until the end of the first Christian millennium, the popes saw themselves primarily as the successors of Saint Peter. The Canadian Dominican theologian J.M.R. Tillard argues that Peter lives on in his diocese of Rome in an almost sacramental, symbolic sense in each of the city's bishops. He says Peter has 'vicars in the see of Rome rather than successors' (*The Bishop of Rome*, p. 97). Another of the primary titles the Roman bishops have claimed for themselves over the centuries is *servus servorum Dei*, first brought into the tradition by Gregory I 'the Great' (590–604), and for the first thousand years the pope did act as 'the servant of the servants of God'. Pope Benedict has already shown by his rhetoric that he understands the important significance of these titles, and that there will be a subtle shift away from grandiose to more traditional designations. He has even dropped the triple papal tiara from the top of his coat of arms. The tiara, which has not been worn by popes since the death of Paul VI in 1978, is the non-liturgical beehive-like crown with three coronets that took on its final form in the late Middle Ages symbolising the papacy's sacred and secular power. In place of it Benedict has retained the mitre, the much more liturgical and priestly headdress worn by a bishop. He has also got rid of thrones, and he goes out into the vestibule to welcome people to his office. He is clearly trying to highlight his role as Bishop of Rome rather than 'vicar of Christ'.

He has also returned to the use of a traditional pallium, a wide band of white woollen material worn over the shoulders and across the upper chest by Metropolitan archbishops; that is, senior archbishops of a province. At his installation Mass he abandoned the rather small, almost insignificant pallium that you would hardly notice, worn by bishops since the late medieval period, and replaced it with the much wider and more spectacular form with a band hanging across both back and front of the left shoulder worn by the bishops of the first millennium and often seen in the great frescos, particularly in churches in Ravenna and Rome. At first sight these symbols seem unimportant, but within the context of the Vatican and the church they take on considerable importance. They signal a subtle but important change in style and emphasis.

This is even clearer in papal liturgies. One of Ratzinger's better books was his *The Spirit of the Liturgy* (2000). In the introduction he acknowledges his debt to Romano Guardini and to his book *The Spirit of the Liturgy* (1918). Ratzinger compares the pre-Vatican II liturgy to a 'fresco … [that] had been preserved from damage, but it had been almost completely overlaid with whitewash by later generations' (p. 7). He says this fresco had been revealed by the Council, but that since then it has been endangered 'by various restorations and reconstructions. In fact, it is threatened with destruction if the necessary steps are not taken to stop these damaging influences' (p. 8), by which he means domesticated worship with bad music that emphasises sentimental dependency and 'togetherness' and a concern with the nurturing of the self, rather than worshiping God. Allowing for his usual tendency to overstate the case, he is right to

say that there is a need for a recovery of reverence and a deep consciousness that we are entering into a sacred space and time that puts us in touch
with the presence of the Spirit of God through contact with Christ. He
makes the point that if liturgy is purely horizontal, that is, purely concerned with the community and relationships, even if the ultimate aim is
social action, it is still a kind of idolatry, a worship of the golden calf of the
self. In his meditations on the Stations of the Cross in the Coliseum on
Good Friday 2005 he said that even in the church 'how often do we celebrate only ourselves, without even realising that he [Jesus] is there!' There
is truth in what he says, but again while expressing a genuine problem,
he goes to the other extreme and dichotomises the situation as though we
were faced with an either-or choice.

To begin with, it is clear that as pope he is going to do something about
papal worship and use that as an exemplar for the rest of the church. For
him worship is connected with the Eucharist, which he sees as a major
responsibility of all bishops. Of course he is right: it is the Eucharist and the
liturgy which create the church and make Christ present to us. Even at his
installation Mass there was a clear change of style and emphasis. Sandro
Magister of *L'Espresso* (28/4/05) says that originally Benedict wanted to celebrate his installation within St Peter's basilica 'because there the architecture better directs the attention towards Christ and not to the pope'. It was
only the size of the crowd that persuaded him to have the open-air Mass in
the piazza. With Pope Wojtyla the liturgy had been much more folksy,
familiar, much more open to the inclusion of extraneous, even foreign symbols. Magister says that 'many of the innovations of showmanship' that
were introduced into the rituals by John Paul will cease with Benedict. The
installation Mass gave immediate expression to a different 'feel' altogether.

To begin with, the new pope received his pallium and fisherman's ring
at the tomb of the apostle Peter beneath the high altar of the basilica. Then
there was the procession. Magister captures the sense of this wonderfully;
you can tell his wife is an art historian with an intimate knowledge of the
Vatican. The pope processed from the high altar of St Peter's along the
nave to the front door behind the processional cross held aloft and the book
of the gospels carried by the deacon. 'The baldacchino with its spiral
columns, another of Bernini's brilliant inventions, framed him in perspective and seemed to move together with him. But what really set the visual
atmosphere was the stained glass depiction of the Holy Spirit in the apse,
set at the centre of rays of light.' Thus Benedict processed along 'the sacred
stage of the church on its journey between heaven and earth'. Given his

Bavarian background with its baroque churches, all this makes eminent sense. The baroque period saw the church building as the forecourt of heaven, the place where we entered into the spectacular and beautiful presence of God. This is the kind of liturgical atmosphere that Benedict breathes in his very being and, as Magister points out, he sees the liturgy as a journey between earth and heaven. For him the focus is not on the celebrant—as it has been in papal worship in the past—but on Christ as the way to God. For Benedict the sense of sacred space and an entry into time beyond time is what is important. Everything that distracts from that must be eliminated.

And then there was the music. The simple reality is that the Vatican choir had become increasingly dreadful as the Wojtyla papacy progressed. But suddenly at this installation Mass they recovered something of their rich tradition. The music was entirely traditional, plain chant and classical polyphony, and as Benedict drove around the piazza in an open vehicle after the Mass the organist played—and it was relayed magnificently by the loudspeakers—the Toccata and Fugue in D minor by Bach. I was present at the time and I must say it lifted my spirits to heaven! I think it is likely that the pope will try to make sure that there is a return to a more sacral and formal approach to liturgy with an emphasis on enhancing the transcendent sensibility of the worship through leaving behind the kind of 'folksy' and sentimental feel that still characterises liturgy in many parishes. Part of this will involve improving both the standards of performance and the types of music used in the Mass. There is much that is worthwhile in this approach.

However, the danger is that the liturgy will become even more clericalised with an over-emphasis on the role of the priest and a neglect of the participation of the laity and other ministries. We have seen something of this in the Roman takeover of the International Committee for English in the Liturgy and the attempt to render the actual language used in worship more formal and less idiomatic and understandable, while at the same time preventing all attempts to introduce gender neutral language.

Certainly the Eucharist will be very much part of the first year of Benedict's papacy with several events leading up to the Synod of Bishops in October with the topic 'The Eucharist, source and summit of the church's life and ministry'. It will interesting to see if the discussion goes beyond safe generalities about the theology of the Eucharist to consider issues like inter-communion with other churches and the crisis that affects the lives and ministry of priests in the developed world. Also the acute shortage of priests in many parts of the world means that many Catholic communities are starved of the Eucharist and are becoming much more like Protestant churches with mere 'Services of the Word'. There are also the problems associated with overwork, the high average age of the clergy (in the United States, the United Kingdom and Australia the average age of the diocesan clergy is just over 60), the increasing number of priests with a homosexual orientation, the radically changed community expectations projected onto priests, the confused spirituality out of which they operate, and the wide range of expectations projected onto them. Put simply, priests face a major identity crisis. One of the litmus tests will be to see if these questions, especially the issue of celibacy, are discussed, or if Benedict explicitly rules them out. In fact, how the new pope performs at this synod may well set the pattern for the rest of his papacy because the Eucharist and priesthood are such central issues for contemporary Catholicism.

As discussed in previous chapters, one of the most acute crises facing the church inherited from the Wojtyla papacy—particularly affecting the United States, the United Kingdom, Canada, Australia and western Europe —is an interconnected series of problems centring around sexuality and the priesthood. The most obvious of these is the sexual abuse of minors. It is hard to predict how Benedict will deal with this complex of problems. On the sexual abuse issue the signs have been mixed. During the Stations of the Cross on Good Friday 2005 he made an extraordinary statement. Reflecting on the ninth station when Jesus fell under the weight of the cross a third time, Ratzinger said: 'How much filth there is in the church, and even amongst those who, in the priesthood, ought to belong entirely to him [Jesus]'. Presumably this referred to the sexual abuse crisis. He seems to be saying the abusers have brought 'filth' into the church and that the time has come for a clean-out of the Augean stables. The danger is that this will focus entirely on homosexual priests and not tackle the underlying issues of clericalism and the hierarchical power structure.

Certainly he is well aware of the issue because the CDF took over the review and management of all cases of sexual abuse of minors from the local bishops in a decree issued on 18 May 2001. The result has been mixed. It seems that the Vatican has only very recently realised the acute nature of the crisis in the English-speaking world, especially the United States. Up until very recently, bishops who tried to deal with problematic priests have been thwarted by a Vatican appeal process that has sometimes reinstated demonstrably abusive men. Some bishops have had the guts to stand and refuse to reinstate these priests. In the United States, which has become the epicentre of the abuse crisis, the draconian US bishops' norms, which remove a priest permanently from ministry for life if there is even one credible allegation of sexual abuse of a minor 'past, present or future', even from as long as forty years ago, have nevertheless been given conditional approval by the CDF and will be reviewed in 2005. The Vatican has particular concerns about what constitutes a 'credible' accusation, the need to protect an accused priest's rights to an assumption of innocence and a fair trial, and the fact that the US bishops seem to have handed over the power of demanding accountability to diocesan and national review boards which are entirely lay in composition. This slight handing over of authority to laity clearly worries the Vatican because it sees it as an abrogation of episcopal authority. At the same time the CDF has done nothing about disciplining bishops who did nothing about abusive priests, and moved them around constantly, protecting them from civil prosecution and refusing to assume responsibility for their behaviour, at the same time doing nothing to support or even care pastorally for those harmed.

Cardinal Francis George of Chicago has said that Benedict XVI told him that he will soon be dealing with the sexual abuse question. This resolution will be tested by the case of the Mexican priest and founder of the religious order, the Legionaries of Christ, Marcial Maciel Degollado. Maciel, 85, is still alive and resides in the order's headquarters in Rome. His influence is considerable in the Vatican, not least through the extraordinary success story of the Legionaries, founded in Mexico City in 1941. Describing themselves on their homepage the Legion says:

> The Legion of Christ is a priestly congregation of pontifical right (that is, fully approved by the pope and the church); it includes 600 priests and 2500 students for the priesthood. 'Regnum Christi' is a predominantly lay association ... with tens of thousands [actually about 30,000] members throughout the world engaged in works of prayer and service to people in all walks of life. Legionary priests offer spiritual guidance to 'Regnum Christi' members and help them organize their works of service.

It runs high schools, universities, media outlets (for instance, the *Zenit* news agency in Rome is a Legionary organisation), parishes and a whole range of other ministries. It is extremely influential in Mexico, especially among the wealthy governing elite including President Vincente Fox, as well as in other Latin American countries, and is found in the English-speaking world mainly in the United States and Ireland. In the United States it has been accused of being secretive and underhanded in the way it operates.

Maciel was one of John Paul's favourites. He had described him as 'an efficacious guide to youth' in 1994, and appointed him as a papal delegate to the Synod for America in 1997. He had travelled four times with the pope to Mexico, although on the fifth trip in 2002 he was nowhere to be seen. By then charges of sexual abuse against Maciel were being publicly aired. Nevertheless, the pope embraced him at a Legionary function in Rome on the sixtieth anniversary of his ordination in 2004.

In January 2005 he was replaced as head of the Legionaries, but the order claimed this had nothing to do with the abuse charges; it was simply a matter of his age. The claims go back to 1976 when the first reports of predatory behaviour against him were sent to the Vatican. Even before that there had been a Vatican investigation of financial mismanagement and drug-taking by Maciel in the 1950s, in which he was cleared. The Legion denies that this had anything to do with sexual abuse and that those now accusing the founder had a chance then to complain. But the fact is they were only adolescents at the time and very much under the influence of Maciel. In the mid-1990s a group of eight men from the 1940s to the 1960s, all ex-Legionaries and Mexicans, got together and claimed they had been abused by Maciel over an extended period when they were young seminarians—some as young as 12—in Spain and Italy. They only went public after they had received no reply from the Vatican to their claims. Maciel denies the claims completely.

Eventually a canonical case of *absolutionis complicis*, absolution in confession by a priest of an accomplice in a sexual act, was formally filed with the CDF in December 1998 by three of the men. Unlike accusations of sexual abuse where claims have to be made within ten years of the victim's eighteenth birthday, this crime does not have a statute of limitations on it in canon law and it incurs an automatic excommunication reserved to the Holy See. The Congregation sat on the case and did nothing until late 2004. All the evidence seemed to point to the fact that Ratzinger and the CDF believed that the claims were malicious and they were unwilling to act, especially given Maciel's influence with Pope Wojtyla.

In the meantime an enormous amount had been written and published in the media about the accusations. Jason Berry, the journalist who first broke the story of child sexual abuse by priests in the United States, and Gerald Renner, a journalist with the *Hartford Courant* newspaper who had been investigating the Legionaries for almost a decade, published a book

Vows of Silence on the case in 2004. By early 2005 it was becoming clear that Ratzinger and the CDF were beginning to take the sexual abuse claims much more seriously. The Promoter of Justice at the CDF (the equivalent of prosecutor), the Maltese Monsignor Charles J. Scicluna, had written an article in which he suggested that the canonical statutes of limitation on sexual abuse cases be waived, as they already had been in many US investigations. Then he contacted the lawyer of the three men who brought the charges against Maciel, asking if they wished to proceed with the case. After an affirmative reply, Scicluna opened a preliminary investigation. According to Sandro Magister (*Chiesa* 20/5/05), Scicluna travelled to the United States and Mexico and interviewed the original eight claimants, plus a number of other ex-Legionaries who have come forward. With Ratzinger now Benedict, it looked as though a canonical process would go ahead. But then on 20 May 2005 the Legionaries suddenly announced that there were no plans for a canonical process to proceed, 'nor is one foreseen in the future'. But as John Allen discovered five days later, this unsigned statement did not come from the CDF, but from the Secretariat of State where Cardinal Angelo Sodano is a long-time supporter of Maciel. So the long and the short of it is that the Secretariat of State will most likely try to block the investigation and at the time of writing the CDF has not made its intentions clear. As a result, Allen thinks 'there are grave doubts within the Holy See about proceeding'. All this seems to throw into doubt the Vatican's—and Benedict XVI's—determination to confront the issue. Jason Berry is right when he said that 'This pope is at a crossroads. He has to resolve the Maciel case or it will stalk him like a shadow in the sun' (ABC News International, 21/5/05).

As to the other issues confronting the priesthood I suspect it is unlikely that a great deal of change can be expected. *The Ratzinger Report* outlines a theology which sees the priest as representing Christ, as someone fulfilling a sacral role rather than a social one. Ratzinger certainly shows an awareness of the kinds of pressure that priests are under and that a man can grow weary and succumb to cultural expectations so that he becomes merely a kind of 'sacred' social worker. Admittedly these are views from twenty years ago and we must allow for some evolution. Ratzinger returned to this theme in a speech at the beginning of the September 1990 Synod on the priesthood. After an interesting introduction in which he outlined the complexity of the emergence of the office of priest in the early church, he again stressed the sacramentality of the priesthood and said that it was not something a man could take upon himself.

The one who receives the sacrament is sent to give what he cannot give
of his own strength; he is sent to act in the person of another, to be his
living instrument. For this reason no human being can declare himself
a priest; for this reason, too, no community can promote a person to this
ministry by its own decree. Only from the sacrament, which belongs to
God, can priesthood be received. Mission can only be received from the
one who sends, from Christ in His sacrament, through which a person
becomes the voice and the hands of Christ in the world. (Synod of
Bishops, 1990)

All this tends to remain in the realm of the theology. He sees the priesthood
as a kind of Christ icon.

But what practical consequences can be drawn from this? He has not
drawn any except to say that women cannot be ordained. So it probably
signals a determination to maintain the status quo. But on the face of it
there is no reason why, in Benedict's theology, a married man, or even a
woman, could not be called to the sacrament of priesthood by God. The
only argument against women is that the church has not done this before.
There is no argument against married men. The Catholic church already
ordains them in the Eastern churches in union with Rome, and has permitted the ordination of some convert clergy. And for the first millennium,
a married priesthood was the norm rather than the exception. So will the
celibacy rule change? It just might, at least a little bit. He may allow the
ordination of some married men as he is certainly not wedded to celibacy
in the sense John Paul II was. The Synod on the Eucharist might give us
some clues, especially if some of the braver bishops speak up and discuss
the issue. As for the ordination of women: given Ratzinger's stance on this
when CDF prefect, I think it entirely unlikely that anything will change.

On 13 May 2005, Benedict spoke informally to the priests of his own
diocese in the cathedral church of Rome, Saint John Lateran. After hearing the Roman priests' comments and questions, which were not recorded
by the Vatican, his response was kindly, but he shifted the focus to his own
preoccupations. Clearly there had been talk about 'the movements', that is
the NRMs such as the Neo-Catechuminate, Focolare, Communion and
Liberation, and the other charismatic groups that have flooded into Rome
parishes over the last two decades to be welcomed by some and treated with
suspicion by others, and almost always causing controversy. Benedict's
reply to his clergy is completely non-committal. The movements, he says,
can offer 'new initiatives, new inspirations, new life', but ultimately the

parish priest 'is responsible for the growth of the parish'. This was hardly a ringing endorsement of the NRMs which had enjoyed such support in the Wojtyla papacy. The evidence seems to be that Benedict will keep his distance from the movements. Their real testing time might be approaching when they lack overwhelming papal sponsorship. As a cardinal and as CDF prefect he does not have much of a record of supporting them.

But Benedict clearly wanted to shift the Roman priests' focus away from parish pump issues to his own preoccupations: Asia, Latin America and especially Africa. In comments that are hard to link with the concerns of his own diocesan clergy, he stressed the need for Christian missionary expansion in Africa, admitting that in the past Europe 'exported not only faith in Christ, but also all of the vices of the old Continent'. Nevertheless he wants a new 'exportation of faith, an answer to the intimate hope of every human being … This seems to me a great responsibility.' He talked about the necessity to 'rebuild a Christian Africa' (possibly a reference to North Africa which was Christian before it was Islamic) so that it can become 'a great Continent of new Humanism'. Given that this is probably an off-the-cuff, even unguarded comment, it does indicate that evangelisation in Africa is very much on his radar. If this kind of missionary activity is taken up aggressively it will have massive consequences for Christian–Muslim relations, especially across sub-Saharan Africa where the two faiths confront each other in countries such as Nigeria and Sudan, as well as in places like Sulawesi (the Celebes Islands) in Indonesia, where Muslims and Christians are in more or less equal numbers—due largely to an influx of fundamentalist-inclined Muslims—and where there has already been serious inter-community violence.

Then, in a convoluted passage (which may have something to do with the translation by the Vatican), he says that the 'language of faith is often very far from today's men and women', but that if they experience Catholicism as a listening religion and see Catholics transformed by it, then it 'can truly be an answer for others'. At the end of his speech he returns to the theme of 'the missionary nature of the church'. He says believers can be tempted to leave others in peace in their own religions and beliefs, or even in their non-belief. The sole aim can be to live with them in harmony as though all religions were as good as each other. For many years Ratzinger has felt that this approach sacrificed the true, unique character of Christianity by making it just one among a number of faiths that for their adherents were salvific. But Benedict returns firmly to the missionary theme. He says (in the contorted Vatican translation):

If we are convinced and we have experienced the fact that without Christ life is incomplete, is missing a reality, the fundamental reality, we must also be convinced we do harm to no one if we show them Christ and we offer them in this way too the possibility to discover their true authenticity, the joy of having discovered life.

This is the real Benedict speaking. While his talk to Rome's priests is much more gentle than the blunt declaration of *Dominus Jesus* (September 2000) that other faiths are 'gravely deficient' and that Christianity alone has 'the fullness of the means of salvation', his words bespeak his real convictions. The theology of pluralism is in for a hard time in the Benedict papacy.

Here we also see the reason for the pursuit of theologians involved in inter-faith dialogue like the late Jacques Dupuis who accepted the fact that non-Christians can be saved outside the church, and was asking how these traditions mediate salvation to their members. More recently, Ratzinger and the CDF have examined the writings of the American Jesuit theologian Roger Haight, specifically his book *Jesus: Symbol of God* (2000). In February 2005 the CDF issued a 'Notification' about Haight's book saying that it contained 'grave doctrinal errors'. Substantially the CDF maintains that the US Jesuit's attempts to talk about the doctrine of Christ in ways that make sense to contemporary, post-modern culture undercut Christian belief in the absolute uniqueness of Christ as the sole, universal saviour of humankind. There is no doubt that the theology of pluralism is in for a rough ride in this papacy, although interreligious dialogue will probably continue.

However, if mission and evangelisation are high on the agenda of Pope Benedict, there are also going to be serious complications with Catholic relationships with the Muslims. Up until now the Vatican has taken a 'softly, softly' approach to militant and fundamentalist Islam in their attacks on the west. Rome has been deeply concerned with protecting minority Christian communities in Muslim countries, especially in Palestine, Israel, Syria and Iraq. But given the extremist attitudes many of the most outspoken Islamists and their unwillingness to enter into genuine dialogue, little has been achieved by this approach. While clearly contacts need to continue between moderate Muslims willing to engage in discussions with Catholics, it looks as though Benedict is suggesting that a more up-front assertion of fundamental Catholic beliefs might get further with the more militant Islamists. At least it has the advantage of being honest, recognising that both are missionary religions. No doubt Benedict would be hoping that on the basis of that a more honest approach and a more vigorous dialogue could ensue. But relations with Islam will remain an issue very much on the agenda of this papacy.

Closely connected to this missionary thrust is Ratzinger's view on what he calls 'relativism', what most would call 'post-modernism'. In his sermon to the cardinals, he claimed that 'We are moving towards a dictatorship of relativism which does not recognise anything as for certain, and which has as its highest goal one's own ego and one's own desires'. At the heart of his critique is a profound concern that God has been banished from public life, especially in Europe. In fact there is a deepening conviction in the Vatican that European secularists are systematically mounting an assault on Christianity and specifically on the Roman church. As Ratzinger said in his speech at Subiaco on 1 April 2005: 'Europe has developed a culture that, in a way previously unknown to humanity, excludes God from public consciousness, either by denying him altogether or by judging that his existence cannot be demonstrated, is uncertain and, therefore, somewhat irrelevant to public life.' He told *La Repubblica* on 19 November 2004:

> We are faced with an aggressive secularism ... It is beginning to turn into an ideology that imposes itself through politics and leaves no public space for the Catholic and Christian vision, which thus risks becoming something purely private and essentially mutilated. We must defend religious freedom ... against an ideology that presents itself as the only voice of rationality.

It is clear that as pope, Benedict will not tolerate this exclusion of God from the public sphere. Whether the situation is as bad as he says is a matter of opinion, and whether the secularism he talks about is as well organised as he suggests remains to be seen. But there certainly is a kind of *sécularisme* on the rise in Europe, especially among the bureaucratic intelligentsia and the political classes. That was why it was so amusing to see them all, including the ultimate secularist Chirac, at the Mass for John Paul's funeral doing their best to look pious! It is clear that one of the priorities of the Benedict papacy will be an attempt to reconvert the secularised masses of Europe, although precisely how this is to be done remains to be seen.

On the issue of relationships with other Christians, in his sermon for the Mass of Installation Benedict seemed to emphasise the importance of ecumenism. He talked about 'an explicit call to unity' and quoted the text from Saint John's gospel '"I have other sheep that are not of this fold; I must lead them too, and they will heed my voice. So there shall be one flock, one shepherd" (John 21:11)'. He continued: 'These are the words of Jesus at the end of his discourse on the Good Shepherd ... Let us do all we can to pursue the path towards unity you have promised ... Grant that we may be one flock and one shepherd ... Help us to be servants of unity'. This certainly seemed like a call for a renewal of the ecumenical movement.

But a note of caution needs to be introduced here. Benedict does not see the Protestants and Anglicans as 'churches' in the proper sense. They are 'ecclesial communities'. He was clear about this when he spoke to a group of church and religious leaders who had come to Rome for his installation in April 2005. He clearly referred to the Orthodox as 'churches', and to the Protestants and Anglicans as 'ecclesial communities'. In the Roman understanding you have a church only when you have valid orders recognised by Catholicism and thus a valid Eucharist. While this may have sounded pedantic, even rude, at least it was a needed retreat from a June 2000 CDF document, 'Note on the Expression "Sister Churches"'. In this Note bishops were told not to use the terms 'sister churches' or 'our two churches' when referring to Catholicism's relationship with other Christian communities. The Note argues that the Catholic church cannot be a 'sister' of any other Christian body, including the Orthodox, because it 'implies a plurality on the level of the one holy, Catholic and apostolic church ... whose real existence is thus obscured ... [She] is not a sister but "mother" of all the particular churches.' The term 'sister churches' had been used mainly to refer to the Orthodox, although it had been first coined by Pope Paul VI in 1970 in reference to the Anglicans. There is no doubt that the CDF 'Note' and to a lesser extent the distinction between 'churches' and 'ecclesial communities' reflects a serious retreat from the unequivocal intentions of the Council, which were essentially ecumenical and attempted to build bridges with the other Christian churches rather than creating divisions over jargon.

Anglican Archbishop Rowan Williams of Canterbury was putting the best interpretation on Benedict's call to unity in his installation sermon and his later reference to 'ecclesial communities'. At a joint press conference in Rome with Cardinal Cormac Murphy-O'Connor of Westminster he said: 'Pope Benedict has gone out of his way to underline his sense of the priority of ecumenical work. He has spoken of being servants of unity.' Given the many divisions in Anglicanism between evangelicals and the high church, and the different understandings of the nature of ministry, worship and ecclesiology reflected in these groups, Williams admitted that the Anglicans 'are struggling as a Communion to find a sustainable, robust doctrine of the Church that will help us deal with the many difficulties we have faced in recent years'. Here Williams, like many Anglicans, uses the word 'communion' to refer to the group of independent national and regional churches that go to make up Anglicanism. In many ways the Anglican–Roman Catholic International Commission (ARCIC) has made more progress than any other international dialogue with agreed statements on ministry, authority and most recently on the Blessed Virgin Mary. But as CDF prefect, Ratzinger remained suspicious, pointing correctly to the 'dispersed' nature of authority in the Anglican communion where no one can really speak for the whole church, and to the problem of the ordination of women which he sees as insuperable. He would see the same problems applying to all the Protestant churches.

But Benedict's real ecumenical priorities are the Orthodox rather than Protestants and Anglicans. The Russian Orthodox particularly have been making very positive noises at the beginning of Benedict's papacy. The reality is that the Vatican feels much more at home with the Orthodox than with other Christians, and vice versa. This was expressed by Patriarch Alexei II of Moscow and All Russia when he said that 'the entire Christian world, including the Orthodox, respects him [Benedict]. Without doubt theological differences exist, but as far as his views on modern society, secularisation and religious relativism are concerned, our points of view are very similar' (ANSA News, 27/4/05). And, one might add, also on sacramental questions like the ordination of women, which the Orthodox strongly oppose. The major theological difficulties that remain are papal primacy and infallibility. The Orthodox consider primacy a negotiable issue, but they see infallibility as heretical. The churches also face practical questions such as 'proselytism' by Catholics in Russia and Ukraine, and the setting up of Catholic dioceses in Orthodox territory. One of the other difficult issues is the status of the so-called 'Uniate' churches, those churches that follow Eastern liturgy and discipline, but are in union with Rome. The word 'Uniate' is insulting to them, and is meant to be when used by the Orthodox. This issue almost reached breaking point in Ukraine in the 1990s when the churches and property of Ukrainian Catholics seized by Stalin and given to the Russian Orthodox were returned to the Catholics after the fall of the Soviets. These problems are now being slowly ironed out and the very diplomatic Metropolitan Kirill of Smolensk and Kaliningrad, who was in Rome for Benedict's installation, felt that the remaining issues between Rome and Russian Orthodoxy can be worked through. The theological difficulties still remain, but with a theologian pope, they will probably be tackled.

The other Orthodox churches, particularly the Greeks, are more cautious about Rome. However, the Ecumenical Patriarch of Orthodoxy, Bartholomew I of Constantinople, visited Rome in July 2004 to celebrate the 1964 lifting of all anathemas between the two churches. The relationship was given further impetus when the Vatican handed over the ancient church of San Teodoro on Rome's Palatine Hill. It was reconsecrated for Greek Orthodox worship. Also the return of the relics of Saint Gregory of Nazianzen and Saint John Chrysostom to the Orthodox was significant. They believe that the relics were stolen during the Fourth Crusade in 1204, when crusaders en route to the Holy Land sacked Constantinople and stole many of the treasures of Eastern Christianity. Catholics, on the other hand, maintain that the relics were brought to Rome by Greek monks during the eighth century, escaping the Iconoclastic persecution in the East. Whatever is true, the relics are now back with Eastern Orthodoxy. There is no doubt that the mainstream Orthodox church has a high regard for Pope Benedict and that relations between Orthodox and Catholics will continue to improve in this papacy. It will be one of the key issues that Benedict, who also has great sympathy for the Orthodox, will make sure is advanced during his papal tenure.

The line along which ecumenism will probably advance in this papacy is that of working towards intercommunion with 'particular churches'. Ratzinger had said that this will happen slowly, and will be clearly with the Orthodox first. However, the former CDF prefect also has a special feeling for the Lutherans. The reformer Martin Luther has been a great influence on him and he has sympathy for the spirituality of the former Augustinian friar. Both were deeply influenced by the theology of Saint Augustine. After an agreed document entitled 'Declaration on the Doctrine of Justification' between the Lutherans and Cardinal Edward Cassidy's Pontifical Council for Christian Unity had been issued on 25 June 1998, the CDF suddenly issued a 'Response' which cut the ground from under the honourable and straightforward Australian Cassidy and threw the whole agreement into doubt.

The issues in debate here are subtle and may well be only about words. Essentially, Luther said that after baptism we all remain *simul justus et peccator*—a person right with God and yet a sinner at the same time. The Catholic doctrine at the Council of Trent declared that the grace that comes in baptism and the sacraments internally transforms us and make us essentially right with God. Luther, on the other hand, would say that the merits and goodness of Christ covers our sinfulness and that we are unable to do anything good except by the redemptive power of Christ. The 'Declaration' got beyond this verbal joust to find a formula acceptable to both parties. So why did Ratzinger torpedo it? One cannot help feeling that he was sour because Cassidy had achieved agreement with the Lutherans when Ratzinger felt this was his area of expertise. He seemed to want to create theological obstacles so that he could introduce himself as the knight in shining armour to save the 'Declaration'. This is exactly what he did in November 1998 and then covered himself with glory as the savour of the agreement. Despite his vigorous denials in German newspapers that he had not sabotaged the Cassidy agreement, it is the only possible interpretation given that not a lot of extra clarity was attained through his intervention.

One of the things predicted by many commentators in Rome at the time of Ratzinger's election was that he would 'deal' with the Roman curia. It is widely felt throughout the church among Catholics of different shades of opinion that the Vatican got right out of control under John Paul II, and that it needed to have a broom put through it to clean out the dead wood. However, as would have been expected of any pope, all curial heads from Wojtyla's time were reappointed immediately after Benedict's election, 'until other provision was made'. This is the key phrase and is a standard procedure. Benedict will gradually appoint his own people. Purges are not the way of the Vatican. People will be slowly moved sideways or out.

His first appointment of Archbishop William Levada of San Francisco to his own old job as the CDF prefect was surprising to many who had no idea who Levada was. He had actually worked in the CDF from 1976 to 1982 and he has remained a friend of Benedict ever since. Here again, loyalty is probably being repaid. Levada is talented and is seen as a reasonably good theologian. He managed to negotiate his way through San Francisco, the gay capital of the world (although Sydney might also put in a claim for that title), without too many confrontations. It is a city famous for its liberal and progressive openness, and Levada is respected there, although he did not win a great deal of affection or support from either clergy or laity. He has a poor reputation among victims and advocates for dealing with sexual abuse cases, and this is important because this constitutes a considerable portion of the work of the contemporary CDF.

An assessment of Levada on the homepage of KTVU, a cable TV station in the San Francisco Bay area, is balanced and gives a feel for

Laveda's tenure as archbishop from a neutral perspective. Talking about the 2004 presidential election controversy over whether Catholic politicians should receive Holy Communion if they supported abortion rights, or even if they were not outspoken against such legislation, KTVU says, 'Levada issued a nuanced statement that emphasized the importance of the abortion issue in evaluating lawmakers, but did not say directly whether he would deny the sacrament to a dissenting candidate'. This is exactly Ratzinger's own position. The KTVU assessment continues:

> Levada, also viewed by many as a conservative, has honed his political skills while representing the church in California and Portland, Oregon, and now nationally as chairman of the U.S. Conference of the Catholic Bishops' Committee on Doctrine. While Portland's archbishop from 1986 to 1995, Levada led an unsuccessful effort to block the voter initiative that made Oregon the first state to legalize physician-assisted suicide. In San Francisco, city officials threatened to cut funding unless Catholic Charities offered benefits to the domestic partners of city employees. Levada brokered a compromise that expanded health care even further: he said anyone in the household of a city employee— including children, parents, even roommates.

The KTVU assessment says Levada has consistently refused to label himself as a conservative or a liberal.

> 'I consider myself to be in the exact middle of the road as to where I should be as a bishop,' he told the *San Francisco Chronicle* in 1995. 'I have a responsibility to uphold the teaching and tradition of the church. I would hope that I would be compassionate, interested in people's situations, their problems, their difficulties.'

It is doubtful whether his self-assessment as 'exact middle of the road' is accurate. He is a conservative, indeed a rigid one, although clearly intelligent. He has not been particularly successful in getting elected to offices in the US Bishops' Conference. It was only after twenty years in 2003 that he was voted in as chair of the Doctrinal Commission. Nevertheless he comes to the CDF with more political skills than Ratzinger did when he arrived from Munich in 1982, and these are the kind of abilities he will need especially when dealing with the English-speaking world. Perhaps he could be labelled as a 'pragmatic conservative'.

Does Levada's appointment mean a better deal for gays and lesbians? This seems unlikely despite the fact he has lived for ten years in one of the gayest cities in the world. His position is probably the same as Ratzinger's and he is unlikely to change as CDF prefect. Certainly Ratzinger has a very confronting record on this issue. In October 1986, for instance, a 'Letter' *Homosexualitatis problema* ('The Problem of Homosexuality') was sent to bishops by the CDF which attacked an 'overly benign interpretation' of homosexuality. It continued: 'Although the particular inclination of the homosexual person is not a sin, it is a more or less strong tendency ordered toward an intrinsic moral evil; and thus the inclination itself must be seen as an objective disorder'. It's a pretty frightening thought: if you're young, gay and insecure about your sexual identity, you have to face the fact that you have a 'more or less' deep-rooted inclination to 'intrinsic moral evil' and 'objective disorder'. While conceding that we are all sinners, no church document says that about heterosexual people. Thus it is hard for gays not to take such comments personally. And even those who have tried to minister to lesbians and gays have been condemned, basically on the grounds that their ministry could be understood as signalling a weakening of church teaching.

Within twelve months of arriving in Rome, Ratzinger tried to have the book *A Challenge to Love: Gay and Lesbian Catholics in the Church* (1983) withdrawn from distribution and he ordered Bishop Walter Sullivan of Richmond, Virginia, to withdraw his name from the cover. The author of the book, Father Robert Nugent, and his colleague, Sister Jeannine Gramick, who together had begun 'New Ways Ministry' in 1977 and who for more than 25 years had carried on an apostolate to gays and lesbians in the United States, were eventually to feel the full force of Ratzinger's rancour about homosexuality. In July 1999 they had lifetime bans imposed on them, forbidding them ever to work with gay people again. Disgraceful attempts were made by the CDF to try to force them to reveal their private conscientious beliefs on homosexual orientation and behaviour. They even tried to impose a 'profession of faith'—along the lines of Tissa Balasuriya —on Bob Nugent because he was a priest. Nugent commented: 'As one letter writer to the *Tablet* in London pointed out, if all the priests in parishes who ministered to heterosexual Catholics had to make a profession of faith in *Humanae vitae* [condemning contraception], we would immediately be very short of priests'.

The CDF's behaviour in the case of Gramick and Nugent can only be described as underhand, dictatorial and disgraceful. Similar treatment was handed out to the Jesuit John McNeill who had published the book *The Church and the Homosexual* in 1976. In 1987 on CDF orders he was expelled from the Jesuits after forty years of service when he refused to abandon his ministry to people with AIDS. It is hard to avoid using the word 'vicious' to describe the attitude of the CDF under Ratzinger to homosexuality.

So it is unlikely that a more caring, pastoral, Christian attitude towards homosexual persons will emerge in the Benedict papacy, no matter how skilful Levada's handling of the issue in San Francisco may have been. The only hopeful sign is that there may be some movement on dealing with AIDS. A number of senior churchmen, including Cardinals Godfried Danneels (Brussels), Cormac Murphy-O'Connor (Westminster), Bishop Kevin Dowling of Rustenburg, South Africa, and Bishop Albert Rouet of Poitiers, France (Dowling and Rouet are the chairs of committees of their episcopal conferences on the AIDS issue), have already talked about the justifiable use of condoms in order to prevent the infection of another person with AIDS. Danneels put it simply in a TV interview in the Netherlands: 'If a person infected with HIV has decided not to respect abstinence, then he has to protect his partner, and he can do that—in this case—by using a condom'. Otherwise, the Cardinal said, he is guilty of murder. Danneels is saying that condom use is justified under the moral principle of double effect when good (the preservation of the life of another) can only be achieved when an evil (the use of condoms) is tolerated.

Clearly the church is right when it says that merely drowning Africa or anywhere else in condoms is not the solution to the spread of AIDS, and may well be counterproductive because it encourages promiscuity. The real challenge is to get people to assume moral responsibility for their sexual behaviour. But the central question for the church is whether it should exclude the use of condoms totally. By completely banning their use, it simply does not acknowledge the situation of the woman who is coerced into sex and whose only protection is a condom. Equally, it does not take into account workers in many parts of Africa who are away from home often for months on end. They consort with prostitutes, get AIDS, and then return to infect their wives and children. When people will not refrain from casual sex then the condom is not a contraceptive but a pro- phylactic. And the church would get more credibility if it disowned the arrant nonsense uttered by people such as Cardinal Alfonso Lopez Trujillo of the Pontifical Council on the Family in the document 'Family Values Versus Safe Sex'. Here he argued that condoms have a 15 to 30 per cent failure rate, which is demonstrably wrong. This was his second foray into this area, and he made a fool of himself on both occasions when he appeared on BBC TV. He is one of the first who should go home in any revamping of the curia.

Perhaps the best thing that could happen is that Vatican and the pope say nothing about condoms and related issues. We don't need a papal statement on everything. People have consciences and are able to sort things out. Allow the moral theologians to work on it and the good sense of the faithful to discern the real ethical issues. They already have, as the excellent series of essays in *Catholic Ethicists on HIV/AIDS Prevention*, edited by James Keenan and Jon Fuller, shows.

Turning to the treatment of theologians and dissenters by the CDF, the Benedict papacy has got off to a very bad start. Just three weeks after his election, Father Thomas Reese, the editor of *America*, the US Jesuits' most prestigious magazine since 1997, was sacked on the orders of the CDF. Reese, who has always been careful to maintain a moderate centrist position between both the right and the left, is the author of *Inside the Vatican* (1996), every intelligent person's guide to that most arcane of organisations, the Roman curia. He was especially prominent in the US media in the days leading up to the death of John Paul and during the election of Benedict. The notes he prepared on the death and election of popes and made available on the Internet for media practitioners were splendid and were widely used in the English-speaking world. He understood that it was very difficult for a journalist with little knowledge of Catholicism to suddenly have to try to cover the Vatican and the papacy with its arcane rituals, 2000-year history, convoluted politics and addiction to secrecy. Reese became a reliable way into this mysterious world and he helped journalists get the story right. I understand how difficult and painstaking this process is, having spent much of my own time over the last ten years doing exactly the same thing in Australia.

The Reese story repeats a pattern with which I am personally very familiar in other ways as well. According to John Allen of the *National Catholic Reporter* (6/5/05), the CDF has had problems with Reese's editing of *America* for over five years. They were not concerned about heresy or deviation from established doctrine, but with matters of editorial choice. Reese was accused of publishing opposing points of view on topics on which the Vatican only wanted its opinion expressed. Thus he published articles outlining the pros and cons of *Dominus Jesus*, essays for and against

the use of condoms in the context of HIV/AIDS, and articles critical of the
attitude of the CDF to homosexuality, and he aired a range of opinions
during the 2004 presidential election on the question of rights and duties
of Catholic politicians regarding legal abortion. Always the coverage was
balanced. Many conservatives were featured, such as Cardinal Avery Dulles
on the rights of accused priests in child sexual abuse cases, and Reese even
published an article by Ratzinger himself (19/11/01) on 'The Local Church
and the Universal Church', replying to the views of Cardinal Walter
Kasper, whose views Reese also published. In a real sense *America* was only
reflecting the actual discussions that were going on among intelligent
Catholics in the wider American church. The notion that somehow people
can't work out orthodoxy for themselves, or that they are all 'simple' souls
who are easily upset by some disagreement in the church is patent nonsense as far as the type of Catholics who read *America* is concerned. They
don't need the protection of Ratzinger, the CDF or the bishops.

Of course, at heart this is not really about doctrine or protecting 'simple'
souls. It is about getting rid of Thomas Reese. The complaints about
America originated in the United States with unnamed bishops. The entire
process went on above Reese's head between the bishops, the CDF and
Peter-Hans Kolvenbach, the Jesuit General. Apparently these bishops
maintained that Reese should not be speaking on church matters to the
general media. They felt that this was their province alone, and clearly
they were jealous that he was media savvy and they were not. The fact is
that the media would not touch any of these bishops with a barge pole,
largely because they lack any ability to communicate effectively, or are so
absolutist and disengaged from a pluralistic world as to be useless in any
form of debate or discussion. One of the best comments on the Reese fiasco
was by the Philadelphia-based *Vaticanista* (a journalist who specialises on
the Vatican) and blogger Rocco Palmo. He says Reese 'decoded the twists
and turns of church politics for a generation of reporters' and that

> his chastisement is but the latest victory for a group of American
> bishops eager to reassert their authority following the devastating
> exposure of cover-ups of clerical sex abuse by bishops and their inner
> circles. The *America* decision marks a new low for those prelates who,
> eager to impose their guilt for their lack of oversight on others, have
> capitalised on the abuse scandal to settle personal vendettas with priests
> [like Reese].

Palmo also indicates the price these bishops will pay for their arrogance.

> But next time a story seen as inaccurate [by the church] the American
> hierarchy has no excuse to continue its cycle of blame. Father Reese was
> always the point-man who ensured that accuracy, and the bishops will
> have no one to blame for his absence but themselves.

Palmo's point is vividly illustrated by the sheer bad timing of Reese's
sacking in the very first month of the Ratzinger papacy. It shows an
unbelievable lack of judgement through the signal it sends. As the magazine *Commonweal* in an editorial on 6 May 2005 said, 'In a church with a
more confident and magnanimous hierarchy, Reese's prominence would
be seen as a great asset, not a threat ... The first thing that many Americans
are now likely to associate with Pope Benedict XVI's papacy will be yet
another act of Vatican repression.' All this does not auger well for a more
open papacy, and it suggests that the situation for theologians and dissenters will be particularly difficult. We have already seen this regarding
the theology of religious pluralism. Of course, an increasing number of
theologians today are lay and many of them are women. The only ones who
will really be able to be controlled are those who are priests or religious, or
those who are working in Catholic institutions of higher learning where
their employment could be in jeopardy if they fall foul of the CDF. Those
working in secular institutions are safer, but it will mean an increasing
decline in the standards of theology in Catholic tertiary institutions, when
all the creative work is done outside the church academy.

Given that it was bishops who persuaded the CDF to sack Thomas
Reese, we should now examine the episcopate that Benedict has inherited
from the John Paul papacy. As I said of the majority of the college of cardinals, many of the bishops appointed by John Paul have been of poor
leadership quality. Quite a few of them obviously lack pastoral sensitivity,
mature spirituality, and even a sound knowledge of Catholic teaching and
theology. This is not to say that there are no good bishops. There are many,
but there are also many whose mediocrity has dragged down the standards
of the worldwide episcopal bench. In the words of *Commonweal*'s editorial,
it is not only the United States that lacks a 'confident and magnanimous
hierarchy'. This is why I now think that, despite my calls in earlier books
such as *Papal Power* for a general council of the church, it would be dangerous to call a council during the Benedict papacy because of the lack of
leadership potential among the present batch of cardinals and bishops.

What is striking about many of these bishops is how dependent they are on papal or Roman approval, and how unwilling they are to assume genuine leadership and make good decisions for the local church. They seem suspended between Rome and their primary obligations to the Catholic community entrusted to their leadership. Consistently it is the good of the local church they abandon in their seeming desperate desire to please Rome. You have the impression of a frightened group of inadequate men anxious to avoid open debate, intellectual inquiry or any form of disagreement. Much of this is the product of the process of appointing bishops by a Roman bureaucracy determined to control the whole church as centrally as possible. Any priest who has said or done anything significant or who has rocked the boat in any way is simply excluded from appointment. Thus, with some notable exceptions, most bishops nowadays are simply too afraid to take initiatives for the good of their own diocese and are constantly looking over their shoulders to Rome. A kind of co-dependency has been set up that is symptomatic of a dysfunctional relationship.

One of the most vivid examples of this was the way the Australian bishops abandoned the widespread use of general absolution on the orders of the Vatican. In the 1980s and 1990s many Catholics found the celebration of reconciliation in a community gathering with general absolution spiritually helpful, as well as a replacement for private confession to a priest which has almost totally disappeared in Australia. But a tiny completely unrepresentative group, the so-called 'Catholics Advocacy Centre', were determined to stamp this out. This same group were also spying on priests' sermons and reporting them for what was perceived as 'deviations' and 'unorthodoxy'. Using the Chilean Cardinal Jorge Medina Estevez as their conduit, they successfully persuaded the Vatican to ambush the Australian bishops at the Synod for Oceania in October–November 1998. General absolution was forbidden, and the bishops left humiliated. The tragedy is the way that almost all of them accepted the humiliation. They simply did not stand up and defend the local church, which was their primary responsibility. The defeat was twofold. Not only was the use of general absolution abandoned—so now hardly anyone receives the sacrament of reconciliation—but the bishops were revealed as inadequate and patently incapable of offering any form of decisive leadership. Many of them were very angry personally, but publicly they accepted their humiliation when, if they had acted as a united group and resisted Rome, they could have given a powerful witness to the whole church.

Thus the question of episcopal collegiality becomes quite complicated. This presupposes a bench of bishops able to assume co-responsibility for the church. So even if Benedict was willing to begin to use a more consultative approach with the bishops in the government of the church, it is doubtful whether many of them would want to take the initiative, or even have much to offer. So perhaps the first problem the pope faces is the gradual replacement of the present bishops with men of better quality and with genuine leadership potential. Given his own intelligence there is some hope that he will appoint more pastorally and theologically able priests as bishops, although with the catastrophic decline in the number of priests he will have a very small pool on which he can draw.

One of the most interesting commentaries on the dilemmas that bishops face today comes from Cardinal Walter Kasper, now president of the Pontifical Council for the Promotion of Christian Unity but, more importantly, from 1989 to 1999, the bishop of Rottenburg-Stuttgart. An equal if not a superior theologian to Ratzinger, Kasper and the pope have been public sparring partners on the questions of collegiality, the relationship of the local church to Rome, and the role of bishops' conferences for several years now. In an article in *America* (23 April 2001) Kasper talks about his experience as the bishop in a large urban diocese facing many difficult pastoral problems and the increasingly wide gap that emerged between the needs and practices of the local church and the edicts issued by Rome under Pope Wojtyla. Local people did not understand the reason for Rome's decisions, so they ignored them. Kasper said: 'This happened concerning ethical issues, sacramental discipline and ecumenical practices. The adamant refusal of Communion to all divorced and remarried persons and the highly restrictive rules for Eucharistic hospitality [with other Christians] are good examples.' What is the local bishop to do? How can he bring the two together

> when their minds are so far apart, even to the point of holding mutually exclusive positions, as happens so often in our days? If the bishop attempts to enforce the general norms ruthlessly—as his Roman superiors sometimes expect—his effort is likely to be useless, even counterproductive. If he remains passive he is quickly judged disobedient. He seems to be caught in an impasse. Yet there is a solution: the bishop must be granted enough vital space to make responsible decisions in the matter of implementing universal laws.

He argues strongly that this is very much within the tradition of the law of the Western church where the virtue of prudence is held in high regard. Kasper goes on to argue that often the communion of the church becomes 'identified with the church of Rome and *de facto* with the pope and the curia'.

He was answered by Ratzinger, also in *America* (19 November 2001). He argues that the universal church takes what he calls 'ontological and temporal priority' over local churches. Kasper had argued that the universal church is composed of local churches and owes its existence to them. What is important here is where each cardinal places his *emphasis*: Kasper on the local church, Ratzinger on the universal. Again this does not necessarily auger well during the Benedict papacy for a recovery of a sense of the local church making as many decisions as possible at the lowest level, choosing its own married or celibate clergy, and the local diocese electing its own bishop.

To this point my comments have been confined to intra-religious and intra-Christian and Catholic issues. That is because this is where the emphasis has been in the previous career of Benedict XVI. But what about the relationship of the church with the wider world and international affairs?

Here I think the pattern of the Wojtyla papacy will continue. In other words, the Vatican will maintain a very dynamic approach to geopolitics, but very much within the parameters of the classical Catholic approach. There will a strong emphasis on peace, firm opposition to military interventions that are not fully justified by the conditions laid down for a just war. Opposition to so-called 'pre-emptive strikes' against possible but not yet real enemies will be maintained, such as the invasion of Iraq in order to neutralise imagined 'weapons of mass destruction'. The Vatican will continue to try to build strong diplomatic relationships with as many countries as possible. One of the testing areas will be relations with the People's Republic of China. Here the Vatican has real concern for the millions of oppressed Chinese Christians and Catholics of both the underground churches and the patriotic church. China will probably not collapse in the foreseeable future as the Soviet Union did, so the Vatican is going to have to negotiate with them.

While it is most likely that Benedict will soon choose a new secretary of state, given that Cardinal Angelo Sodano will be 78 in November 2005, he is likely to keep on Archbishop Leonardo Sandri, the substitute (secretary) for ordinary affairs, and Archbishop Giovanni Lajolo, the Secretary for

Relations with States, effectively the Vatican's foreign minister. One or other of these might well become secretary of state, although Cardinals Giovanni Battista Re at the Congregation of Bishops, and Crescenzio Sepe at the Congregation for Evangelisation are both ambitious for the job.

So, finally, what are we to expect from this pope? First, the simple fact of Benedict's age means that this will not be a long papacy. And the cardinals who elected him clearly did not mean it to be. Second, I suspect it will be a bridging papacy, away from the extremes of high notions of the papacy under John Paul II to a more modest and traditional exercise of the papal role. We do not need any more 'super popes', pontiffs who see themselves as 'bishop of the world'. Benedict is clearly a more modest man and for that Catholics can be thankful. Third, this pope brings a lot of baggage to the papacy and we have already seen some of it. Leopards do not change their spots, although they might fade a bit with age. It is all very well to say that his previous job was to be an 'inquisitor', but now it is to be a reconciling presence in the church. People do not change that radically, especially at an advanced age. So I suspect that this will not be a comfortable papacy for those perceived as 'dissenters' of any sort and it will not be an easy time for those who think that the church's cause is advanced by open discussion of contentious issues. Fourth, this is going to be a 'missionary' papacy, a time when Catholicism will be encouraged to be on the march again. The consequences of this for relations with Muslims remains to be seen. Fifth, he probably will be more consultative, more open to the bishops, more prepared to listen, especially to those he respects. John Paul listened to no one—except perhaps to Ratzinger. Sixth, there will be a lot fewer 'saints' and 'blesseds', and a trimmed down church bureaucracy.

Seven, there will be a call for a better celebration of the liturgy, a greater sensitivity to the presence of God in Christ at Mass and in the sacraments, a focus on the transcendent rather than the horizontal. But this does not mean it will not be joyful, with beautiful music and colour. Benedict is a man who loves poetry, music, art, nature, the mountains. Above all he loves Beethoven and especially Mozart.

That is a big recommendation for me.

NOTES

INTRODUCTION

For an introduction of John XXIII, see EEY Hales, *Pope John and His Revolution*, Doubleday, New York, 1965. A multi-volume history of the Council is being published at present; see Giuseppe Alberigo and Joseph A Komonchak, *History of Vatican II*, Orbis, Maryknoll, NY, in press. To date, five volumes have been published in English, in 1995, 1997, 1998, 2000, 2002. For a popular but accurate account of the Council, see Xavier Rynne, *Letters from Vatican City*, Faber, London, 1963; *The Second Session*, Faber, London, 1963; *The Third Session*, Faber, London, 1965; *The Fourth Session*, Faber, London, 1966.

Peter Hebblethwaite called Paul VI 'the first modern pope' in *Paul VI: The First Modern Pope*, HarperCollins, London, 1993.

George Weigel has published a massive biography of John Paul II, *Witness to Hope: The Biography of John Paul II*, HarperCollins, New York, 1999. He discusses his 'greatness', pp. 843–64.

My investigation by the CDF is described in *From Inquisition to Freedom: Seven Prominent Catholics and Their Struggle with the Vatican*, Simon and Schuster, Sydney, (Continuum, London) 2001, pp. 208–44. The book was published in the United States with the title *The Modern Inquisition*, Overlook Press, New York, 2002.

1. LAST DAYS IN THE PAPAL *APPARTAMENTO*

This chapter is based on several personal discussions in Rome with well-informed Vatican sources. I have also used articles of Italian journalist Sandro Magister, who writes for *L'Espresso*; see particularly 'The Pope is Ill', *L'Espresso*, 10–16 October 2003; and 'A Thousand Curial Manoeuvres', *L'Espresso*, 24–30 October 2003. Both can be found in English at his website, www.chiesa.espressonline.it.

For the comments of Mexican Discalced Carmelite, Father Camilo Macisse, see *The Tablet*, 22 November 2003, p. 26.

The John Henry Newman references can be found in *Certain Difficulties Felt by Anglicans in Catholic Teaching*, vol. 2, Longmans Green, London, 1901, p. 297; and Charles Stephen Dessain (ed.), *The Letters and Diaries of John Henry Newman*, vol. 29, Oxford University Press, 1961–72, p. 167.

2. THE IMPACT OF THE PAPAL TRAVELS

For the Ramzi Yousef plot, see Simon Reeve, *The New Jackals: Ramzi Yousef, Osama bin Laden, and the Future of Terrorism*, André Deutsch, London, 1999, pp. 73–93; George Weigel, *Witness to Hope: The Biography of Pope John Paul II*, HarperCollins, New

York, pp. 750–1; Doug Struck, 'Borderless Network of Terror', *Washington Post*, 23 September 2001; Matthew Brzezinski, 'Operation Bajinka's Bombshell', *Toronto Star*, 2 January 2002.

For papal trips, see my 'The Peripatetic Pope: A New Centralising of Power', in Hans Küng and Leonard Swidler (eds), *The Church in Anguish: Has the Vatican Betrayed Vatican II?*, Harper and Row, San Francisco, 1987, pp. 52–7.

See my book *Papal Power: A Proposal for Change in Catholicism's Third Millennium*, HarperCollins Religious, Melbourne, (Collins/Fount, London), 1997. For an account of Vatican Council I, see my *Upon This Rock: The Popes and Their Changing Role*, Melbourne University Press, 2000, pp. 239–50; and *Papal Power*, pp. 44–61.

The term 'runaway church' comes from the title of the late Peter Hebblethwaite's *The Runaway Church*, Collins/Fount, London, 1995.

I discuss Wojtyla's intellectual formation in my *Mixed Blessings: John Paul II and the Church of the Eighties*, Penguin, Melbourne, 1986, pp. 154–76.

3. A CRISIS OF LEADERSHIP

This chapter is based on a wide range of different sources and a long experience of observing and dealing with bishops and those priests who have been promoted to the episcopate, or passed over by the process. The details of the story of the misrepresentation of the state of the Australian Catholic church is set out at some length in my book *Between the Rock and a Hard Place: Being Catholic Today*, ABC Books, Sydney, 2004, pp. 7–11.

John L Allen's interview with Cardinal Franz König is from *National Catholic Reporter*, 8 October 1999; see the *NCR* online archives.

For the election of bishops, see Thomas J Reese, *A Flock of Shepherds: The National Conference of Catholic Bishops*, Sheed and Ward, Kansas City, 1992; and Reese, *Inside the Vatican: The Politics and Organization of the Catholic Church*, Harvard University Press, Cambridge, Mass., 1996, pp. 231–42.

For episcopal ambition in the United States, see Andrew Greeley, 'Look Out for Ambitious Clerics', *National Catholic Reporter*, 9 September 1995.

In his theological biography of Cardinal Joseph Ratzinger, John Allen describes the CDF Prefect's theological trajectory clearly and shows how Ratzinger's opinions have shifted on central doctrinal issues; see John Allen, *Cardinal Ratzinger: The Vatican's Enforcer of the Faith*, Continuum, New York, 2002, p. 64 (for the Synod of Bishops). This book has been reissued as *The Rise of Benedict XVI*, (Doubleday, United States, and Penguin, United Kingdom, 2005) with a discussion of the politics of the papal election. Note that Ratzinger usually spells his Christian name 'Joseph', not the German form 'Josef'.

4. LINES OF DIVISION

For the role of Ratzinger and Frings at Vatican II, see Giuseppe Alberigo and Joseph A Komonchak, *History of Vatican II*, vol. 2, Orbis, Maryknoll, NY (see index for names 'Frings' and 'Ratzinger'); and Xavier Rynne, *Letters from Vatican City*, Farrar, Straus & Co., New York, 1963 (see index for Frings). Again, John Allen's book on Ratzinger (*Cardinal Ratzinger: The Vatican's Enforcer of the Faith*, Continuum, New York, 2002) is also important and helpful here.

For the Lefebvre schism and Paul VI, see Peter Hebblethwaite, *Paul VI: The First Modern Pope*, HarperCollins, London, 1993, pp. 670–4. For the activities of the CDF under Ratzinger, see my *From Inquisition to Freedom*, Simon and Schuster, Sydney, 2001, pp. 20–31 (US edition: *The Modern Inquisition*, Overlook Press, New York, 2002).

The story of the birth control encyclical is told in Bob Kaiser, *The Politics of Sex and Religion: A Case History in the Development of Doctrine 1962–1985*, Leaven Press, Kansas City, 1985. There is a summary of the whole story in my *Mixed Blessings: John Paul II and the Church of the Eighties*, Penguin, Melbourne, 1986, pp. 114–19.

For a comprehensive treatment of Rahner's theology, see Louis Roberts, *The Achievement of Karl Rahner*, Herder and Herder, New York, 1967; and especially William V Dych, *Karl Rahner*, 'Outstanding Christian Thinkers', Geoffrey Chapman, London, 1992.

A good treatment of Balthasar's theology is in David L Schindler (ed.), *Hans Urs von Balthasar: His Life and Work*, Ignatius Press, San Francisco, 1991.

Aidan Nichols, 'An Introduction to Balthasar' *New Blackfriars*, January 1998.

Philip Kennedy, 'Rome and Relativism: *Dominus Jesus* and the CDF', *Commonweal*, 20 October 2000.

Ratzinger's book, *Fede, verità, tolleranza: Il cristianesimo e le altre religioni del mondo*, Unilibro Italia, 2004, is translated into English: *Christian Belief and World Religions*, Ignatius Press, San Francisco, 2004.

The whole story of Father Tissa Balasuriya is told in my *From Inquisition to Freedom*, Simon and Schuster, Sydney, 2001, pp. 80–108. See also, Jacques Dupuis, *Towards a Theology of Religious Pluralism*, Orbis, Maryknoll, NY, 1997; Roger Haight, *Jesus Symbol of God*, Orbis, Maryknoll, NY, 2000; John Hick, *God Has Many Names*, Pan Macmillan, London, 1980.

Michael Walsh, Review of *From Inquisition to Freedom*, *The Tablet*, 24 March 2001, p. 418.

For Lopez Trujillo, see John Allen, *Conclave: The Politics, Personalities, and Process of the Next Papal Election*, Doubleday, New York, 2002, p. 190; Peter Hebblethwaite, *The Next Pope*, HarperSanFrancisco, 2000, pp. 117–18.

For Lopez Trujillo's attack on liberation theology, see my *Mixed Blessings: John Paul II and the Church of the Eighties*, Penguin, Melbourne, 1986, pp. 142–9, especially pp. 146–8.

On the liturgy wars, an excellent article is Austin Ivereigh's 'A war of words', *The Tablet*, 17 January 2004.

Both Hans Küng and Charles Curran have pieces in my *From Inquisition to Freedom*, (Simon and Schuster, Sydney, 2001) describing their experiences, pp. 189–207 and pp. 46–79 respectively. For the history of the Roman curia, see pp. 1–45.

5. THE HEART OF THE CHURCH

Talbot's comment comes from a letter to Henry Edward Manning, Archbishop of Westminster (later cardinal), dated 25 April 1867. The letter is quoted in Edmund Sheridan Purcell, *Life of Cardinal Manning: Archbishop of Westminster*, vol. 2, Macmillan, London, 1895, p. 318.

Between 5 September 1979 and 4 July 1984, John Paul II gave a series of talks at general audiences on the subject of sexuality. These have subsequently been gathered into a book, *Theology of the Body According to John Paul II*, Pauline Books and Media, Boston, 1997.

For the problems inherent in the Vatican II decree on the priesthood, see Christian Ducocq, 'Clerical Reform', in Giuseppe Alberigo (ed.), *The Reception of Vatican II*, Catholic University of America Press, Washington, DC, 1987, pp. 297–308.

For statistics on homosexual clergy, see Donald B Cozzens' excellent book, *The Changing Face of the Priesthood: A Reflection on the Priest's Crisis of Soul*, The Liturgical Press, Collegeville, 2000, pp. 98–9. See also Jane Anderson, *Priests in Love: Australian Catholic Clergy and Their Intimate Relationships*, John Garrett Publishing, Mulgrave (and Continuum, New York), 2005.

For church statistics, see *Annuario Pontificio* (the Vatican Year Book) for 2003. It shows that the 1.07 billion Catholics in the world are served by 4549 bishops, 405 058 priests, 30 097 permanent deacons, 782 932 religious sisters and 54 828 religious brothers. The statistics in the *Annuario* are usually very reliable and are compiled by the Central Statistical Office of the Vatican.

For the Indonesian bishops, see Thomas B Fox, 'Indonesian Bishops Take the Lead', *National Catholic Reporter*, 10 September 1999.

The sexual abuse crisis is discussed in Jason Berry, *Lead Us Not Into Temptation: Catholic Priests and the Sexual Abuse of Children*, Image/Doubleday, New York, 1994. For the crisis in Australia, see Muriel Porter, *Sex, Power and the Clergy*, Hardie Grant Books, Melbourne, 2003. Porter's chapter on the media is especially good. For another view on the United States abuse crisis that is more forgiving of the church, see Phillip Jenkins, *Paedophiles and Priests*, Oxford University Press, New York, 1996.

See Jason Berry and Gerard Renner, *Vows of Silence: The Abuse of Power in the Papacy of John Paul II*, Hodder Headline, Sydney, 2004.

Cardinal Julian Herranz's comments to *La Repubblica* were reported by John Allen in the *National Catholic Reporter*, 25 August 2003.

The last chapter of my *Between the Rock and a Hard Place* (ABC Books, Sydney, 2004) deals in detail with the NRMs.

Ron Rolheiser, 'The abuse scandal as a dark night of the soul', *The Tidings*, 22 August 2003.

For Weigel's estimate of John Paul's significance, see *Witness to Hope: The Biography of John Paul II*, HarperCollins, New York, 1999, pp. 850–60. Eamon Duffy's assessment is in *The Tablet*, 18 October 2003.

6. THE EMPTY CHAIR

Information about the size of the crowd and the world leaders attending Pope Wojtyla's funeral comes from widespread media sources.

The source for Richard John Neuhaus' comments is his 'Rome diary', *First Things*, 11 April 2005.

For the rules governing the *Sede vacante* and conclave period, see the Apostolic Constitution *Universi Dominici gregis*, 22 February 1996. Available in English on the Holy See website, www.vatican.va.

For Andrew Greeley's article on papal elections, see his column in the *Chicago Sun Times*, 22 April 2005.

For the John Allen argument about the need for secrecy, see 'Church in Transition', *National Catholic Reporter*, 9 April 2005. He discusses the *de facto* exclusion of some cardinals from the pre-conclave discussions in 'Church in Transition', 17 April 2005.

For the papacy in the tenth century in Rome, see my *Upon This Rock: The Popes and Their Changing Role*, Melbourne University Press, 2000, pp. 95–117. For the Council of Constance, see pp. 172–7.

Thomas Reese points up the difficulties in the new papal voting procedure in *Inside the Vatican: The Politics and Organization of the Catholic Church*, Harvard University Press, Cambridge, Mass., 1996, p. 87; see also pp. 81–9.

I constructed the probable scenario for the election of Benedict XVI and the groups and people involved from a wide range of sources and from discussions with a number of people. The proposed reconstruction of what happened both before and during the conclave is my own.

For the Subiaco speech of Ratzinger, see a translation of extracts in *Seattle Catholic*, 17 April 2005. Full text will be published in Italian by Catagelli Editore.

Sando Magister discusses the influence of Richard John Neuhaus in the newsletter *Chiesa*, 11 June 2004. His 'What Really Happened in the Conclave' is in *Chiesa*, 2 May 2005.

7. THE ORIGINS OF BENEDICT XVI

The material on the German newspaper response to Benedict XVI's election comes from the homepage of the English service of Deutsche Welle, www.dw-world.de.

The Frei Betto comments are from 'We Are Church UK'. The translation from the Portuguese is by Helen Hughes.

Uta Ranke-Heinemann's comments are quoted at www.somareview.com/humbleintellect.

Ratzinger has written a major reflection on his childhood and youth in *Milestones: Memoirs 1927–1977*, Ignatius Press, San Francisco, 1998.

Erich Przywara, *An Augustine Synthesis*, Harper and Row, New York. 1958.

Robert A Krieg, *Catholic Theologians in Nazi Germany*, Continuum, New York/London, 2004.

For Heinrich Brüning, see William L Patch, *Heinrich Brüning and the Dissolution of the Weimar Republic*, Cambridge University Press, New York, 1998, p. 295.

An English translation of Rahner and Ratzinger's *The Episcopate and the Primacy* was published (Herder, New York) in 1966.

The quotation from Beozzo is from Giuseppe Alberigo and Joseph A Komonchak, *History of Vatican II*, vol. 1, Orbis, Maryknoll, NY, p. 376.

Hans Küng, *My Struggle for Freedom: Memoirs*, trans. John Bowden, Wm B Eerdmans Publishing Company, Grand Rapids, Michigan, 2003.

The quotations from Cardinal Frings are from Xavier Rynne, *Letters From Vatican City: Vatican Council II (First Session): Background and Debates*, Farrar, Straus & Co., New York, 1963, pp. 143–4.

The books by Ratzinger mentioned in the text are: *Revelation and Tradition*, Herder, New York, 1965; *Introduction to Christianity*, Ignatius Press, San Francisco, 2004; *Eschatology: Death and Eternal Life*, Franciscan Herald Press, Chicago, 1988; and with Balthasar, *Two Say Why: Why I am Still a Christian*, Search Press, London, 1973.

Vittorio Messori's interviews in *The Ratzinger Report: An Exclusive Interview on the State of the Church* (Ignatius Press, San Francisco, 1985) quickly became the major source for Ratzinger's views.

Andrew Greeley has written extensively about the 'Catholic imagination'; see *The Catholic Myth: The Behavior and Beliefs of American Catholics*, Charles Scribner's Sons, New York, 1990; and *The Catholic Imagination*, University of California Press, Berkeley, 2000.

8. PREFECT OF THE CDF

Ratzinger says that before his ordination as Archbishop he was 'in rather poor health' (*Milestones: Memoirs 1927–1977*, Ignatius Press, San Francisco, 1998, p. 152), but that the day itself was 'radiant'.

John Cornwall, *A Thief in the Night: The Death of Pope John Paul I*, Penguin, London. 1989.

David Yallop, *In God's Name: An Investigation into the Murder of Pope John Paul I*, Jonathan Cape, London, 1984.

The German journalist interviewed Ratzinger in 1996 and the result was *Salt of the Earth: The Church at the End of the Millennium: An Interview with Peter Seewald*, Ignatius Press, San Francisco, 1997.

For the Küng case see my *From Inquisition to Freedom*, Simon and Schuster, Sydney, 2001, pp. 189–207.

The translation of the Barbara Engl speech comes from Peter Hebblethwaite, *Introducing John Paul II*, Fount, London, 1982, p. 117.

The Edward Schillebeeckx book is *Ministry, Leadership in the Community of Jesus Christ*, English trans., Crossroad, New York, 1981.

Leonardo Boff, *Church, Charism and Power*, English trans., Crossroad, New York, 1985.

For the Charles Curran 'case', see my *From Inquisition to Freedom*, Simon and Schuster, Sydney, 2001, pp. 46–79.

Richard McCormack's comments on the Curran case are found in *Theological Studies*, 50(1989), p. 17.

For Tissa Balasuriya's own description of what happened to him, see my *From Inquisition to Freedom*, Simon and Schuster, Sydney, 2001, pp. 80–108. His books *Christ and Human Liberation* and *Mary and Human Liberation* are obtainable through the Centre for Society and Religion, 81 Deans Road, Colombo, Sri Lanka.

Jacques Dupuis, *Toward a Christian Theology of Religious Pluralism*, English trans., Orbis, Maryknoll, NY, 1999.

For Lavinia Byrne's experiences, see my *From Inquisition to Freedom*, Simon and Schuster, Sydney, 2001, pp. 162–88.

Ladislas Orsy's article is in *Doctrine and Life*, 48 (1998), pp. 453–65.

Avery Dulles, *The Catholicity of the Church*, Clarendon Press, Oxford, 1985.

John May's article is one of a series of essays in Michael Rainer (ed.), *Dominus Jesus: Anstoessige Wahrheit oder anstoessige Kirche*, Lit Verlag, Munster-Hamburg-London, 2001.

9. FIRST DAYS IN THE PAPAL *APPARTAMENTO*

It has been widely reported in the media that Ingrid Stampa is affiliated with the Schoenstatt Movement. However, after checking with the Movement it is clear that she is being confused with Sister Brigid Wansing, who is a Schoenstatt Sister of Mary who worked with Ratzinger in the CDF.

Cardinal Errázuriz Ossa's comments can be found on the homepage of the Schoenstatt Movement, www.schoenstatt.de.

JMR Tillard's views can be found in *The Bishop of Rome*, English trans., Michael Glazier, Wilmington, Del., 1983.

Joseph Ratzinger, *The Spirit of the Liturgy*, trans. John Saward, Ignatius Press, San Francisco, 2000.

The full story of the Maciel affair is told in Jason Berry and Gerald Renner, *Vows of Silence: The Abuse of Power in the Papacy of John Paul II*, Hodder Headline, Sydney, 2004. For John Allen's story about the canonical case against Maciel proceeding, see *NCR*, Breaking News, 25 May 2005.

For Ratzinger's views of priests, see *Ratzinger Report: An Exclusive Interview on the State of the Church*, Ignatius Press, San Francisco. 1985, pp. 55–8.

The KTVU assessment of Levada can be found at the station's website, www.ktvu.com.

Robert Nugent's comments can be found in my *From Inquisition to Freedom*, Simon and Schuster, Sydney, 2001, p. 149.

John McNeill, *The Church and the Homosexual*, Beacon Books, Boston, 1976.

On the AIDS issue, see James Keenan and Jon Fuller (eds), *Catholic Ethicists on HIV/AIDS Prevention*, Continuum, New York, 2000.

INDEX